We should revere Sven Lindqvist.
than an historic document. Its pre
Lindqvist's insights speak direct
against ignorance as well as the ....g
knowledge and institutions. *Dig Where You Stand* is a practical
primer which shows how we can change things for the better.

Paul Gilroy, author of *Darker Than Blue*

There are many Sven Lindqvists. The experimental essayist, the
astute chronicler of revolutionary China and Latin America, the
radical historian whose excoriations of European barbarism are
still revelatory. *Dig Where You Stand*, more locally attuned, is a
wonderful toolkit — a work of barefoot research — that shows us
how to investigate our own jobs, communities and lives with one
simple goal: social transformation.

Sukhdev Sandhu, Director, Colloquium for
Unpopular Culture, New York University

Sven Lindqvist's call to "Dig Where You Stand" has been a lasting
inspiration for me, an influence leading me to combine international
oral history in parallel with local community projects, revealing
the amazing richness of the life stories which — once you learn to
listen — you can discover right around you.

Paul Thompson, author of *The Voice of the Past*

Do not mistake this for an ordinary handbook or a dated analysis
of working-class conditions. Lindqvist's book shows with vivid
clarity how capitalism permeates society, our homes, lungs and
our children's future. And yet, at the end, there is not despair and
hopelessness but an empowering sense that things can and will be
changed.

Catharina Thörn, Professor of Cultural Studies,
University of Gothenburg

A sharp reminder that we are in danger of losing the art of research, bamboozled by the sheer immediacy of what passes for information and data today. Sven Lindqvist quietly insists that the practice of finding out how our worlds are put together can be — should be — an integral part of political work. This book is a gift for new generations of radical activists who grasp exactly how much we have to change.

Vron Ware, author of *Return of a Native*

Dig Where You Stand has long had mythic status as a self-help manual for oral and community historians. By putting ordinary workers at the centre of history it became an important influence on the History Workshop movement. Now at last we have a definitive English-language version of this ground-breaking book. Though forty-four years after its first publication, its appearance today can hardly be more timely or relevant. It should be on every activist's bookshelf.

Jerry White, Emeritus Professor of History, Birkbeck

"History does not disappear," Sven Lindqvist argues, when asking why we need to keep remembering the past, "it lives on in capital." This pioneering work is as relevant today as it was on first publication, as capital continues unceasingly to move around the world, desperate to avoid accountability for its disastrous social and environmental consequences. Lindqvist bears witness, and he demonstrates to us how we can too.

Ken Worpole, Writer and Social Historian

At last we have an English translation of this much-rumoured book, written to help workers develop an autonomous, convivial and also empowering understanding of their industry and workplace. Half a century old but still vivid, it is to be welcomed as a fearless and ambitious manual on how to live and think as well as research, write and make connections in an apparently disjointed time.

Patrick Wright, author of *The Sea View Has Me Again*

DIG WHERE YOU STAND

DIG WHERE YOU STAND

HOW TO RESEARCH A JOB

SVEN LINDQVIST

EDITED BY
ANDREW FLINN
AND
ASTRID VON ROSEN

TRANSLATED BY
ANN HENNING JOCELYN
(REVISED 2017)

Published by Repeater Books

An imprint of Watkins Media Ltd

Unit 11 Shepperton House

89-93 Shepperton Road

London

N1 3DF

United Kingdom

www.repeaterbooks.com

A Repeater Books paperback original 2023

1

Distributed in the United States by Random House, Inc., New York.

ISBN: 9781914420955

Ebook ISBN: 9781914420962

Printed and bound in the United Kingdom by TJ Books Limited

CONTENTS

AN INTRODUCTION TO THE LONG-AWAITED ENGLISH TRANSLATION OF *DIG WHERE YOU STAND*

Andrew Flinn and Astrid von Rosen

Finally the long-awaited English translation of Sven Lindqvist's key activist research manual and manifesto *Gräv där du står / Dig Where You Stand* has arrived! When first published in Swedish in 1978 the book was a critical intervention into the conflict between the competing narratives of workers' histories and more dominant and pervasive elite histories. Today the book makes for a powerful entry into the urgent and pressing task of critically addressing the increasingly complex, painfully precarious work conditions of human lives in global-local economies, as well as for all "barefoot researchers" working to research and write counter-histories which challenge other dominant and often exclusionary narratives.

Sven Lindqvist: Writer and Activist

Lindqvist, born in Stockholm in 1932 and died in 2019, was a prolific and award-winning writer, journalist, historian and activist. While Lindqvist, in the Swedish context, is not usually described as an activist, drawing on our 2016 interviews with him we suggest that activism is a crucial part of his legacy. Described by Patrick Wright in 2001 as a "citizen-writer with socialist roots and an open mind" (Wright 2001), Lindqvist wrote to educate and facilitate change through the knowledge and understanding gained. Particularly in relation to *Dig Where You Stand*, readily described as an activist manual for history-from-below research, understanding the activist dimension of Lindqvist's work facilitates accessing and using the book. In the case of *Dig Where You Stand*, Lindqvist's longstanding interest in profound social and economic change is manifested through his recognition of the importance of history (and history-making) and understanding the past as a foundation for transformation in the present.

When interviewed, Lindqvist explained to us that he used the money from one of his prestigious literary awards to fund his extensive research and writing of *Dig Where You Stand*. He did so because not only did he see an acute lack of worker's history in Sweden and beyond, but also because he wanted to empower workers (and others) to do the liberatory work of researching and writing that history themselves. Featuring cement workers as a prominent industrial group of the time (with which he had family connections via his grandfather), but owing to the prevalence of industrial illness also making a very poignant case study, Lindqvist exposes the elitist and exclusionary practices of history-making. When academic historians, companies and professional museums produced industrial history, workers were frequently absent, and their perspectives and expertise by and large ignored. Lindqvist saw the urgent need for a comprehensive and usable manual for conducting historical research that workers could readily read and implement, and invested the time to produce one himself.

Both Lindqvist's parents were public school teachers and his upbringing can be described as bourgeois. When attending the upper secondary school Södra Latin in Stockholm, Lindqvist turned to writing as a way of competing for girls, and in particular a very popular one named Cecilia Norman. The initial reason for this was, as he told us, his inability to conduct social dancing. Suffering from what he described as immobility, stiffness and a frozen heart, he discovered his skill with words when writing letters to Cecilia. Looking back, Lindqvist said that if he could write to a woman such as her, he could write anything, comprehend and change the whole world with his words. This was the confidence and feeling that everything is possible that was necessary for an author to dare leaving already trodden paths and invest in a new kind of personal, political and activist literature, such as *Dig Where You Stand*.

After graduating in 1951, Lindqvist started working as a literary critic for the daily paper *Dagens Nyheter*. A pacifist choosing to do alternative military service, he ended up doing manual labour in a Swedish creosote factory and published his first book, *A Proposal* (1955), aged twenty-three. Writing in the first person, the non-fiction documentary essay combining his own experiences of labour with use of diaries, signalled the development of the first-person, problem-oriented, socially engaged and creative style and voice that would characterise much of his writing right from the start. At the same time as publishing *A Proposal* he also joined the SAP, the Swedish Social Democratic Party. The following year he married Cecilia, who was to become a writer, photographer and highly acclaimed sinologist. Cecilia's work was an important component of *Dig Where You Stand*, with the original Swedish edition featuring many of her photographs, helping to illustrate crucial parts of the text. In 1986 the couple divorced, and Lindqvist subsequently married economist and author Agneta Stark, with whom he lived until his death in 2019.

Drawing on the young financially poor family's daily life experiences, Lindqvist's second book, *Advertising is Lethal* (1957), addressed the relationship between media, marketing and consumerism. The book received mixed reviews and criticism, which resulted in Lindqvist being sacked from the daily paper he was then writing for. Entering academic education at Stockholm University, Lindqvist first completed a licentiate degree, and in 1966 received his doctorate in comparative literature, with a dissertation on the Swedish poet Vilhelm Ekelund, who was also a great source of inspiration for him. In parallel he studied Chinese and Chinese literature, which resulted in him travelling to China and being appointed as cultural attaché in Beijing from 1961-62. This Chinese experience sparked Lindqvist's international career. Sven and Cecilia's account of life in Mao's China was carried by leading international newspapers, reaching a global audience. A few years later, *The Myth of Wu Tao-tzu* (1967, in English 2012), now a modern classic, combined a personal approach with a fierce discussion about painful realities, politics in relation to art and dreams. Throughout the 1970s (and after) Lindqvist continued to travel the world, his writing addressing from an often first-person and creative stance issues of political history, racism and Western imperialism in Europe, Latin America, and Africa. The English reader might be familiar with *Exterminate All the Brutes* (1992), *A History of Bombing* (1999) and *Terra Nullius* (2005). Indeed, Raoul Peck's outstanding TV-series of *Exterminate All the Brutes* for HBO Max draws on Lindqvist's original text and provides access to another important part of his authorship, namely his views on history and desire to prompt meaningful change. When first published in 1978, *Dig Where You Stand* was equally a globally-influenced activist manifesto and a practical manual firmly anchored in the realities of Swedish industrial life, prompting workers and others to take charge of the telling of their own history.

The "Dig Movement" and *Gräv där du står*

The first Swedish edition unexpectedly sold out quickly and a second edition had to be printed very rapidly. Several factors explain the book's immediate success and impact. *Dig Where You Stand* was not published in a vacuum. First, there already existed a fertile ground for the *Dig Where You Stand* initiative of worker-led research and local history practice. Sweden has a long tradition of independent workers' education, rooted in nineteenth-century social movements concerned with temperance, labour rights, education and religious belief. The establishment in 1912 of the *Arbetarnas Bildningsförbund* (Workers' Educational Association) (ABF) formalised the place of independent working-class education within the Swedish labour movement and the *Sveriges socialdemokratiska arbetareparti* or Social Democratic Workers' Party (SAP). The early twentieth century also saw the development of organisations and processes for gathering and preserving peasant culture (*allmogekultur*) and the growth of the homestead movement (*hembygdsrörelsen*), which celebrated local place, culture and traditions.

Second, in the 1960s industry underwent a major structural upheaval, with many smaller factories merging into larger conglomerates. One result of this process was the urgent need to salvage the local industrial cultural heritage at risk of disappearing, including significant employers such as the cement factories Lindqvist describes in *Dig Where You Stand*. Lindqvist was very aware of these developments, attending conferences on industrial archaeology and maintaining a continuous dialogue with the research community. At the same time, local governments addressed these changes by promoting the establishment and work of local history study circles, and by the early 1970s the media were helping to popularise historical research and distributing study materials for producing local history.

It is in this context that Lindqvist's *Dig Where You Stand* was published, and soon became the core text of the hugely popular *Grävrörelsen* or "Dig-movement", a social movement at its most popular and widespread between 1975 and 1985, with hundreds of thousands of people becoming involved in their local study circles (Alzén 2011). Many of the people engaged in this social movement shared the same social democratic values and collective identity, and were motivated to take action to react to and accomplish social change. Importantly, the Dig-movement consisted of thousands of local study circles aimed at fostering local democracy, conducting local and industrial historical research, producing worker's theatre and lots of other aesthetic activities resulting in exhibitions, oral history sessions and writing workshops. Considering and describing these "Dig" groups (and indeed the wider international oral history community) as a "movement" connects this collective activity with the labour and social movements of the early twentieth century, as well as the 1960s movement politics of many of the leading participants (Konig, 2019, 59 & 79).

In this environment Lindqvist's *Dig Where You Stand* functioned as a detailed practical manual and activist manifesto showing workers (and others) how to empower themselves and their community by researching their hitherto excluded and devalued histories, particularly within their factories and workplaces. Throughout *Dig Where You Stand* Lindqvist demonstrates how industrial history and archaeology have been conducted and produced without workers' voices being represented or their perspectives and experiences included, and how damaging this was. The book not only managed to summarise and articulate the Dig-movement's central ideas, but crucially it also delivered substantial instructions on how anyone interested could conduct historical research. Even if not everyone involved in the Dig-movement read the book in its entirety, it was widely taken up and the research methods taught by the study circle leaders.

The text and ethos of *Dig Where You Stand* managed to unite the prevailing aspiration on the left to further democratise cultural and knowledge production — Lindqvist (1979, 25) himself credited the participatory turn in theatre and the arts in the early 1970s as an influence on *Dig Where You Stand* — with practical instructions on how workers and others might empower themselves by researching and documenting their own history. In doing so, the title "Dig Where You Stand" developed a wider metaphoric force, a motto prompting people to become historians themselves. The book and the motto were thus adopted by Dig Where You Stand study circles promoted by the Labour Movement across Sweden and the other Nordic countries in the 1970s and early 1980s and connecting with international "history from below" and oral history movements more broadly (Thompson 2000, 18, Konig 2019, 69 & 79). While it is difficult to establish exactly how many Dig study circles and history-from-below research groups were created, it is commonly held that more than ten thousand groups existed in Sweden and neighbouring countries, with hundreds of thousands of members involved over the period (Lindqvist 2014). By the late 1970s it seems that in Sweden "everybody was digging" for their history.

The popularity of the book was certainly helped by the fact that Sven and Cecilia Lindqvist were a well-known couple, with a high and generally positive media profile. Lindqvist in particular was perceived as "a modern man", a proponent of leftist ideas but also a highly acclaimed author, whose books were consequently able to reach a large audience. In this way *Dig Where You Stand* became one of the most important and influential texts from the "history from below" movement, which was characterised by radical, socialist and feminist approaches to history and knowledge-production beginning in the 1960s, peaking in the late 1970s and declining in widespread popular influence and interest during the 1980s.

Digging as Workers' Inquiry

The central idea underpinning *Dig Where You Stand* is that doing history work is a necessary and significant contributory factor in achieving social, political and industrial change, and indeed in fashioning a new world. The book conveys the key idea that everyone — not just academics — can learn how to (and benefit from) critically and rigorously explore history, especially their own. It provides clear, comprehensive and engaging instructions on how everyone can systematically research the history of their workplace and industry, employ a multiplicity of sources (official records as well as more informal oral and personal sources) in a critical fashion and choose research methods relevant to the subject of the research. It instructs the reader how to formulate and pose urgent and critical research questions — questions about power and the lived legacies of the past in the present still relevant today — and provides the researcher with the tools to research and answer those questions. Without a proper question, you are ill-equipped to enter the archive and commence the act of research, warns Lindqvist, and you will get lost. Today, in our global precarious economy, and the resulting indeterminate archives, the warning is more relevant than ever.

Dig Where You Stand prompts workers to become researchers, to follow the money and the power it represents, confers and reproduces. It invites them to take on the role as experts on their job and industry and "dig" out its hidden histories to produce a new picture and understanding of that industry and their position within it as a vital step towards social and economic transformation. Written in an engaging and clear language that everyone can understand, *Dig Where You Stand* challenges the arbitrary and harmful boundaries between the public and the academy, workers and experts, "amateur" and "professional" researchers. In so doing, *Dig Where You Stand* was aligning itself with a long-standing intellectual and political tradition. Lindqvist himself described the roots of workers "digging" being located in the writings of Friedrich Nietzsche (*"Wo du stehst, grab tief hinein!"* / "Where you stand, dig in deeply") and also in practices undertaken after the Russian and Chinese revolutions (Lindqvist 2014). Digging practice has also strong echoes of the "Workers' Inquiry" advocated by Marx and the Workers' Enquiry movement in Italy in the 1950s and 1960s, not to mention the approach encouraged by inter-war Pan-Africanists like Arthur Schomburg for African Americans to dig up their past (McAllister 2022, Wright 2017, Schomburg 1925).

According to Lindqvist, experts (academics, industrial leaders and the likes) are not to be automatically feared and deferred to, because a worker is the expert on their job. Lindqvist concludes his preface, "That is why *your own job* is such a good starting point for your research. Dig where you stand!" These short and to-the-point sentences neatly capture what we argue is a key distinguishing feature in and for *Dig Where You Stand*, namely embodied and situated action. Making "your own job" the point of departure in becoming a researcher, Lindqvist firmly grounds and situates the practitioner (in his case, the cement worker) in real life, material space and the human body. When adding the imperative "dig where you stand!", this research stance is charged with a call to take action, enter the explorative stage empowered as practitioner-scholar, and to do so without shame and fear.

In line with previous as well as current perspectives in feminist research, Lindqvist's real-life case studies situate, embody and visualise rather than merely describe how workers (and other communities) can on their own or in collaboration with others create this "new picture" and use it as tool for change. His exposition of politically engaged and counter-history-making is still known and acts as an inspiration to many interested in radical history practices within social movement and activist environments today (see for instance the international History from Below network and the influence of Dig, "a mass history movement" (Ball and Box, 2015)).

Starting by looking out from one's local setting to the world and ending with a vision of the future (set sometime in the 2020s) where activist scholars collaborate with academics to work for social change, the book's thirty chapters of "materials and methods, which anyone can use to trace their own history and that of their workmates", together create a montage of possible ways to explore a job and the workplace. History is set in motion in a multitude of dynamic and critically fruitful approaches engaging oral history, visual analysis, archival research, memory work, spatial explorations and critical reflection. The results of such research could be equally dynamic, with Lindqvist warning that "research is not mainly a defensive but an offensive weapon. It's more suited for conquest than for defence."

International Reception

The book was translated into Norwegian, Danish, German and French, and it inspired similar movements in these countries. Its influence was strongly felt in the English-speaking world through Lindqvist's close contacts with the oral history and History Workshop movements and in summary accounts published in the *Oral History* journal (1979) and in *Our Common History* (Thompson 1982) and reports in US radical history publications, but a full English translation has not been published until now. For many years the only access to the full English text was via a translation prepared in the 1970s and 1980s, held in the International Institute of Social History archives in Amsterdam. As a result, in English the legacy of the book and the ideas it contained has been the strength of the metaphor and the exhortation to Dig Where You Stand!, the inspiration of a basic approach, communities taking responsibility for researching and writing their own history, which has remained influential to this day. In the words of Ken Worpole (2008, 7), a London-based advocate of people's history and working-class writing and autobiography, *Dig Where You Stand* was the "rallying cry" and ethos of the History Workshop movement, and its influence is clear (if indirect) in long-running community-based documentary and history groups like the Living Archive of Milton Keynes (Kitchen, 2012, Croall, 1992).

This history is important, because to consider *Dig Where You Stand* as just a how-to-do manual for conducting local community or even workers' history does *not* reflect its full essence. It is that — a detailed guide to researching history from below — but it is much more as well. Inspired by the understanding that "History is dangerous... History is important because the results of history are still with us", Lindqvist's book was a manifesto and critical montage in support of the empowerment of workers and of historical research and activist learning as a tool for social and economic transformation. For Lindqvist — echoing previous workers' inquiry movements but with an historical emphasis — "factory history could and should be written from a fresh point of view — by workers investigating their own workplaces", because "those who are to conquer the company must first conquer the picture of the company... A new picture must be created, a picture that puts workers and their work in the foreground". *Dig Where You Stand* has a prompting quality, operating through the dynamic juxtapositions of imperative instructions, documentary photographs, inspiring witness accounts, blunt economic tables and revealing archival materials.

Since the initial publication of *Dig Where You Stand*, historical research has been transformed by developments in digital technology, which can make some of Lindqvist's case studies and research methodologies seem dated. We suggest, however, that the recognition of the importance of histories and the "useful past" within political and social movements, and the thought-provoking ideas contained within *Dig Where You Stand*, are as important and relevant as ever, as are Lindqvist's contemporary critiques of the absences and marginalisation of workers and other under-voiced communities and peoples in formal archives, museums, popular and academic histories and the value of identifying other oral and informal sources to provide a corrective to these unreliable narratives. In fact, our period sees a widespread revival of interest in democratised knowledge-production, participatory and community-based research practices seeking to overcome rigid and arbitrary binaries between public and academic research, community-based critical education and learning.

In terms of impact and visual agency, the original 1978 Swedish cover is particularly interesting and significant. The original cover-collage, composed by graphic designer Bo Berling using Cecilia Lindqvist's photography, features the head of a large-scale male worker, looking up from behind a cement factory on a smaller scale. Wearing a cap, and looking the reader straight in the eye, the worker oversees and takes control of the image of the factory and its history. Even if we do not see his entire body, we can sense the firmness with which he is standing on the factory ground, as a powerful digger. He is about to rise higher, above the factory, becoming even bigger.

The system of signs in operation in the collage resonates with well-known worker's iconography such as the gesture of the big figure, one giant representing the many workers, as well as the singular raised fist, empowered by myriads of workers.

We wish to acknowledge the importance of the original cover for understanding and accessing the book. In respect of the original cover and at the same time wanting to update it in recognition of today's more diverse and inclusive perspectives and "diggers", Repeater Books have here designed a new cover which resonates strongly with the spirit of Berling's 1978 collage.

Dig Where You Stand: An Activist and Prompting Text

It is our argument that *Dig Where You Stand* is a unique book, fusing different styles and motivations in a fashion that leaves it with few clear comparisons. It is both a detailed manual on how to research one's own history (as a worker but also as any individual or community) but also an imperative and provocative account of why history is important in supporting struggles for transformative change. All the chapters of *Dig Where You Stand* provide the reader with engaging empirical evidence and theory-driven arguments conveying its main message about the necessity to conquer the picture of the company. Lindqvist's book presents research methods and materials concerning thirty different areas which anyone can use to trace his or her own history and that of their fellow workers. Each chapter draws out key critical questions, suggests historiographical approaches and exemplifies where and how archival and other materials can be accessed. Even though the examples belong to a different period of time and place, and do not provide updated details and digital resources, the point they continue to make today is a powerful impetus to "dig where you stand". Firmly grounded in critical thinking, we believe the detailed examples can still be transposed to other contexts and research challenges to convey the material and embodied nature of any research activity. "You have to do it, you have to be there!"

The person engaging with the book can — in resonance with contexts and ambiences — get a sense of being prompted to *become an activist digger* by embodied examples and frictions that create the necessary critical questions guiding the history-production. The book is thus more than a manual; it can better be understood as an instigator and motivator of activism. It prompts DIY-engagement, urges the practitioner-researcher to conduct research in collaboration with others. Thus, *Dig Where You Stand* can be understood as a directly instructive agent, an active text not to be passively consumed, that can be operationalised anew in very different context, bound and grounded ways by people engaging with it, learning as they go along.

Lindqvist's way of writing, the examples he uses, effectively operationalize an active embodied understanding and activist capability into body and mind. *Dig Where You Stand* prompts and enables the practitioner-researcher to critically engage with their history from one specific perspective and challenge and change the dominant narrative and picture. Its thirty chapters all contribute to this transformative process. Taken as a whole, we suggest that one key characteristic is embodied and affectively charged empowerment. As Lindqvist states: "you are there!", physically, actively, as explorer-practitioner-expert, to explore experience, memories and physical features, such as ruined lungs, food shortages and dangerous spaces.

Whilst there are books which advise on local or community history techniques (*Writing Local History*, Beckett 2007), and there are others which look at the significance of democratised history practice (Iles and Roberts, 2012), there are few that mix the continuing influence of the DIY "history-from-below" approach of *Dig Where You Stand* with the clear sense of political engagement and change. Other social movement or local community history manuals, such as these from the US, South Africa and the UK (Brecher, 1986; Witz, 1988,

Croall 1992), take a similar approach and commitment without replicating the detail and depth of the guidance. Paul Thompson's oral history classic and near contemporary *The Voice of the Past* (latest edition 2016, but originally published in 1978) combines detailed discussion of oral history practice with a similarly clear advocacy of the democratising and transformative power of the approach and historical research. Indeed, Thompson references Lindqvist and the Dig-movement as influential work comparable to his own. David Rosenberg's recent excellent *Rebel Footprints* is different but shares very similar perspectives on the value of engaging and doing history-from-below work for oneself or for one's community. There are also parallels with the 2015 publication by MIT Press — for the first time in English — of a translation of another in its time very influential, stimulating and practical manual from the same period as *Gräv där du står*, namely Umberto Eco's *How to Write a Thesis* (1977). Nonetheless, *Dig Where You Stand* remains a unique text that was until to now unavailable in its full form to English readers.

This Edition and *Dig Where You Stand* Today

Andrew Flinn and Sven Lindqvist in Stockholm, May 2016.
Photo credit: Astrid von Rosen

In recent years there has been a significant revival of interest in Sweden and elsewhere (Olofsson, Hilborn & Nilsson Mohammadi (2022), von Rosen (2022), Flinn & Sexton (2018)) in studying the history of the Dig Where You Stand movement in the 1970s and 1980s. The continued relevance of these ideas today in a range of different contexts is also at the centre of the research we have been doing at the Centre for Critical Heritage Studies (CCHS) at the University of Gothenburg and University College London. Together, we — the editors — interviewed Lindqvist in February and May 2016, exploring his *Dig Where You Stand* history and philosophy, and subsequently arranged several Dig Where You Stand workshops, including "Digging Across Borders: Historicising Dig Where You Stand in Sweden and Internationally" (November 2016), attended by Lindqvist himself. Lindqvist generously contributed a new text on the history and motivations behind *Dig Where You Stand*, which he read to the workshop participants. In September 2018 we arranged a two-day workshop to celebrate the fortieth anniversary of the first publication of *Dig Where You Stand*, reading and discussing the book from current critical stances. Scholars engaged in Dig Where You Stand work concluded with expressing their gratitude to Lindqvist for his generosity, engagement and the critical digging method that is still with us.

In February 2016, Astrid von Rosen first contacted Ann Henning Jocelyn, who shortly after the Swedish original was published worked with Lindqvist on an English translation of *Gräv där du står*. A copy of this translation, never finalised or published, was as we have already noted kept in the International Institute of Social History archive in Amsterdam. Sections of the manuscript were full of comments, suggestions and further edits by Ann Henning Jocelyn, Sven Lindqvist and perhaps others unknown. Before Ann Henning Jocelyn could rework the manuscript, von Rosen took on the difficult and time-consuming task of providing a clean copy of the Amsterdam manuscript. Ann Henning Jocelyn then revised the copy and provided some updates. The Archives Cluster paid for Ann Henning Jocelyn's work. As far as possible we have left the text as close to the original and the translation, making only very minor changes including making some of the language more gender neutral. Otherwise the text is as originally written by Lindqvist in 1978.

The 1978 cover

With the encouragement of Professor of Comparative Literature Mats Malm, who knew Lindqvist personally, and the active support of Sven Lindqvist and Agneta Stark themselves, we then sought to find a first English publisher for the translation. We are extremely grateful to Gareth Evans and Repeater Books for recognising the importance of Lindqvist and *Dig Where You Stand* and the continued relevance of the ideas and approaches advocated by the text.

For the current publication we have made every effort to reproduce Lindqvist's distinctive language. Together with Repeater we have been careful to make the publication resemble the original layout of the book and make it as readable and open to new audiences as possible. The images contained within the original Swedish version were an important and powerful part of that volume, and as far as possible we have included reproductions of these images to form part on an equal basis with the translated text. Indeed, it can be argued that a strong component in what makes the book function and inspire is the visual aspect, in combination with arguments and content. It is not exclusively the textual content of the "published" archival documents, but also the visualising of them as examples that creates the powerful affect that the book provokes. The visual aspects are strongly communicative: they perform, they instruct, they provoke and seduce, and structure the reader experience.

What you hold in your hands or read on a screen is the fruit of much dedicated work to make this classic text of radical history practice and critical heritage available to English-speaking audiences for the first time. More than just an interesting product of the creative political and intellectual ferment of the times, we believe that this book, Lindqvist's own engaged writing and its overall message remain hugely relevant and important to today's readers. Whilst Lindqvist (2014) himself recognised that, in its original form, *Dig Where You Stand* may have had limited success in its primary aim of increasing workers' power in the workplace, he did see significant achievement in contributing to making "the working life of the working classes part of a permanently broadened concept of history", and suggested the method's continued relevance in terms of examining the processes and decision-making which lie behind globalisation, industrial change and restructuring which result in the precariousness of so many lives and the environmental damage and climate crisis which surrounds us. Whatever the changes in society and in the practices of research, understanding how these histories remain alive and at work today and the structures of power that these histories can reveal remains as important and urgent today as it was when Lindqvist's *Dig Where You Stand* was first published in 1978. We must keep digging in order to fashion a new and better world for all.

Bibliography

Annika Alzén (2011), *Kulturarv i rörelse: en studie av "gräv där du står"-rörelsen. (Cultural Heritage in Motion: A Study of the "Dig Where You Stand Movement")* Brutus Östlings bokförlag Symposion, Mölndal.

Roger Ball & Peter Box (2015), "History is the New Punk", talk given at conference at Manchester Metropolitan University 11 May 2015 and available at https://radical.history-from-below.net/. Accessed September 2022.

John Beckett (2007), *Writing Local History*. MUP, Manchester.

Jeremy Brecher (1986), *History from Below: How to Uncover and Tell the Story of Your Community, Association, or Union*. Commonwork / Advocate Press, West Cornwall.

Jonathan Croall (1992), *Dig for History: Active Learning Across the Curriculum*. Southgate Publishers, Devon

Umberto Eco (1977), *How to Write a Thesis*. MIT Press, Cambridge (translation 2015).

Andrew Flinn & Anna Sexton (2018). "Research on Community Heritage: Moving from Collaborative Research to Participatory and Co-Designed Research Practice". In *Heritage and Interpretation*, eds Sheila Watson, Amy Barnes, Katy Bunning, Routledge, Abingdon.

Antony Iles & Tom Roberts (2012), *All Knees and Elbows of Susceptibility and Refusal: Reading History From Below*. Transmission Gallery, London.

Christian Konig (2109), "Movement and Solidarity". In *Giving*

Voice to the Oppressed, edited by Agnes Arp, Annette Leo and Franka Maubach. De Gruyter, Oldenbourg.

Roger Kitchen (2012), "Dig Where You Stand: Using Local Lives to Generate Community in Milton Keynes". In Oral History Vol. 40 No. 2.

Sven Lindqvist (1978), *Gräv där du står. Hur man utforskar ett job.* Bonners, Stockholm.

--- (1979), "Dig Where You Stand". *Oral History.* Vol 7 No 2

--- (1982), "Dig Where You Stand". In *Our Common History: The Transformation of Europe.* Edited by Paul Thompson. Pluto Books, London.

--- (2014), "Dig Where You Stand Movement". In *The SAGE Encyclopaedia of Action Research.* SAGE Publications Ltd, London

Craig McAllister (2022), *Karl Marx's Workers' Inquiry: International History, Reception, and Responses.* Notes from Below, London.

M. Olofsson, E. Hilborn & R. Nilsson Mohammadi (2022), "Gräv där du står! Vad kan vi lära oss av grävrörelsen?" In *Arbetarhistoria: meddelande från arbetarrörelsens arkiv och bibliotek,* 181-182, (1-2), 92-101.

Astrid von Rosen (2022), "Affect and Digital Caregiving: Challenging the Performing Arts Canon with a 'Dig Where You Stand' Database". *Archives and Records,* 43:2, 128-142.

David Rosenburg (2019), *Rebel Footprints.* Pluto Press, London.

Paul Thompson (2000), *The Voice of the Past.* OUP, Oxford.

Arthur Schomburg (1925), "The Negro Digs Up His Past". In A. Locke, *The New Negro.* Simon and Schuster, New York (reprint 1997).

Leslie Witz (1988), *Write Your Own History.* Raven Press / SACHED Trust, Johannesburg

Ken Worpole (2008), *Dockers and Detectives.* Five Leaves Publication, Nottingham

Patrick Wright (2001), "Dropping Their Eggs". *London Review of Books,* Vol. 23 No. 16, 23 August.

Steve Wright (2017), *Storming Heaven.* Pluto Books, London.

DIG WHERE YOU STAND

HOW TO RESEARCH
A JOB

SVEN LINDQVIST

PREFACE

This is a research handbook for non-professional researchers. It describes thirty different ways of investigating a job and a place of work.

For this I needed a concrete example: a job going back roughly as far as the Swedish industrial society. I needed a basic industry that is represented in most countries. Determined to avoid glamorous branches and romantic products, and not opting for an easy way out, I chose the cement industry as my example.

The book is aimed at anyone who wants to try and research their own job. But it is of course equally suitable for people who want to investigate their future or their past job. Secondarily, the book is aimed at teachers, students, journalists, authors and others who may have a professional ambition to find out more about jobs in Swedish industry.

I do not intend any single reader to do all the things suggested in this book. Life is not long enough for that. Treat the book as if it were a seed catalogue or a brochure from a travel agent. Choose whatever suits you! Do co-operate with others and divide the tasks up between you. Concentrate on whatever applies to your particular problems.

It would be easy to point out another thirty, perhaps even more interesting ways to research a job. I never meant this book to be the final word. But as far as I can see, it is still the most comprehensive demonstration available in any language of possible ways to research a job.

This comprehensiveness has its price. In each of the areas I discuss there are specialists who would have written a much better handbook than I — on that particular subject. I have a word for them too: Please do! No one would appreciate it more than I.

And my word to other readers is this: Do not fear the experts. You know your job. Your professional experience is a firm basis on which to stand when judging other people's activities — and non-activities. They may be experts, each one in their own area, but when they discuss your job, you are the expert. That is why your own job is such a good starting-point for your research. Dig where you stand!

Sven Lindqvist

A JOB...

1. IN THE WORLD

You have a job. In other places, in other countries, other people have the same job. What is their experience of it? Are they annoyed by some things, amused by others? What are their hopes and dreams? How much money do they earn, what is their work environment like? Do they have a right to participate?

Let's say you work in a cement factory. If all the cement workers of the world could go and see each other and compare notes, what, do you think, would dominate? Similarities or differences? What would be the cause of the differences?

"All large companies in this particular industry are fairly similar — only the level of technology varies."

"Oh no, it all depends on the unions — if the trade unions aren't strong enough, others will take advantage of the improved technology."

"The decisive factor is surely the owners of the means of production, those who have the power in the economical-political system."

"What does it matter — the great difference is between industrial and developing nations. The general level of development within a country decides what can be got out of the jobs."

Who is right? It's difficult to tell, because most cement workers of the world have never met each other. Do you know what your workmates in England or Germany, in Yugoslavia or the Soviet Union, really discuss and believe in? Do you know what they strive for in Mexico and enjoy in Nigeria? Do you know how the Chinese regard their jobs and lives?

Your job is international. In thousands of factories all over the world your unknown workmates are doing the same job as you. But they know nothing about you. You know nothing about them.

Why is that?

Travelogues

It's partly due to travelogues and reports from abroad.

All sorts of people have travelled and then given an account of their experiences. They have visited Europe and Asia, Africa and Australia, North and South America. Some of them have just flown from one major city to another, whereas others have travelled along dusty country lanes. Some have rubbed shoulders with the social elite, others have met inhabitants of slums and ghettos. Briefly, they seem to have been everywhere and to have seen everything.

But has any traveller to another country ever seen and described a cement factory?

It's a well-known fact that travel writers won't be daunted by hardship. In the most terrible conditions they struggle across polar expanses or penetrate the rain forest in order to describe its secrets to their readers. Loaded with cameras and tape recorders, they will reach even the most savage, inaccessible Indian tribes, just to be able to report on their living conditions.

So why hasn't even one of them, on some occasion, in some country, had something to say about cement workers?

I have been a keen reader of travelogues and foreign reports for over twenty-five years. I've seen them change — from being exotic to becoming socially aware, from being picturesque to becoming political. But I have yet to read a travelogue which tells anything about a cement factory. So far I have never seen a press or television report that touches upon the conditions of cement workers.

Other industries are almost as rare in the world of travel writers and foreign correspondents. You may catch a glimpse of a place of work, but that's all. The chance is greater if the report comes from a developing nation or the states behind the Iron Curtain, where visits to factories are often obligatorily included in the programmes. But these descriptions are usually affected by the ignorance of the visitor and the limitations of the visit, and so offer very little.

In the 1920s a Swedish author, Ivar Lo-Johansson, had the ambitious plan to describe all the countries of the world by describing their places of work. Today that plan is further than ever from realization. You can only give a good account of a place of work in a foreign country if you have your own experience, in your own country, of its equivalent, Those who write usually lack that experience. Those who have the experience don't usually write. They don't even travel for that reason.

• What have you read about your own job in travelogues or in foreign reports?

Aid: Travelogues can be found in public libraries under "N" (in Sweden). As far as I know, no one has yet systematically examined travelogues from different periods to establish what impression they give of work and industries. It would be interesting to do this for a few selected typical countries.

• Write to your local paper, your trade union journal, to radio or television and suggest that they report on the industry that involves your job in some of the countries that interest you. Emphasize your opinion that such reports should be made with the assistance of Swedish workers.

Trips Abroad

The fact that we know so little about our workmates in other countries is also due to the way we travel. Few things have changed as fundamentally as the travel habits of the Swedes.

In the old days, all travel was connected with work. Journeying was part of a craftsman's education. Many journeymen crossed the borders to get to know places and conditions of work in foreign countries. These habits survived the guild-system. Even when I was a child there were a surprising amount of older workers who had had some professional experience abroad before settling down. Some had tried their luck in America, others had spent their years as journeymen in Finland or Russia or on the Continent.

In the 1960s, mobility in the European labour markets was greater than ever before. But now it involved almost exclusively people coming to us. We had work to offer, we had the highest salaries. That was fine. But it stopped us making contact with working life in other countries.

Trips abroad have become part of our leisure and recreation. Swedish people go on holiday abroad. We no longer work our way through foreign countries — we arrive with the money in our pocket, in cars and caravans, on chartered flights. We don't get to know the factories but the beaches and nightclubs. We don't go there to work but to be waited upon. It costs us about 3 billion kronor each year.

I realize as well as anyone that sunshine is nice after a long winter, that you want to spend the holiday with your family and forget about work. But it is true that the holiday trip will often turn into escapism. It certainly gives a distorted picture of the countries you visit.

Twenty-five years ago it might have been a possible to control this development. We would have been able to consider the matter and then consciously choose between several different alternatives, such as:

1. Do we want to build up a tourist industry which aims at giving Swedes access to a mass version of international playboy life? In that case, we want to make sure that the cement workers in Degerhamn can go easily and cheaply

by chartered flights to foreign resorts and experience barbecues, nightclubs and tax-free liquor.

2. Or do we want to build up a tourist industry which concentrates on giving Swedish workers a chance to get to know their workmates in foreign countries and gain access to international occupational communication? In that case, we want to make sure that the cement workers in Degerhamn can go easily and cheaply by chartered flights to Germany or India or Japan to meet other cement workers, observe their environment and discuss mutual problems.

3. Or do we want to build up a tourist industry which would enable workers in the export industry to see how the products they make are used in other countries? Or enable them to follow the products back towards the raw material stage and meet those who produce these materials? In that case we want that access to be cheap and easy.

4. Or do we want to organize an exchange system which would enable Swedish workers to take a job for a year or two in some other country in some other part of the world? Instead of spending a week on a crowded beach in Majorca, you and your family could have moved to the US or the Soviet Union, to England or France, to work there, to get into a circle of friends and get to know the country.

5. Or do we want to concentrate on increased contact and understanding between Swedes and immigrants in different industries? In that case we want to make sure that the Swedes can go easily and cheaply with their foreign workmates to Greece and Turkey, to Yugoslavia and Finland — to meet them on their home ground, where their language and nationality are not a handicap but an asset.

You may still have chosen the beach. But I'm not so sure. I have spoken to several Swedish cement workers who sneaked around cement factories during their holiday in Spain or Italy.

But without an interpreter and any previous arrangements or support from their surroundings, they never plucked up the courage to enter the building.

One thing is certain: if we had shown a little more foresight, the Swedish tourist billions could have realised other dreams than those presently encouraged and exploited by travel agents. But we never had any well-considered alternatives. We never made a conscious choice. We simply followed the law of least resistance and let ourselves be ruled by market forces.

• Have you ever visited the equivalent of your own place of work in another country?

• Write to your union and suggest that they arrange chartered trips for their members according to the alternative which appeals to you most.

Aid: In his book *Sötebrödet* (Halcyon) (Sthlm 1975), Billy Ehn describes getting to know a group of Yugoslav papermill workers in the village of Åsen in the province of Dalsland, and then going to see their home province of Serbia. This investigation was initiated by Swedish papermill workers who wanted to get to know the background of their Yugoslav workmates. At the end of the book is a chapter describing the process for making such investigations.

Foreign cement factories can be found in the *World Cement Directory*, which is in the Cement Library and can be ordered at public libraries. Many other industries have similar catalogues. Your trade union will help you contact the union of the foreign factory. The trip itself can be arranged by taking a chartered flight to the place that is closest to your destination. On request, some travel agents will help find an interpreter and pre-arrange a special programme for a small group.

The Return Journey

In the *World Cement Directory* we found Cliffe. It looked exciting on the map — a small, isolated village on a headland jutting out into the Thames estuary.

We took a chartered flight from Sweden to London. The local travel agent informed us that we should take a train from Waterloo Station to Gravesend. It was one of those slow, tatty commuter trains with plush seats and views over thousands of backyards and sitting-rooms. The bus to Cliffe went every two hours. However, when we arrived, it turned out that the factory had closed down.

After travelling so far we wanted at least to see it. Three kilns, wet method, annual capacity of 355,000 tons, according to the catalogue. The chimneys still rose above the water some miles away from the village. We asked at the local post office. No, there were no buses going that way anymore.

It was a nice day, though, a cool wind and blazing sunshine, so we started to walk. A yellow Mini pulled up next to us.

"I was in the post office and I heard where you wanted to go," the driver said. "I'm on my way to do some shopping in Gravesend but I have time to give you a lift to the factory."

His name was Cyril Edwards. When we arrived at the gates, it suddenly occurred to him that he had left his thermos flask behind in the canteen when the factory closed in 1969. He decided to come in with us to see whether it was still there. He told us he had worked there as a burner for twenty-five years.

Cyril Edwards. The factory is sort of his again since the company left it.

William Aspdin's kiln in Northfleet, where the Portland cement was created — accidentally. See Chapter 27.

He had now been transferred to the new factory in Northfleet. Although he still lived in Cliffe and had his own car, he hadn't visited the factory since it closed down. We went to the canteen by the burner's platform to look for his flask. Everything had been ripped away.

"Just imagine, this was the place for the washbasin. I've been standing here so many times, looking out over the river. In the control room at Northfleet you see neither sun nor moon. It was nice here, you know, especially at night when we were left alone, no bosses, just mates, on summer nights we'd go out and sit on the steps, with the wind coming from the sea..."

It was all coming back to him, as if the factory was his again, since the company left it. He went up to the hole in the kiln where he used to stand staring into the glowing mass. All he could see now was cold darkness. Out of habit he checked the instrument panel. It had been torn from the wall and the indicators swung forlornly back and forth in the draught...

This affected him more than anything else. These indicators that he had been observing so keenly for twenty-five years, strongly aware of his responsibility, prepared to react at the slightest deviation! These indicators which used to be so important — here they were, swinging in the wind, meaning nothing at all!

Having forgotten all about his thermos flask, about the shopping he was to do in Gravesend, he now wanted to go and see the clinker cooler, he wanted to see everything: the coal mill, the cement mills, the canteen, all of it. Memories appeared — the heat under the kilns, the experiments with water to cool red spots, the explosions in the coal chamber, the faces of his mates. The whole of his life came back to him: the war, the Thirties, the stories of older workers in those days, so many generations that had been making cement there before him. "Wait, I must show you…"

And before we knew what was happening, we were back in his yellow Mini and driving to his present job (although he goes there by moped, he won't ruin the paint on the car by leaving it in the car park with all its factory dust) and stopped in front of a mass of warehouses in Northfleet.

"It should be somewhere in here," he said, and we went back and forth through meandering corridors until finally we found a back door and entered a tiny yard where an old brick shaft kiln rose, surrounded by the metal walls of the warehouses. "This is Aspdin's kiln. This is where the Portland cement was made the first time."

We are in the classical country of origin for cement, and he drives us back and forth between Swanscombe, West Thurrock and Dartford, through what seemed to be a cemetery of closed-down factories — each collapsed chimney, each broken lump of concrete has its own story and behind him generations of cement workers appear, to his surprise as much as ours, until the day has passed and he suddenly remembers that…

"Blimey, I was going bloody shopping in Gravesend!"

- The job you are doing has been done by others before you. Who were they? What did they hope for, what did they fight for, and what did they achieve? How can you get to know them?

Aid: This book.

The deserted rotary kiln in Cliffe.

2. THE COMPANY

All Swedish cement factories now belong to the same company: The Industri AB Euroc. Its origin is the Skånska Cement Company, founded in 1871. Its history has been recorded frequently and comprehensively for the first time in:

GRANSTRÖM, G.A.
The Swedish Cement Sales Company 1893-1922.
A memorial publication, Sthlm 1923.

The company selling cement, called Cementa, was a cartel dominated by Skånska Cement to control the prices on the Swedish cement market. The author, a mining engineer, was a retired director of one of the companies in this cartel. He had been Managing Director of Ölands Cement for twenty-five years and a board member of Cementa for twenty years. A reliable man, he was given the task of writing the history of the cartel.

The book describes fairly comprehensively the seven companies that were then the members of Cementa. They are presented as a large happy group of siblings — not a mention is made of the fact that they had all been forced on to their knees by Skånska Cement. The author concentrates mainly on the technical problems in the factories at Lomma, Limhamn, Degerhamn, Visby, Hällekis, Maltesholm, Klagshamn and Bromölla. The book has plenty of illustrations: factory facades and portraits of directors and technicians.

It is possible that these factories also employed workers. Not that there is any mention of them in the text — but a couple of photographs contain a few diffuse figures which could be workers. In one picture from the limestone quarry in Maltesholm in 1910, for example, there is a suggestion in the background of a man pushing a wheelbarrow loaded with stone.

In 1931, Skånska Cement had its sixtieth anniversary. A bold proposal was then made, and a Social Democrat economist was asked to write the jubilee publication:

KOCK, Karin
Skånska Cementaktiebolaget 1871-1931.
Memorial. Uppsala 1932.

One sole worker can be found in Karin Kock's memorial of 1932. He is nameless and leans decoratively against a clean, quiet, inoperative cement mill.

Kock's book follows the usual pattern, describing economy and technology. The only work revealed to us is that done by company management and technicians. They look out from their portraits, it's their work that we are invited to admire in all the pictures. One sole worker can be found. Nameless, he leans decoratively against an inoperative cement mill in a factory free from dust and noise. The final chapter of the book pays homage to the cement company as a social builder and exemplary employer.

As early as 1903, Skånska Cement founded The Scania Employers' Federation in the Building Materials Industry. Thanks to its dominant position within this federation, the company was able to take over the management of the General Employers' Federation and in 1907 guided this federation into the Swedish Employers' Federation, where Skånska Cement was one of the main members. The company then led the employers in building materials out of the General Employers' Federation and into a new national federation, The Building Materials Federation, where the part played by Skånska Cement was even more dominant.

The creation and development of these organizations are described in:

BJURLING, Oscar
The General Employers' Federation 1922-1932.
Malmö 1933.

BJURLING, Oscar
The Building Materials Federation, 1908-1933.
Malmö 1933.

It's a distinctive feature of an employers' federation that the members are often competitors until they manage to tie down or swallow each other. With the cartel, Skånska Cement had succeeded in tying down all the major members of the Building Materials Federation even before it was founded. By and by, the members were overpowered and taken over. Many smaller companies met with the same fate. How did Skånska Cement take advantage of its dominant position within the employers' federation when the company established its empire? What tensions did this create within the organization?

No such questions are ever mentioned in the memorials. The whole account is dominated by the fight against the mutual enemy — the workers.

Three years later the cement factory in Degerhamn celebrated its fiftieth anniversary and published:

KILLIG, Fr.
Ölands Cement Company 1886-1936.
The history. Kalmar 1936.

Killig was Managing Director of the factory. Keen on history, he had done some research into the traditional craft of local stonemasons (Acta Oleandica, 5). He also appreciated "the peace of the endless expanses on the island and the blue sea surrounding it". But when it came to cement he couldn't see anything but financial prospects and technical problems. Not a word or a picture indicate that any workers existed in the factory during these fifty years.

In the midst of the Second World War, Skånska Cement's subsidiary in Slite celebrated its twenty-fifth anniversary:

SLITE
Cement and Lime AB 1917-1942.

The book has some proud pictures of buildings erected with cement from the factory, such as Södersjukhuset, a Stockholm hospital, and the concrete "umbrella" in Stureplan, a square in Stockholm. A few lines also suggest that cement is actually made by humans. But all we are told about these humans is the various ways in which the company caters for them: "There is of course a sauna, and we are building an 'interest office'." Apart from this, the whole stage is taken by owners and management.

Are they worthy of all this attention? Hardly. The one person within the Swedish cement industry with some kind of personal luminosity is R.F. Berg.

He was a versatile, far-sighted man. There is plenty of material on him, of course. He wrote articles and delivered speeches, he presented motions to the City Council in Malmö and to many of the associations that counted him as a member; he wrote memoranda to the Board of the company and to his own colleagues and corresponded profusely with family and friends.

If Mr R.F. Berg had been a politician, artist or author, academic research would have taken an interest in the documents he left behind. These would have been subject to much critical discussion. Berg's contribution would have been analysed and evaluated from different angles. But since he happened to be an industrial company director, any critical examination is considered either superfluous or irrelevant.

The only man who wanted to and was allowed to go through the material left behind by Berg was a writer of detective stories commissioned to do so by the company. The main feature of this publication is the absolutely boundless admiration the writer has for the object of his biography.

MELLVIG, Folke
An Industrialist and an Idealist.
The book about R.F. Berg written for the 100th anniversary of his birth on 31 May 1946. Malmö 1945.

In 1950, the first issue of Skånska Cement's internal journal, *Around the Rotary Kiln*, was published. It has changed its name several times since then but is now named *The Rotary Kiln*. During its first two decades, this journal often contained articles about the history of the company and its subsidiaries — always seen through the eyes of the management.

In 1954, Slite Cement changed its name and became, in name as well as in practice, part of Skånska Cement. To "commemorate the transition to a new era", the company hired two professional writers of memorials and published:

HÅKANSSON, L-M and AHLGREN, Arvid
The Burning Kilns at Slite: A Book About the History of Gotland's Cement Industry
Slite Cement and Lime Co. Slite 1954.

The cement factories at Visby, Valleviken and Slite whirl past —
again in the shape of facades and leading personages. But in the
very last few pages, for the first time in the history of cement
industry anniversaries, the names of five workers are mentioned.
It's the trade union's local committee of management in Slite.
"Relations between management and trade unions in Slite are
distinguished by trust and mutual understanding."

Skånska Cement still had one competitor to deal with:
Gullhögens bruk. Its history was written by a retired director
to commemorate the fiftieth anniversary of the works:

GLISE, Hjalmar
Gullhögens bruk 1916-1966.
Skövde 1966.

The usual official photographs of the "workforce" are here
complemented by the odd picture of men at work. Everything
is of course seen loyally from the point of view of owners
and management, but there is some room for criticism from
outsiders, e.g. concerning the environment. At least it's
mentioned and discussed. This may have been the reason why
the book was reserved for internal distribution within the
company, "to employees with many years of employment".

We are now approaching our own time. The centenary of
Skånska Cement takes place in 1971. The company has now
changed its name and calls itself Cementa, after the old cartel,
whose original members have all been swallowed up. A new
Board makes fresh efforts, turning straight to the employees
with a publication that is supposed to contain critical views of
the company:

CEMENTA.
*Insight — Opinion. A Cross-Section of a Company. As It Is and
as We Would Like It to Be. Facts and Attitudes in Articles and
Interviews.*
Kristianstad 1971.

The articles have been written by different managers within the company. The interviews have been made by Marketing Konsult in Solna. The book was produced by PR Konsult in Malmö in collaboration with Gumaelius' advertising agency. It laid a foundation for study groups with three thousand participants, producing a total of eight thousand suggestions for improvements. These suggestions were then processed by the Personnel Administration Service in Malmö.

Many people were disappointed that this jubilee campaign did not lead to any concrete measures being taken. Still, the effort in itself was encouraging.

The past, however, that which can't be undone, was not suitable for experiments. This had to be entrusted to a reliable conservative historian who wrote the traditional commemorative publication:

ÅBERG, Alf
Cement Over 100 Years: A Chronicle of the Skånska Cement Company — AB Cementa.
Malmö 1972.

It's a long time since the history of our country was that of its kings. But in Åberg's book the history of Swedish industry is still that of its directors.

The Past Started Yesterday

"So what? Let the companies keep their history — we're taking over the future!"

I don't believe in that attitude. If there was anything I learnt in Latin America, it was the fact that the future in fact started yesterday. History is not past, it continues tomorrow.

I toured Latin America, visiting and examining North American companies, finding that these huge multinationals rule as they like in many Latin American states. And all that was written about them was controlled by themselves. This astonished me at first:

Every minor poet these days qualifies for a biography. But who will write a biography of the Marcona Mining Company? Who is currently studying the influence of the Southern Peru Copper Corporation? Who is researching the history of the Cerro de Pasco Corporation? These giant companies that move mountains, create cities and level them once more to the ground, that intervene in the lives of millions, whose influence extends over centuries and continents — what makes them so uninteresting from a scientific point of view?

At most they have been the subject of a commissioned work commemorating some anniversary or a romanticized brochure from the company's PR department.

Sven Lindqvist, *The Shadow*, p. 201

The company's representatives were happy to talk at length about present problems and future prospects. But they were clearly annoyed whenever historical aspects were brought up.

"We want to get away from the past," Bookers in Guyana said. This company established itself with the help of the slave trade.

"We are still being accused of the sins of the past," DEMBA said. This company acquired its riches for peanuts from poor peasants who had no idea of the assets of their land.

Both found it unfair that the sins of the past should still be held against them.

But *the result* of the sins of the past — the land, the buildings, the machines, in brief: the capital — that of course they wanted to hold on to. That was holy private property that must not be touched.

History is important because *the result* of it remains. That's what I learnt in Latin America. The past still yields dividends. The past still holds power.

Therefore, companies take great care to keep control of their history. Therefore, it appears to be the same, whether it is written by faithful servants, professional supporters or reliable academics. Throughout eleven memorials the basic features of the history of the Industri AB Euroc constantly remain the same:

1. The company management is wise and far-sighted. It has never made a mistake.
2. The company management is fair. Its decisions have never been worthy of any blame.
3. The company belongs to its shareholders. Their contribution to production has been far more important than that of the workers.
4. The workers' contribution to the development of the cement industry has been mainly twofold: They have made unrealistic claims. They have enjoyed the company's consideration.
5. For more than a hundred years, nothing has ever occurred that could possibly have given cement workers a justified reason to register pride or fury.

- Has any book been written about the company that you work for? What picture does it give of your place of work, of your job, of the contribution of your predecessors? Whose history is being *recorded*?

Aids: Books about local companies should be available at your local public library (in Sweden under the library code Qz). The list of the latest memorials usually includes earlier ones. Remember that the history of the company may also be described in publications of employers' federations, related companies, suppliers and competitors.

Where Swedish industrial history is concerned, reference is always made to two main books: Arthur Montgomery's *The Breakthrough of Industrialism in Sweden* (4th ed. Surte 1970) and Torsten Gardlund's *The Industrial Society* (Stockholm 1942). They give the general background but are written more

---

or less from the same directors' point of view as the companies' own publications.

General books on Swedish history don't mention jobs in many words. So far I have only found one that even mentions the word cement — Carlsson and Rosén, *Swedish History II*, which summarizes the contribution of the cement workers in one single sentence: "The Swedish cement industry was founded in 1871 with the appearance of Skånska Cement, the largest company in this industry." Those most likely to find facts about their predecessors in books of general history are workers in the metal, wood or textile industries.

3. THE UNION

"But it's only natural that the company management should be at the centre of a story commissioned and paid for by the company! In the same way, the staff journal is the natural organ of the management. The workers have their own organizations to publish journals and write their history!"

Let's examine this objection. Most of the workers employed by the Industri AB Euroc are members of the Swedish Factory Workers' Union. The union journal, *The Factory Worker*, previously called *The Union Comrade*, was first published in 1898 under the name of *The Labourer*. I went through all annual editions to find out what the journal had written about the companies now forming part of Euroc. That took me a week. It appeared to me that four periods could be discerned in the history of the journal:

During the first years, the journal often had concrete and highly critical descriptions of agitation activities at different places of work:

The Labourer. Journal of the Swedish Labourers Union.

Degerhamn, Öland.

"On July 13th, I gave a talk in the Hall of Good Templars. It lasted for an hour and a half and was attentively received by a little more than one hundred and fifty workers. Because work at the cement factory goes on night and day with very irregular working hours, it was impossible to get all labourers to come to a meeting, even if it were arranged in the daytime. The workers present at the meeting urged me to stay on until Sunday to enable everyone to hear me, in the interest of the success of the union. On Sunday 17th, I gave another speech on the above mentioned premises, which was received with great interest by those present.

I must say that the workers' conditions are very poor in this place. Women and children are exploited to the point of exhaustion, the work is unhealthy, the working hours much too long and the pay poor.

Women work at the lime and cement pits, excavating, and they roll coke and work in the stamp house. These women handle their wheel-barrows with surprising skill. Plenty of accidents occur in the factory. While I was there, a young girl had her fingers caught under a press. A doctor had to be called in to amputate them. Some time ago, a man was buried alive by cement powder falling over him. A couple of other workers who rushed to assist him were close to being hit by a cement wagon, which was being lowered from a considerable height. Better protection for the life and limb of workers here is necessary. The area surrounding the factory is constantly engulfed by a thick cloud of smoke and dust, obviously harmful to the health and development of the children. But the income of the breadwinners is small, and in order to exist, they have to let their children drudge in the company's factories."

(November 1898)

There are other examples from this period, such as:

Working conditions at the Limhamn lime pit. 1901:no. 3
The fight for Union rights at the cement factory in
Visby. 1908:nos. 2,3,8.
Workers' Solidarity (Hällekis). 1914, p. 6.
Whip it out! (Limhamn). 1915, p. 81.

After 1915 came a new period, which was to last for about a quarter of the new century. In this time the journal announced hardly any news from a single factory, at least not from any cement factory.

The third period covers the years 1940-1968. A large number of factory reports were then printed, which could have been included in any employers' journal. For example:

Cement, 1941, p. 76.
A walk with the engineers around the new factory in Köping. Only criticism: the workers are messy on the toilets. "With such bad manners it is often a waste of money and effort to procure perfect lavatory equipment." Comrade Gottfrid Hill complains about poor interest in the union.

Jubilee in Slite. 1943, p. 60.
A short report on the 25th anniversary of company and union.

Cement Manufacture and Accommodation Problems. 1944, p. 156
Another walk round the Köping factory, this time together with the chairman and treasurer of the union's local branch. They are very pleased with everything. "What is not quite satisfactory, however, is the passive stance taken to the union by far too many of his workmates."

Limhamn-cement. 194 9:no. 1.
An impressed reporter walks round the "foggy bank of smoke resting like a dome over the whole great plant". In passing he runs into some workers who claim that they enjoy good co-operation with the company management. "The roar of machinery does not permit a longer interview. Lind only has time to say that they are very bothered by the noise..."

Close-up of company Board. 1952, p. 11.
A comprehensive, very positive report of a meeting with the company Board in Limhamn.

Three men operating the fully automated factory in Slite. 1964:no. 11.
Delighted praise of the new factory.

From Suspicion to Co-Operation. 1967:no. 16.
Very positive report of company health care at Gullhögen.

Cement: A Key Product in Modern Society. 1968, p. 22.
An enthusiastic presentation of the new Limhamn factory.

The fourth period starts in 1969. The headlines now often contain direct quotations. The tone is sharper, there is more criticism against the company. Workers who have objections to the union are also given space. For example:

"I wouldn't like to see my children working here." 1970:12, A report from Limhamn. "I have nothing to say", is Jensen's point of view. "Nothing at all, really. I can tell off the person packing the sacks, tell him it's going too fast, which may get him to slow down a little. And I can tell off the shop steward, but he won't take any notice of what I say. I don't call that participation... I believe we need a union but it

should be a union that has the time to listen to what we workers have to say. After all, it's our problems."
"They should be forced to stop the crusher." 1971:15.
A critical report of a place of work at the Cementa stone crusher at Tegene. Dust level:115. Maximum permitted value:1.

"What about the wages gap?"
A report from Limhamn about monthly salaries for workers.

Protection works fine here (but it has been better...) 1971:20.
Protection at Stora Vika is held up as an example.

"Why are we on the Board if we aren't told anything?" 1973:13.
A critical report about the take-over of Gullhögen by Cementa.

I shall not continue this list, which would soon become too long, especially since the closure of the Hällekis cement factory and the asbestos cement factory at Lomma. These examples will do to illustrate the fourth period, when, for the first time in over fifty years, the Factory Workers' Union journal resumes its critical attitude to the separate companies.

For this reason, the union journal does not represent the history of the cement workers. Neither do separate factories play a part in the memorials of the union, written by the editor of the union journal:

KARLBOM, Torvald e.a.
The History of the Swedish Labourers' and Factory Workers' Union. 1-2.
Sthlm 1941, 1944.

KARLBOM, Torvald e.a.
The Swedish Factory Workers' Union: 60 Years.
Sthlm 19 51.
This regional jubilee book is somewhat more rewarding:

UHLÉN, Axel
The Fight of the Unions in Malmö During Seven Decades.
Malmö 1949.

This book has a comprehensive index, referring to descriptions of many conflicts at Lomma, Limhamn and Klagshamn.

The commemorative publications of the local branches of trade unions give the most vivid descriptions of the company. Some examples:

LIMHAMN
The Swedish Labourers' and Factory Workers' Union.
Local union 60 1898-1948. Arlöv 1948.

LOMMA
The Swedish Labourers and Factory Workers' Union.
Local union 30 1900-1940. Malmö 1940.
Local union 30 1900-1950. Malmö 1950.
Local union 30 1900-1960. Malmö 1960.

HÄLLEKIS
The Swedish Labourers' and Factory Workers' Union.
Local union 225 1906-1935. Sthlm 1937.
Local union 225 1906-1946. Lidköping 1946.
Local union 225 1906-1956. Falköping 1956.

BROMÖLLA
The Swedish Labourers' and Factory Workers' Union
Local union 227 1906-1946. Kristianstad 1946.

The first thing you notice is the small, modest format of local union booklets, in comparison to the splendid publications of the company. The impression the company management present of themselves has been paid out of production, whereas that of the union is financed by members' fees. The union could not afford to employ academics or professional writers. The sparse photographs are of poor quality.

The local memorials contain much valuable information, especially from the early years of the local trade unions, describing conflicts over union rights, strikes and lockouts. But they also give cause for some critical reflections:

All of them are jubilee publications, written in the solemn vein usually employed for jubilees. Any search for everyday, concrete details yields very little.

They also seem to follow the same pattern. If a previous publication has been written about the same department, this is repeated, in a watered-down version in the following. The trade union movement does not seem anxious to create new patterns.

The main sources are protocols and agreements. Only by exception have the authors used letters, newspaper reports and other documents or interviews.

Very little is said about the people, in most cases only names and positions are mentioned. Where did they come from, where did they go, what did they do, what were they like, how did they change, why were they remembered?

Union work is not related to politics. How, for example, did the change in power balance between local government and the company affect the position of the unions? How did the union fight for different laws and reforms? What did these come to mean to the activities of the union?

Pay negotiations are at the centre. But what do the figures mean? Where did the money go? How did the union's fight for a better quality of living for its members affect the activities of the union?

The memorials say very little about the work itself, about premises and machinery, about work organization, time studies, working environment, external environment, etc. The image of the company is entrusted to the company management.

The deficiencies of the memorials reflect the fact that local trade union branches have long been regarded as fairly unimportant within the trade union movement as a whole, where the central organizations are quite dominant.

Now, however, this development is changing direction. Legislation for work environment and workers' participation are for the first time handing over important tasks to local branches. The conquest of a workplace can only be done locally. The centrally suggested workers' funds aim even further: to a conquest of the whole company.

One important step in this conquest is the creation of a new company image, an image with work and workers at the centre. For this we need a new kind of research, and this book attempts to provide some of the tools for it.

- What is told in your union's jubilee publication about your work, your place of work and the people working in it? What would you like to know of the things not covered by the book? What do you know that you think ought to be included?

- If you want to penetrate this point more deeply — examine how your place of work has been treated in the union journal and in the history of the union. What concrete problems at your place of work have been dealt with at the union congresses?

Aids: A list of local memorials is included in *Yearbook for Cultural-Historical Societies of Workers 1963-1965*. The yearbook is a continuation of *Notices from the Cultural-Historical Societies*

---

of Workers, which was first published in 1926. This journal contains much valid material on the history of the workers and for the years 1936-1951, regular lists of similar material in other journals.

The Yearbook of the Workers' Movement can be sent for by paying the annual subscription of 20 kronor to The Workers' Cultural-Historical Society, number 1725-1. The yearbook is published in collaboration with the *Workers' Movement's Archive* (Upplandsgatan 5, Box 1124, 111 81 Sthlm, tel. 08/24 17 60). They can assist you with both material and methods if you want to explore the history of your trade union. On request, the archive will send, free of charge, a list of about fifty *local workers' and popular movement archives* throughout the country.

Old files of the *union journal* should be available at your local library, if not it can be ordered there. The Labourers and Factory Workers' Union's congress protocols have been printed since 1897, with a subject index since 1906, also with a motion index since 1913, and with a name index since 1920. In the *union archive* you will find the correspondence with local branches on microfilm, which can be ordered by the local library.

Start by finding your own local trade union's old protocols, letters and other documents. They can be found in the most unexpected places — in Slite, I found them in the boiler-room of the home of a former Board member. Now they have been removed to the District Archive in Visby.

Sylve Hägvall, the union chairman in Slite, reading old protocols at the Visby District Archive.

4. THE WORKERS' COMMUNE

"This is not a matter for trade unions. It's a political task. The issue of the ownership of means of production has been the decisive watershed in Swedish politics, ever since the first Social Democrat party programme in 1897. Go to the local organizations of the party, the workers' communes. There you will find a view of the company quite different from the one presented by the management."

Let's examine this statement. The history of the workers' commune has been written in two of the places dominated by the Industri AB Euroc:

JACOBSSON, Eric
The History of the 50-Year-Old Workers' Commune in Slite
Slite 1967.

SVENSSON, Nils A.
Lomma Workers' Commune: 70th Anniversary 1901-1971.
Arlöv 1971

Both of these publications are small and modest compared to those of the company. They are both so similar that we only need to discuss one of them, Eric Jacobsson's book.

Slite is a little village on the east coast of Gotland. At the beginning of the twentieth century, lime burning and the export of butter and eggs to England were the main sources of income. Eric Jacobsson writes:

Politically, the Nyström company "ruled" at the beginning of the twentieth century, then the Degerman company, when the county was ruled by the office manager, Mr Olsson. At the beginning of the century, the "fyrk" taxation system was applied, but when this was abolished, there were still ways of keeping the workers from voting, such as making the tax collection between 10 and 12am and then writing a poll register, where people who had not paid their taxes lost their right to vote.

It was the cement industry that created the conditions for an organized workers' movement in this place.

When the building of the factory commenced, a large number of labourers and factory workers, carpenters, smiths, mechanics and others came to live in Slite. On the 11 August 1917, the Slite workers' commune was formed after a speech given by the Social Democratic party agitator Himdén.

PROGRAMME
for
The Swedish Social Democrat Party
agreed on the 4th party congress in Stockholm
July, 4th, 1897.

General principles.
Social Democracy differs from other political parties in as much as it wants to completely transform the economic organisation of the Capitalist society and achieve the social liberation of the working classes, securing and developing spiritual and material culture.

The main reason for the defects that cripple today's civilisation is the private Capitalist production method, which has dismissed old petty-bourgeois social conditions, gathered the capital in the hands of a small number of people and divided the society into workers and Capitalists, the layer in between consisting partly of vanishing social groups — peasants, craftsmen and small merchants — partly of new groups being formed.

In the old days, the right to private ownership of means of production used to be a natural condition for production, since it assured the producer of his product. But at the same time as large-scale production exceeds crafts, machines replace tools, world trade and mass production abolish all market limits, the real producers turn into a class of salaried workers, who in [...]

PROGRAM

. . för . .

Sverges Socialdemokratiska Arbetareparti

antaget på 4:de partikongressen i Stockholm

den 4 juli 1897.

Allmänna grundsatser.

Socialdemokratin skiljer sig från andra politiska partier därigenom, att den vill helt omdana det borgerliga samhällets ekonomiska organisation och genomföra arbetareklassens sociala frigörelse, till betryggande och utveckling af den andliga och materiella kulturen.

Hufvudorsaken till de lyten, som vidhäfta våra dagars civilisation, är nämligen det privatkapitalistiska produktionssättet, som upplöst de gamla småborgerliga samhällsförhållandena, samlat förmögenheten i ett mindretals händer och delat samhället i arbetare och kapitalister, med mellanliggande lager af dels försvinnande äldre samhällsklasser — småbönder, handtverkare och småhandlande — dels uppkommande nya.

Den privata eganderätten till produktionsmedlet var i förra tider en naturlig betingelse för produktion, i det den tillförsäkrade producenten hans produkt. Men i samma mån stordriften undantränger handtverket, arbetsmaskinen verktyget, världshandeln och massproduktionen nedbryta alla marknadsgränser, i samma mån blifva de verkliga producenterna förvandlade i en klass af lönarbetare, som i sig

The programme assumed by the workers in Slite started like this:

> Social Democracy differs from other political parties, in as much as it wants to completely transform the economical organization of the Capitalist society and achieve the social liberation of the working classes, securing and developing spiritual and material culture.
>
> The main reason for the defects that cripple today's civilisation is the private Capitalist production method, which has dismissed old petty-bourgeois social conditions, gathered the capital in the hands of a small number of people and made the opposition between workers and Capitalists the distinguishing feature of today's society.

The Slite workers must have recognized themselves easily in this description. But other issues were seen as more urgent — such as the lack of provisions. The young organization also discussed the cottage hospital, the arranging of a Civic Park and a Civic Hall, the need for a new school and candidates for different tasks. But there is no evidence that the take-over of power in the Slite Cement and Lime Co. was ever discussed.

In 1920, the Social Democracy assumed a new programme which took a sharper attitude to the companies. The concept of exploitation became a central issue:

> The right to private ownership of means of production in the old days used to be a means to assure the producer that he could have his product. But the Capitalist private property has instead become a means for the owners to rob the workers of the fruits of their labour. This Capitalist exploitation dominates, although to a varying degree, modern society and leaves no aspect of it unaffected...
>
> The class struggle between the exploited and the exploiters have a modern distinguishing feature: The

working classes are aware of their historic mission to carry a new production method, liberated of the profit interest, and emerge as the leading class among the exploited, who have been made dependent and insecure by Capitalism.

Whether the workers' commune ever discussed the new party programme, is not clear. It's doubtful whether the working-class people of Slite were really aware of their historic mission. Did anyone really explain to each member the way in which workers, especially in Slite, were robbed of the fruits of their labour? I doubt it. The main company of the town is mentioned only once during the entire 1920s:

> The issue of a Civic Park was resolved that year, as Slite Cement through Captain Nyström allocated 5,000 square metres of land to the west of Solklint.

The exploitation remained a theoretical problem, whereas the practical difficulty in Slite was the fact that many people could not find an employer willing to exploit them. 1931: "Unemployment had grown worse." 1932: "This year unemployment was the most urgent issue and it called for extra meetings. Work subsidized by the government was initiated along with local council work. Piecework rates were introduced for some jobs. At the end of the year, eighty registered workers were still unemployed." 1933-34: "During these years unemployment was the main issue, causing a lot of ill feeling."

It is not mentioned at whom this ill feeling was directed, only in passing that the main company of the place had changed hands — not to be nationalized but to become part of Skånska Cement:

> The cement company changes hands, as Skånska Cement has taken over share majority. As the Chair became vacant, Herman Engström was elected Chairman.

Meanwhile, the number of votes for the Social Democrats had increased from 87 in 1922 to 203 in 1923 and 347 in 1930. In 1934, the Social Democrats had their political breakthrough in Slite:

> Due to the majority gained at the local government elections in 1934, some desirable reforms could be carried out. The workers now were in majority and held the Chairmanship of County Council, District Council, Board of Guardians and other Boards.

This takeover of political power led to many new tasks: medical examination of school children, free dental care, elementary school amounting to seven years, the buying of land for a public beach, supplementary pensions paid by the County Council, etc. It is understandable that the workers' commune temporarily abandoned the more fundamental issues as yet beyond their control. The company is only mentioned a couple of times in the historical description of these years:

> 1939-42: These years an extension of the sewage was discussed, as well as the building of an old people's home and a civic hall, which, however, were referred to a future date, since Slite Cement and Gotland's power station had formed a new company to build a cinema and a hall for meetings.
>
> Slite Cement offered the County to buy the hotel, as they were going to build a new one. This offer was, however, withdrawn... Slite Cement gave 15,000 kronor as a basic contribution to a civic hall at the 25th anniversary of the company. This was done before they decided to build a cinema.

In 1944, the Social Democrat Party adopted a new programme, written by Ernst Wigforss. It starts like this:

The aim of Social Democracy is to transform the economic organisation of the Capitalist society, handing over the right to decide about production to the people, liberating most of the population from the dependence of a small number of Capitalists and replacing the social system based on economical classes with a system of co-operation based on freedom and equality, for all citizens.

Power concentration in industry, rather than exploitation, was here emphasized:

Even more prominent than the accumulation of riches is the concentration of economic power. Even where the right to ownership is divided into somewhat wider circles, the power to decide about the administration of the capital is gathered into the hands of a few, whilst most people depend for their survival on decisions made by these few on the basis of their own personal interest or their personal judgement regarding the interests of society.

The records reveal that the Slite Workers' Commune discussed the 1944 party programme. The workers in Slite had illuminating material close by. Skånska Cement had bought and closed down the cement factories at Maltesholm in 1928, at Klagshamn in 1939, at Bromölla and Visby in 1940. Cement production at Valleviken was already discontinued, and the workers were transferred to Slite in 1947. All these decisions had been made by a few on the basis of their own personal interest or personal judgement regarding the interest of society. Slite's future fate was in the hands of the same few.

But judging by the history of the Workers' Commune, the power of these few never seems to have been discussed at all during the 1940s and 50s. Quite different matters were highlighted: a laundry, a vocational school, the licensing of restaurants, electric heating of the church. Fewer people were joining in the May Day demonstrations and these were completely cancelled at the end of the 1950s.

In 1960 a new party programme was assumed, which established:

> The effective democratic control of power positions in industry is still lacking. The great number of wage-earners in private industry depends on decisions formed by a few mainly guided by their own personal interests.

In the Slite Workers' Commune, these decisions seem to have been criticized on two occasions in the 1960s:

> Regarding Cement's tipping of refuse and ashes in Vägomeviken, it was stated that the Health authorities ought to step in.

> There was a complaint that only some children were allowed to take the school bus to Visby. This bus was, however, privately arranged by the Cement company, but the matter was referred to the County Council for investigation.

We arrive at the fiftieth anniversary of the Slite Workers' Commune; celebrated on 30 September 1967 at the Slite Bath Hotel with a speech by the Minister of the Interior, Hans Gustavsson, and dance music by the Playboys. Eric Jacobsson wrote his history for this occasion. In retrospect, he was quite pleased with what he saw:

> As of 1935, the Slite community, has been truly reformed, both where schooling is concerned, with a new school and a new athletics hall, as well as socially, with old people's homes, flats for old age pensioners, health visitors and council-employed home helps. Waterworks have been built, and sewage and pumping stations have been established.

The building of a number of blocks of flats has been initiated by a council-owned housing trust. A holiday village has also been built and proved very popular. A large contribution has been made towards an artificial skating rink which also costs money to maintain.

Sure, the Slite Workers' Commune has a lot to be proud of. But the basis for it all has always been and still is one single company, whose leaders' decisions mean life or death to the community.

When you read the party programme, this fact emerges strongly. But when you read Jacobsson's history of the Workers' Commune, it seems to be of secondary importance; an accepted, self-evident fact which does not even need to be mentioned.

It is possible that the author wanted to avoid controversial issues on a festive occasion like this. If I went through the old protocol once more and sat down to talk to the older members of the Workers' Commune, I might be able to produce material for a new history, which put more emphasis on the power over the factories and the company.

One thing is certain — the history of the Slite Workers' Commune, as it is written, does not offer an alternative to the picture of work and company presented by the company management.

This is serious. If the party programme claims for economic democracy are to be carried out, its criticism of the company must be well established in the local awareness. Each person must be able to refer the generalized sentences in the programme to their own conditions, his own history — in the job he has, in the place where he lives.

But as far as I know, no Swedish company has yet been examined on that basis.

- Has the history of your particular political organization been written? What picture does it give of conditions at your place of work? Is there another picture preserved by protocols and living memory?

Aids: There are many books which give the general background of the development of the workers' movement at your own workplace. The ideas of the movement have been described from a Social Democrat point of view by Jan Lindhagen in *The Social Democratic Program 1-2* (Karlskrona 1972,1974), from the communist point of view by Knut Bäckström in *The Workers' Movement in Sweden 1-2* (3rd ed. Kungalv 1977) and from a liberal point of view by Herbert Tingsten in *The Ideological Development of Swedish Social Democracy 1-2* (latest ed. Sthlm 1967).

The first issue of *A Message from the Workers' Movement's Records and Library* (1977:1) includes a list of over two hundred present research projects associated with the history of the workers' movement. Some of this research can be followed in the journal *Archive for Studies of the History of the Workers' Movement*. More accessible journals taking up similar subjects are *Then and Now* and *Journal of the Archive of Popular History*. The Records of the Popular History Society (PO Box 16213, 103 24 Stockholm, tel:08/21 20 94, Saturdays 12-15) has local branches in Göteborg, Lund and Uppsala.

5. LOCAL HISTORY

"Trade unions and political organisations are certainly not geared towards research. They've got better things to attend to. But there is a large popular movement with up to 300,000 members, busy investigating the past, including local industry. You should go to an association of local history to find an independent view of your company."

Let's examine that statement. The local history movement consists of twenty-four regional local history associations and over five hundred local history societies. Most of them are organized in the National Association for Local History, founded in 1916. More or less each association produces some publication and many of them publish large annual reports or books describing the results of local research. Altogether, the literature on local history in Sweden increases by about thirty metres of bookshelves per year.

The movement for local history thus makes a great contribution based mainly on voluntary work by non-professional researchers. It is very important in the way it effects people's view of themselves and their immediate environment.

The movement for local history originally had a critical social aspect which was also directed at the companies. Advancing industrialism was regarded as an invasion from outside. The character of the environment was ruined when old, handmade, beautiful objects for everyday use were replaced by cheap goods coming from outside. Local independence was lost when the people turned into workers for "foreign" company managers.

Why was the native forest devastated? Because it had been bought up by people who themselves did not live in its vicinity but only saw its inherent monetary value. Why were waterfalls drained and old buildings demolished? Because decisions were made outside the local cultural community by unsympathetic strangers. Why were sulphate mills allowed to pollute miles of land, and ore concentrating plants permitted to ruin the water in lakes full of fish? Because those who made the decisions did not have to suffer the consequences themselves:

> And they accept this, a whole local population accepts such tyranny, accepts the destruction of its environment and the exposure to health risks, by some *industrial princes, usually strangers living far from them.*

This was written by Karl Erik Forsslund in his 1914 book *Care of Local Environment*, a polemic pamphlet which became the igniting spark for the movement for local history. Many arguments of his have been resumed in the present debate: those ecologically inclined criticize pollution by the industries, village communities demand local control of their immediate environment, trade unions criticize the multi-nationals.

But social criticism never became the aim of the movement for local history. Instead its members gathered round their rural halls — often built as direct equivalents of the Civic Halls — and preserved the relics of a lost peasant culture. This emphasis is also prevalent in the handbooks for research used within the movement, such as:

NIHLÉN, John
Discovering Our Local Environment.
Hälsingborg 1971.

GUSTAFSON, KG Jan e.a.
Chasing a Local Environment.
Sthlm 1976.

These books contain many useful tips, such as how to use records and maps. But their attempts to modernize a basically traditional attitude to local environment are feeble. They still focus on the farm and the church, the spinning wheel and the flail. Both were written for farmers and the middle classes, who are the main members of the movement of local history. Where is the industrial community? Where is the social criticism? Almost as far away as it was thirty years ago when Sigurd Erixon and his assistants published the monumental work of the local history movement, *Swedish Country and Popular Culture in Collection, Research and Care*. 1-4 (Sthlm 1946-48).

The cities' local history associations likewise are mainly concerned with memories from the pre-industrial era. The Limhamn Museum Association is a typical example. What did they choose to restore and preserve in a typical industrial place such as Limhamn? An old soldier's croft and a farm. And when the annual journal *Limhamniana*, which has been published since 1959, for once takes an interest in the cement industry that created the town — who holds the pen? Naturally one of Cementa's directors:

LAURELL, Gunnar Chr.
The Cement Factory in Limhamn.
Limhamniana 1972.

The essay is accompanied by huge advertisements for Cementa. Generally, *Limhamniana*, like many other similar annual journals, is to a large extent financed by advertisements. And when it comes to preserving anything from the past, the local history associations become even more dependent on the support of the companies.

The companies won't pay for a critical appraisal of themselves. They won't pay for a realization of the original programme of the local history movement. They pay for the movement to avoid today's problems and to render the past harmless.

The Lomma Case

"Isn't it only natural for a movement aiming to attract all residents of a place to avoid politically controversial issues? One has to appeal to the mutual interest in local affairs that goes beyond politics."

This is a common attitude. The problem with it is simply that if you evade the politically controversial issues, you also evade almost everything that is important and engaging.

One example: out of the thirteen places that have or have had a cement factory at its centre, Lomma is the only one to be subject to a more extensive description in local historical terms:

NORDENGREN, Sven
The History of Lomma Parish and Congregation.
Malmö 1973

When you sit down with such a book in your hand, you may feel motivated to ask certain questions:

1. Who wrote this book? The preface states that Mr Nordengren is a doctor of economic history. The library catalogue will reveal what he has written before, which will give a better idea of the author.
2. Who commissioned this book? Local history is often written on commission. In this case the Lomma Parish Council commissioned the work. If someone takes on a commission, he often needs to achieve something to satisfy the commissioners. Therefore, it is inevitable that the expectations of the commissioners will affect the work. Generally, Nordengren has sought and found the history the Parish Council had hoped for.
3. What problems did the commissioners want to illuminate? It is possible, for example, that the Parish Council worried about the isolation of the church in Lomma today. How did that come about? Did it have anything to do with the

church appearing in the social battle during the years of breakthrough of the workers' movement? Perhaps it is related to the social control formerly exercised by the church? Or are there other reasons?

It is also conceivable that the Parish Council had been surprised by the sudden influx of thousands of Malmö residents into a community which so far had been reasonably static. Had similar changes taken place in the past? Had they occurred anywhere else? What happened then? What can be done about them now?

The Parish Council could also have been surprised by the class differences in Lomma and asked for an historical illumination of their origin. The Parish Council could also have been involved in the issue of asbestos risks and the future of the local industry. There are a thousand and one issues which could have given the Parish Council a reason to explore Lomma's history.

But what was the real reason? The usual one — a jubilee. The church was a hundred years old. The old church that had been on the same site was demolished in 1871. "What did the old church look like, why was it pulled down?" These questions gave rise to others: "How many people lived and worked in Lomma at that time, what were their means of supporting themselves? What is known generally about Lomma over the centuries?"

The answers follow the questions. Sven Nordengren is not an historian who would unnecessarily seek out the problems his commissioners haven't asked him to examine. He glides past them as quickly and comfortably as possible:

Where industry is concerned, capital and initiative to a large extent came from Malmö. The workers accepted low pay and most of their money was spent on consumer goods. Profits from the Lomma companies were distributed throughout the country or taken to Malmö to be invested in new companies not located at Lomma.

That's it. But *how* large were the profits taken away over the decades? What *did it mean* to the place that the main industry was not an independent unit but part of a cement concern? What *possibilities* does a small community have *to act* when it ends up in the same situation as a developing nation in relation to a large multi-national company?

These are some of the main issues in Lomma's modern history. But they aren't even questioned.

4. What sources has the author used? For the pre-industrial era in Lomma, Nordengren's research is relatively comprehensive. He has used the archives for dialect and local names and for local conditions in Lund, as well as the National Archives and the survey department of the District Council. He has studied parcelling maps, district bailiff documents and protocols of catechism attendance.

For the industrial era, he has had access to a worker's diary, more annual than diurnal, written by the engine driver Jöns Nilsson (see Chapter 15). This is a unique document, but Nordengren uses it only for the odd quotation.

The development of industry is described with the assistance of the Managing Director of Scandinavian Eternit, Bertil Kylberg. Apart from this, everything is taken directly from the commemorative publications of Cementa and R.F. Berg. These have been the basis of descriptions of the trade union and the Workers' Commune as well. Nordengren imposes the frozen history drawn from these four commemorative publications on the church.

Four jubilee speakers are talking through a fifth. Nobody wants to be slow to forget an injury. "When Kylberg succeeded Scharengrad, Lomma was a pretty, sleepy little idyll." Nobody wants to disturb the atmosphere. "The relationship between company management and workers was always personal and favourable in this time." Reconciliation hovers like a mist over the past:

During the fifteen years following 1925, no great conflicts erupted in Lomma. The workers' movement was consolidated and affiliated to the Social Democrat Party, whose aim was to change society by reforms and education. This was fulfilled in Lomma, to a great extent. The library was developed and played an important part, and the same can be said about the Story-Telling Movement.

That was in 1973. All's well that ends well!

But a few years later, in 1975, the company management, appointed by the owners of the Industri AB Euroc, announced that the company's activities at Lomma, due to work environment legislation against asbestos risks, no longer yielded any profits that could be distributed over the country and be taken to Malmö to be invested in new companies not located at Lomma and that the Lomma factory was to close down — then there were a few Lomma citizens who had reason to ask: What was really the Story-Telling-Movement? In other words, the Lomma factory was to close down. Then there were a few Lomma citizens who had reason to ask: What was all this about the "Story-Telling-Movement"? Could that have been the final goal of the struggle of the Lomma workers? Or were there possibly other goals which have been lost on the way?

The past is not a thing to parade on festive occasions. That only serves to paralyse history. When you need a push forward, it helps to take a step back. To break the paralysis, you need to turn to history with concrete problems. It makes the past more relevant than the Story-Telling Movement.

- Is there an historical description of your local environment? What picture does it give of your place of work and the company that you work for?

- Are you a member of the association of local history? If so, suggest that they form a research group for investigating the local places of work. Try to co-operate with the local union branches and with local history associations in other places where your company is active.

Aids: TRU's (*Kommittén för Tv och Radio i Utbildningen* [TV and Radio in Education]) study material *Changing Environment* (1973) is an attempt to direct local history research towards the environment and problems of industrial communities. It can be ordered from Brevskolan, 126 12 Stockholm, tel. 08/ 744 25 00.

Literature about your community can be found in your local library. See Chapter 6.

In Norway, research into local history has a stronger position than in Sweden. The national association for the history of town and country has published *Local History in Research and Cultural Work over 200 Years* (Trondheim 1970) with a comprehensive bibliography. Topical publications from the Norwegian Local History Institute in Oslo include *Local History at School* (Orkanger 1975) and Rolf Fladby e.a. *Local History from Farm to Town* (Oslo 1974).

There are some excellent English handbooks, such as W.G. Hoskins *Local History in England* (2nd ed. London 1972) and *Fieldwork in Local History* (2nd ed. London 1969). The cheapest handbook is David Iredale *Discovering Local History* (Aylesbury 1973). Experiments with local history at school are described in H.P.R. Finberg, *Local History: Objective and Pursuit* (2nd ed. Newton Abbott 1973).

Both Norwegian and English handbooks are written by definitely conservative people. I have been unable to find a socialist equivalent to these handbooks. But it may be on the way. At the end of Gunnar Sillén *We Go Towards the Light* (Malmö 1977), published on the initiative of the Workers Educational Association and the National Association for Local History, there is also a Marxist pattern for local historical research. See Chapter 21.

6. AT THE LIBRARY

During a few years around 1970, Sweden's view of the rest of the world changed. Old loyalties were broken, new ones were created. During the Vietnam War, the powerful US propaganda system was overcome by study groups, stencils and leaflets. Developing nations and liberation movements emerged from the darkness of ignorance. A new view of the world was formed.

When will the picture of our local community change in a similar fashion?

In those years, I spent a lot of time travelling around Sweden, lecturing about Latin America. People would listen for hours to the story of trade unions in a little Chilean town called Molina. To them it appeared to be the turning point of the world. But the story of the trade unions in their own home town was as unknown to them as it was to me.

People would listen for hours to the analysis of Marcona Mining or Anaconda Copper. But they knew very little about the large industry in their own county. I knew even less.

Some of these lectures I gave in libraries. We used to check there what was written about them. What people had written about them? What interests did they represent? What subjects were dealt with? What values were prevalent?

It was usually the vicar or the retired works manager who had written about the town or the company. The Latin teacher and the local editor of the conservative newspaper might also have contributed. The County Council had paid for indifferent commissions. The pillars of society wrote their own history.

For how long will people who have acquired a critical view of the world be satisfied with an outdated picture of their own conditions?

The new view of the world was not served on a platter. It grew out of a deep suspicion against established authorities. People started to ask questions themselves, to investigate and draw conclusions. They learnt to compare today's lies to those of yesterday and expose both of them. Facts that had been buried for decades were produced to create a new type of awareness.

The new view of ourselves must be produced in the same way. By our own questions, our own investigations and our own conclusions.

The County Library

When you want to start an investigation, the county library is the natural starting-point. A great deal of the work on this book was done at the Malmö City Library. Systematically I went through the different departments of that library to establish what they could offer a cement worker from Limhamn keen to research his job.

It was the summer of 1974 — quite a good summer for me. I used to eat at Ringbaren on the other side of the cemetery, and in the evenings often walk back and forth under the trees along the canal, excited by my discoveries. With each passing day my respect for the public library as a research centre for the people increased. It does, in fact, provide information on most things.

The Malmö City Library is the main library in Malmö County and the district library of the Malmöhus district. Most such libraries have a special room or a department with books associated with its own county and district. Sometimes they also keep a list of books and articles about the towns and villages. For example: *Literature about Limhamn in the Malmö City Library*, Malmö 1959 (Stencil). There are printed lists for larger towns, such as:

HEINTZE, Ingeborg e.a.
Literature about Malmö.
Bibliography. Malmö 1977.

If you can't find such a list for the place where you live, there may be one for your province. One example is Cappelin, O., *Where is Scania Described?* Helsingborg 1909.

These literature lists (bibliographies) are in Sweden placed on the first shelf of the library, and their code is Aa. They may also be kept by the information desk as an aid to librarians.

Many libraries also make up lists of other subjects. Because they know that many people are interested in horses, they make up lists of horse books. And because they know that many people are interested in detective stories, many libraries create a special department for thrillers, to make them easy to find. It ought to be equally important for the libraries to create a special department with books and articles about the main places of work in the area.

Most librarians are in my experience friendly towards borrowers and happy to be of help, which is exactly what they are paid to be. Their interest in your particular subject may of course vary. If you want the assistance of a librarian with socialist inclinations, you can contact BIS.

BIS is an abbreviation for a Swedish association — Library in Society — which publishes a journal with the same name. This journal should be available at the county library. If not, it can be ordered from:

BIS, c/o Birgitta Bengtsson
Uddevallagatan 33, 41-6 70 Göteborg.
Tel: 051/80 25 31.

Each issue includes the names and addresses of contacts in different parts of the country.

- Is there any list of literature about the place where you live? Does the county library have a local collection? What picture does it give of your place of work, of the company where you work? Who has created that image?

> • Does the county library have a special department for books and articles about conditions at your place of work? If not — get them to arrange for such a department through your union and political representatives.

Loans from Other Libraries

All the books you need may not be available at your county library. In that case, your library can get the books by ordering them from some other library. This service is provided by the libraries free of cost. *Any book available at any swedish library can be ordered to your library.*

How do you know what books are available in other libraries? You simply look them up in two large bibliographies. *The Swedish Book List* has been published annually since 1866 (although the first hundred years it was called *The Swedish Book Catalogue*) and lists all printed books published that year in Sweden. (Except so-called small prints, see below). The *Accession Catalogue* (in Sweden often abbreviated as AK) is published annually since 1686 and lists all foreign books bought by public libraries that year.

If you know what year a Swedish book was published, you can look for it in *The Swedish Book List*. If you know the publishing year of a foreign book, you can look it up in the *Accession Catalogue* — if a Swedish library has bought it. If so, it can be ordered to your library.

It is often possible to produce books which are not listed in either of these two bibliographies. Large libraries for example can order books straight from abroad. But the thumb rule is: any book listed in *Swedish Book List* or the *Accession Catalogue* can be ordered for you by your local library, free of charge.

Research Libraries

When you investigate a place of work or a company, you need more than books. You may be interested in fly-sheets or a poster from the year of the general strike, 1909, in a telephone directory or an advertising brochure from the 1920s, in the annual report or workshop regulations from the year the last war broke out, 1939. Such material, called *small prints*, is available in special research libraries, mainly at the Royal Library in Stockholm and the university libraries in Uppsala and Lund.

If you need small prints or have some other problem, with which the county library can't assist you, don't hesitate, go to a research library. They are not just there for the sake of universities but just as much for researchers like yourself. Believe me — many of the people busy with research in these libraries have tasks less important than yours.

Each research library has its own special interests, so don't be afraid of asking. Most people who come to the libraries need help. Asking for it is only natural.

One common reason why people go to research libraries is to study the catalogues. At the Royal Library in Stockholm there is for example a *Catchphrase Catalogue* of books published before 1956 and a *Systematic Catalogue* of books published in 1956 and after 1956. In a matter of hours, these two catalogues can help you gain a general idea of Swedish books published on a certain subject, such as time studies, or a certain place, such as Slite. In the catchphrase catalogue, cards are arranged according to the same principle as in an encyclopaedia. In other words, you can look up the word "time studies" directly. The Swedish systematic catalogue arranges cards with the names of books on time studies under the code Q Economy, subdivision Qibc Studies of work. It takes some time to learn to find things in the systematic catalogue and to begin with it is a good idea to ask the librarian for assistance.

At the county library you can take books straight from the shelf yourself. This is a great advantage. The research libraries, on the other hand, keep almost all of their books stored away, and you must first find them in the catalogue and then hand in a written order. Normally the ordered material is produced within a few hours, but it may take even longer.

Aids: If you live far from a research library it may be a good idea to write to them in advance. If you know exactly what you're after, the librarians can produce the material in advance and it will be ready when you arrive, to save your time. You can formulate the letter in many different ways, for example like this:

The Royal Library, PO Box 5039, 102 41 Stockholm.
We are a few workmates at the Köping cement factory who are going to Stockholm next week. We would like to have a look at our union journal *The Labourer* for 1909, also the telephone directory for Köping of 1940 and the staff journal at Skånska Cement, *Around the Rotary Kiln* of 1955. Could you please order this material for us so that it is available when we arrive on Thursday 22 May 22?
Yours faithfully...

Remember that you have a right to ask for this. You and your workmates have helped to pay for research libraries for years without using them — now it is your turn

---

Company Libraries

Most large companies have their own libraries. They are listed in:

BERG, BRIT
Swedish specialised libraries and documentation centres
Sthlm 1971. (*Handbook of the Society of Technical Literature*)

It says, for example, the following about Cementa's library:

AB Cementa
PO Box, 210 10 Malmö. Tel: 040/736 60. Telex 3316.
Chief librarian: Anna Greta Winderup
Other staff: 1
Number of books: about 20,000
Running journals: about 400; 200 of which are foreign
Classification system: UDK
Subjects: cement, concrete, lime
Xerox copying — lists of new acquisitions 8-9 / year — list of journals

Other company libraries within this concern are the Iföverken library in Bromölla and the Cement and Concrete Laboratory library in Malmö. Since Cementa became Euroc, the above information is no longer valid. The financial and legal department of the Cementa library is still with the management of the concern in Malmö, whilst the technical department has been amalgamated with the library of the cement laboratory and moved to Limhamn. The work force has been invited there through the house journal:

> This is a good suggestion for people who want to know more than they do already about building materials generally and cement and lime in particular. Contact the superb library housed in the Cement and Concrete Laboratory building in Limhamn... They have now got themselves organised and welcome all borrowers.
> There is even a place reserved for researchers [i.e. you!] who want to study literature at the library. If you want to know more about some special subject and are unable to visit the library, you can send for a literature list to begin with...
> (*Cementa News*, 19/1/6).

By ringing round some large company libraries I could state that all of them do not have this welcoming attitude. The libraries are said to be used more or less exclusively by senior officials. They won't exactly say that it would be strictly forbidden for other members of the workforce to use the company library. Instead they say that most employees in their jobs have no reason to go to the library.

It ought to be self-evident that a research group among workers should have access to the company library's resources, if they consider it necessary. The costs for the library are after all taken from production and contributes to decreasing the pay available. You and your workmates have contributed to financing the company library just as well as the public libraries.

If you are not permitted or if you don't want to use the company library directly, you can sometimes use it via your county library. The Malmö City Library, for example, regularly receives lists of books bought by the company libraries in the city and they have prepared an alphabetical *co-catalogue* of the books of the Malmö industries, which can also be ordered to the city library.

- Does the company where you work have a library? If so, have you visited it? Are you allowed to visit it? Can books from the company library be ordered to the county library?

How It's Done

When I start to investigate a subject, I usually do it like this: I get a ring file in the A5 format, in which I collect notes about books, articles in journals, interviews and other material associated with the subject. I write down the name of only one book on each page. A stiff piece of card marks the limit between things already read or done and things waiting to be done.

Just like the libraries, I write down the author's surname and first name. Then follow the full title of the book, its place of print and year of print. If the book is part of a series of some kind, I add information about this within brackets.

If the book has no author or has been written by several authors, I start with the title. Where articles from newspapers and journals are concerned, it is important always to give the name of the paper, its number and/or page and the year.

I arrange the pages alphabetically in the ring file. If I have more than about fifty pages, they become difficult to survey and should be divided into subject groups. The material on a factory, for example, can be divided into "people", "buildings", "machines", "work organization", etc. The method of division depends on my own interests — what I want to find out. On the first page in the file I describe the subject groups.

I also make a note on each leaf what in the book or article is important to my subject and what I think about it. Don't think you'll remember such things — you won't. And if you work in a group, others will be able to use your notes.

I usually take photocopies of interesting material — that is a service provided by most libraries. I'll then write a reference (e.g., "see Copy 5") on the page in the ring file. The copies are kept in numerical order in a special file, which is larger.

In a research group, one member ought to be responsible for keeping such notes on the material used by the group. The notes are an important result of the group's work and should definitely be kept even after the actual research work has been concluded. They may be needed again in a few years' time.

The library is a good start for all kinds of research. But don't be depressed if you don't discover very much about your particular place of work or the company employing you. To know that there is nothing written about a certain subject is in itself a result. And, as we shall see, there are many more sources of knowledge than the library.

7. IN THE ARCHIVE

It took me forty-two years before I first visited an archive. Most people never do.

A few old researchers sneak around the archives, as familiar as house cats. The odd student will look in to search for documents for exams. Some archives are much visited by people researching their family tree (See Chapter 12). But there are rarely queues forming on the steps of an archive.

Those who work in archives naturally will be disappointed if people don't go there. They collect all these documents, classify and care for their papers, make up long lists to show where each can be found. But where are the visitors for whom all this work is done? Some documents have been kept for hundreds of years, in the hope that someone some day will come and ask for them. But no one does.

On occasion they will feel very despondent, asking themselves whether it is necessary to keep old documents that nobody seems to require. But it is necessary. It's a good thing that these papers are kept for the day when people will discover their archives and realize how they should be used.

The fact that only a few people have got to that point has of course one advantage. Being one of the first, you can expect to be well received. Those who work in archives are friendly and helpful. They look as though they would offer you a cup of coffee if they dared. Each visitor does make their role in life more meaningful. You may of course be unlucky and run into the odd person with a different attitude. But I myself have never been so well received anywhere as I have been in the archives.

Beginners are usually given the advice to leave record studies until they have gone through all the printed material on their subject. I disagree: don't wait too long! The archive can give you an experience to deepen and stimulate your interest.

You Are There

Let's assume that you work at the cement factory at Slite. Some time when you happen to be in Visby, you go into the archive (the address is in the telephone directory). To the left inside the front door is a large room with books and catalogues. You ask the person sitting by the desk if the office keeps any documents on the cement industry in Gotland.

It's a good idea to look in the staff journal or memorial publication in advance and make notes of any people who have been important to the history of the company, e.g. Jan Myrsten and Fredrik Nyström.

"Yes," she will say when she looks at your notes, "we have just received some documents from Major Nyström. There may be something for you in them."

She helps you fill in an order form whilst apologizing for not yet having arranged and sorted the documents, just the way you would apologize to visitors to your home if you hadn't made your bed. She soon returns and puts the first plastic carrier bag with Nyström's documents in front of you.

You dig into the heap, and the first thing you find is Myrsten's and Nyström's correspondence as they planned the cement factory. What profits they aimed at, what wild aspirations they had! Then follow the secret documents from the 1920s, when the cartel around Skånska Cement forced them down on their knees and the companies divided the market between themselves. At the end of the 1920s, Cementa has Slite Cement in a stranglehold. You can see how Nyström tried to defend himself by entering an agreement with his workers — lower wages in return for greater transparency and security of employment.

Then he sells out to Cementa, which leads to reduced operations and redundancies. The matter is taken up by the Labour Court. You have the letter where Nyström is given the task of stabbing his former workers in the back.

He himself has been moved to the Visby Cement Factory, but only for a short period of grace. The outbreak of war gives Skånska Cement the long-awaited excuse to close down the Visby factory. Then follows the struggle to create a substitute industry in the old premises of the cement factory. It was turned into a plant for hemp dressing, which never proved viable.

This is Nyström's story. But it is also the story of two places of work and many hundred workmates. The old cement factory in Visby was demolished in 1974 to make way for a new motorway. Soon very few people will remember that it ever existed. Even today many people have forgotten how Industri AB Euroc earned its millions. But the evidence is there. At the District Archive in Visby the papers are on the table — for you as well as for me.

You won't have to leaf through them for long before realising that a archive is something quite different from and more interesting than a library. A book is after all just a report *on* something, e.g., the decision to close down the cement factory in Visby. But the document provided by the archive *is* the very decision. It's a fantastic difference.

Historians usually talk about *relics*, which is an expressive word. One letter from Wehtje giving orders to close down the factory is more than a story: it is the very order sent to Nyström. The piece of paper you're holding in your hand *is* the very piece of paper Nyström held in his moments after receiving it. Your eyes see what he saw. You are there.

There are other "relics" of the same decision. What Skånska Cement gained from robbing Visby of its one industry, what Skånska Cement gained from unemployment and early retirement — that money is not gone. It's still here. It grew with accumulated interest and today forms part of Industrial AB Euroc´s capital.

History does not disappear. It lives on in capital. The archive is a good place for realizing this.

Company Archives

The type of documents left by Major Nyström to the District Archive in Visby — the internal correspondence of the company management, minutes of Board meetings, information about staff, reports, calculations, estimates — are usually kept in the archive of the company.

Euroc's archive for Gotland is in Slite. In the spring of 1973, it was visited by an official from the District Archive in Visby. He wrote: "The archive is situated in the basement of the office block in the southern and northern vaults. The records are comprehensive and include material from all Gotland cement factories..." (hand-written report to the District Archive in Visby, 5 July 1973).

Even if you are employed by the cement factory in Slite, you're unlikely to be given access to that basement. Their own records are the companies' most strictly kept secrets. It is generally opened only to absolutely reliable researchers, i.e., people with a guaranteed uncritical attitude to the company. Therefore company history in Sweden looks rather like party history in the Soviet Union — what the company does is always right.

The workers' legal right to participation (in Sweden called MBL) creates new possibilities for the staff to gain insight into the companies. This right is useful mainly to gain insight into material associated with actual problems of the company.

However, in the long term it is equally important to destroy the old image of the company and replace it with a new one, based on the experience and research of the workers themselves. They should be able to use the right to participate on behalf of the workers. Only then will company history be written seriously.

- Does the company where you work have a archive? Do you have access to it? How can the workers' right to participate be used to open the company archive?

Public Archives

A company archive is still a secret of the company. But each place of work comes under its County Council and the company maintains links with the local authorities: it writes letters, gives out information, is subject to investigations and decisions. All this leaves traces in the County Archive. Each Swedish citizen has a right to inspect the documents there on request.

If, for example, you are interested in the Hällekis cement factory, you ring the County Council offices in Götene and make an appointment to visit the County Archive, located in the basement of an old people's home in Gössäter. There you look under "Österplana County Council", which Hällekis used to come under. You will find "protocols of County Council meetings" 1907-51, "incoming documents and correspondence" 1887-1951 and "documents" 1919-1951, in all eight volumes, plus a lot of old calculations and verifications of less interest to you.

There is not much space down there and the air is stuffy, but you can always go out and get some fresh air together with the old boys in the room next door, who have a carpentry workshop with a lovely fresh smell. And you will find that in small counties, completely dominated by one single company, such as Österplana, the County Archive has a lot to offer to anyone researching a company.

The letters and information from the companies to the different local authorities can be examined in a similar fashion in the District Archives, located in Härnösand, Östersund, Uppsala, Vadstena, Visby, Göteborg and Lund.

A huge concern such as Industri AB Euroc also has had many occasions to correspond with and give out information to different national authorities and investigations. These documents are kept and eventually end up at the National Archives in Stockholm, where they can be examined.

Aids: At the National Archives, (Fyrverkarbacken 13-17, PO Box, 100 26 Stockholm, tel: 08/54 02 00), you can find Otto Walde's *Catalogue of Private Archives*. This gives information about privately recorded material associated with *people* (such as K.F. Berg and B.H. Fahnehielm), *companies* (such as Lanna Eastern Lime Bit company) and *villages* and *farms* (such as Hällekis and Maltesholm, to mention two associated with Euroc). Walde's catalogue formed the basis of *The National Archives' National Directory of Private Archives*. You can write to this national directory and ask whether there is any material of relevance to the subject you are researching.

Many *county libraries* have a right to borrow documents from public archives. All that is required is a fire-proof safe in the library to keep the documents in. Some county libraries have copies of important records associated with the county in question.

The best *handbooks* for records research by ordinary people are intended for genealogists (see Chapter 12). Many archives have stencilled small guides for visitors. The National Archive, for example, on request will send free of cost a copy of *How to Research in the National Archive*. But that is only fourteen pages and the information is neither comprehensive nor inspiring. It is an important task for anyone working in an archive to write relatively comprehensive, practically useful directions on how to use the archive for a certain purpose, e.g., to research the company where you work.

How reliable is the information taken from records? If it is contradictory, what should you believe? This type of question is called "source criticism". An easy orientation in source criticism is given by Torsten Thurén in *Is It Really True?* (Stockholm 1976).

"Official Documents"

The archives do not receive documents from the authorities until they are many years old. But you have a right to inspect them even before they go to the archive, even on the day when they are written.

Anything written by national or local authorities is namely an "official document". This also goes for all letters received or sent by them. This means that *any citizen at any time can go into any authority's offices and demand to see any document.*

A small number of documents are classified as secret. A small number of authorities (such as the Price and Cartel Board) have almost exclusively secret documents. But the main rule is that authorities are legally obliged to let you see their documents.

You don't even have to tell them who you are. You don't have to explain why you want to see a certain document. You are not obliged to answer any questions. Just ask them back: "Is this an 'official document' or isn't it?" The authority is under obligation to hand you any official document without objections.

Today it is mainly journalists who know and exploit this right. Most other people would consider the principle of "officialness" an empty word. It shouldn't be like that. The right to partake of official documents is relatively unique and one of the most important civil rights in Sweden. Children ought to be trained at school to use this right: they shouldn't be allowed to leave school without having been to the authorities, at least on one occasion, to demand to see such documents.

Aids: The exact regulations for the authorities' obligation to give out official documents are included in *The Principle of Officiality and the Authorities* (8th ed. Lund 1976). Practical examples of the use of this right can be found in chapters 10 and 13.

Start at Home!

A person investigating a company can also use some very important special records such as museum records, local history movement records and insurance company records. It is useful to know these possibilities. But be careful not to be overwhelmed. You could certainly go to an archive with the general aim to see "if there is anything" referring to the company or the work. But you should establish as early as possible what exactly you're looking for — what questions you want to ask the material.

And don't go further afield than necessary. Most people keep their own private "records" — old letters and photographs, diaries with notes, perhaps old cash-books. The largest, most inexhaustible "records" are the experience you and your workmates have — and the memories of old workers. That's where you should begin. Dig where you stand!

Aids: A records list for anyone searching for material on places of work and companies is *Industrial and Transport Memories: A Catalogue of Essays, Inventories and Records*. Sthlm 1973. Letters, see Chapter 15. Memories, see Chapter 17.

Students from the intermediate school in Sian making steel in the schoolyard.

8. IN SCHOOL

In China, crèches, schools and leisure premises are often located on the site of a factory, in close proximity to the parents' place of work. This has many advantages. Parents and children can see each other several times a day. The parents can take turns to partake in the tasks of social workers. In that way they get variety in their daily routines and better connection with their children's life. Likewise, the children become familiar with their parents' work environment. Via simple little jobs they can be brought into the working life.

What? Surely, children shouldn't be working?

In China I saw many who did. They cleaned their classroom. They swept the schoolyard. They dug the gardens. They helped cook the food at school and wash up afterwards.

After the Cultural Revolution in the mid-1960s, these aspects of school life have increased further. The children have a workshop next door to their classroom, where they learn to make finished products or collate parts which will then go on to the factories for mounting. Great efforts are made to find suitable tasks for children of different ages. The teaching of practical work is discussed and planned as carefully as the theoretical education.

This may appear shocking. Abolishing child labour in industry was one of the first demands of the Swedish workers' movement. But that referred to the exploitation of children, unreasonably long working days, tough and hazardous working conditions, and child labour as a means to keep adults' wages down — this was what they wanted to abolish. The idea wasn't exactly to stop children learning how to work.

However, urbanization, rationalization and more and more years of schooling have made practical work disappear from the world of Swedish children. What is left is called "handicraft".

This should preferably be "creative" — i.e., children are encouraged to make silly little ornaments. It is not considered creative to learn to sew on a button, stitch up a pair of trousers or do something else that would increase the child's ability to cope with the practical problems they are constantly facing.

And what about cleaning? Is it really right that the school from the very start teaches children that they are free to make any mess they like and then leave it to others — low-paid, inferior adults — to clean it up? Should the school teach the children that food is something that is simply served, something they do not need to help prepare or wash up after?

Is it right that people during the first fifteen, twenty, twenty-five years of life should grow up with a pure consumer's attitude to life — in a world where goods seem to appear by some sort of self-generation on the shelves in the shops, and that they themselves never ever have to help produce them?

I don't think this is right. On the contrary, I believe the Chinese attempt to interweave work and play as early as in nursery school gives the children a healthier attitude to life.

School and Company

In Sweden the interaction between school and working life has a different face. *Company and School* (1971), published by the Swedish Employers' Federation and the Confederation of Swedish Industry, describes how this interaction has been planned. It is a loose leaf collection with detailed instructions as to how companies in a certain area should arrange their relations with the school. From the preface:

> More than one Swede in six now goes to school. One million in elementary schools and a quarter of a million in high school. 125,006 are university students.
>
> The new school will therefore be the natural entrance gate for information to young people about the many aspects on industry. The gate is open for concrete, relevant and versatile information.

The suggestion is made that the companies in one place should create so-called "control groups" to handle contacts with the school. The member companies undertake among other things to produce material on their companies, directed at students, and to allocate money so that the control group can produce joint material on the local industries.

The control group should plan things like the students' educational visits to the companies. The impression the students get can be controlled by the material supplied in advance, such as "company presentations, brochures, staff journals, annual reports, films, slides, posters etc." There are also other ways to give the visit a certain slant in advance:

> The school teachers like to be tipped off about questions the students can prepare to ask during the visit to the company. Therefore, try to complement the different types of material with questions directing the attention of the students on particularly important conditions.

The person responsible at the company should also agree with the teacher in advance on who should be in charge during the visit. "I don't suppose I have to point out that you are in charge?" The person showing the company to the students is well instructed as to how to treat them: "Establish eye contact, use the student's name and move close to him to improve contact and strengthen your leadership."

"*Company and school*" goes through the elementary school's educational plan and points out a number of different aspects on subjects, such as sociology, economy and history, which relate to industry. The companies, it says, should make sure their representatives take part in school conferences in order to enter "direct agreements on dispersal of information relating to relevant courses."

> • What is the picture given of the company where you work to students in the local school? Is it correct? Is it comprehensive? Is there any material for the school giving the workers' views on the job and the company?
>
> **Aids:** Publishing Distribution of Industry (Box 16120, 103 23 Stockholm, tel: 08/ 22 75 60) and The Trade Union Congress Information Department (105 53 Stockholm, tel: 08/22 89 80) on request will send free of cost catalogues of material offered to the schools. When I ordered these catalogues in 1974, the Employers' Federation offered almost twice as much material as the National Union. A great deal of the EF material was produced directly for use in schools, though the material on the whole was more difficult to use. The EF had far more audio-visual material, which is extremely effective. More EF than TUC material was given out free of cost. The TUC covered two special areas, which the EF material did not take up. The EF had material on twenty-six special areas which the TUC material did not take up — unemployment, motor industry, computers, the EU, export, finance, fusions, company history, company law, people with disablties information, inflation, calculation, alimentary additives, market economy, ecology, multinational companies, staff policy, regional politics, advertising, taxation, schools, structural rationalization, profits and vocational guidance. And moreover, it was easier for the teacher to order material from the EF. What is it like today? What local material is there on your place of work?

Workers' Training

To teach the children to work, like the Chinese, has one basic obstacle in our society. Work to us has a fundamentally different role than in a socialist society. We can't teach our children to take part in one great communal task to the common good —

in reality we send them out after finishing school to the labour market, to sell their manpower.

That is why our crèches can't not be built adjoining the industries — where a small number of capitalists have the power. That is why we don't teach our children to work at school — the school can't take on the task of getting the children used to their future roles as manpower for the capitalists of the 1990s.

Or maybe this is the very task of modern education?

Let's see how a cement worker is supposed to be trained. From now on this will be done at the so called secondary stage. The training is described in:

EDUCATIONAL PLAN
for the secondary stage. Lgy 70. Part II, Supplement.
2 year-course, process technology; Stockholm 1971.

The educational plan first presents a schedule describing the number of hours per week to be devoted to each subject:

Schedule for Course in Building Material/Technology

Subject	First year	Second year
Process technique	27-30	32-35
Orientation of working life	1	1
Gymnastics	2	2
Swedish	4	0
Extra hour	1	0
English or other languages or religion or psychology or sociology or maths or art	3	3
Total	**38**	**38**

In other words, as you can see, the subject "process technology" is completely dominant. It encompasses 78-86% of the study time. The aim of teaching this subject is the following:

SVEN LINDQVIST

Process Technology: Aim

By being taught process technique, the student should:

- learn about constructional principles, effects, areas of use and names of production equipment in the processing industry;
- acquire basic skills at different stages of work applied in processing industry;
- develop his skill in operating, starting and stopping, and in correcting and resetting operations;
- practise observation of instruments and apparatus and quickly trace faults and intervene and correct possible faults;
- develop the ability to take in information by directions, instructions, etc.;
- gain insight into different kinds of safety regulations and their application;
- develop the ability to observe and analyse social conditions at his place of work and gain insight into the changeability of professional and industrial conditions.

The first aim includes a certain amount of basic knowledge. Aims two to five refer to skills needed in daily routines. Note that the student should learn to "take in information" by understanding the "directions" of the company and the "instructions" from superiors — but this seems to be the only information he needs to take in.

The sixth aim refers to safety. The student should learn to apply current safety regulations — but there is no question of an independent assessment or investigation of the security of the place of work.

The last two aims differ from the others. For one thing, they don't seem absolutely necessary from the point of view of the employer; secondly, they are formulated in a more general, vague manner. What does it really mean to learn to

97

"observe and analyse social conditions at the place of work"? *How* should they be analysed?

What type of "insight into the changeability of professional and industrial conditions" are the students supposed to gain? Are they to be prepared to adjust to fresh demands from employers brought on by technological development and concentration of capital? Or are they supposed to gain insight into measures they themselves could take to change their occupational and working conditions?

The "directions and notes" of the educational plan have been written to provide the answer to such questions. 113 of the 120 pages of the plan are directions and describe in detail the different parts of the plan. A few examples:

Aim and Contents
Location of Faults (25 hours)
Correcting faults in simple mechanical and electrical systems, in chemical apparatus, lifting equipment, transport equipment, etc. Exchange of spares. Operational test. Equipment taken from the processing industry should be used for practising location of faults. The exercises are done systematically and taking the time factor into consideration. Students should be made aware of the huge financial values represented by the plants of the processing industry, and they should realize the importance of proper handling and care. Emphasize the accident risks.

Production Knowledge: Cement Industry (150 hours)
Excavating, drilling, blasting, loading, coarse crushing, cleaning, carburizing, grinding, screening, chemical adjustment, transport of slurry, chemical control, automatic analysis and adjustment of raw material composition, process control by computer.

Work Procedures: Cement Industry (800 hours)
Buffer container for slurry levelling, burning in rotary kilns, clinker cooling, clinker transport and clinker storage,

cement grinding, cement storage and loading, Process control of kiln operation, laboratory control, distribution of cement.

To achieve the aim of these studies, great care is required at the planning. The basis of the planning should be to make the studies an extension of the knowledge the students acquire at school. Intimate co-operation between school and company is necessary to achieve this. The students should be given jobs which test their attention and observation.

Product Knowledge: Cement (60 hours)
Knowledge of raw materials, areas of use for cement, cement chemistry, cement norms.

Aims and Contents
Material Testing: Cement Industry

Testing of Raw Material
Analysis of the composition of the slurry from the chemical and physical points of view.

Testing of Clinker
Chemical analysis, such as contents of "free CaO".

Testing of Finished Product
Establishing the binder time, the screening rest, establishing the compressing, bending, pulling strength, according to present national standard chemical analysis, especially for CaO, SiO2, A1203, Fe203 and S03.

The educational plan gives detailed directions as to how the first six aims of the teaching of process technology should be achieved. But there is no explanation as to how the last two aims of the lessons could be attained. These aims have not given cause for a special entry. They have not been allocated any hours. They are not even mentioned — except under the headline "general views" where it says:

> The school should undertake to stimulate the students to develop their observational skills and to analyse the social conditions at a place of work and to gain insight into the changeability of professional and industrial life.

So the description of the aims is repeated. But how should it be done? Nothing is said about that. The distinct impression is that these two aims have been included merely as decoration.

The course in process technology should be one of several equal courses within the secondary stage. It should have the same general aims and direction as the rest of the secondary stage education. These aims are described in Part 1 of the *Educational Plan for the Secondary Stage* as follows:

> The main objective of the courses in the secondary stage is to develop the student's independent and critical powers of observation. The result can vary widely, but from the very start, students should get used to an investigatory attitude to the knowledge and the information offered to them inside and outside school. They should check whether facts are correct, how argumentation is structured, and assess whether conclusions, drawn by others as well as themselves, are reliable.

Beautiful. Very wise. But in what way could the teaching of process technology contribute to attaining these goals? In what way does the school attempt to give a future cement worker a critical, investigatory faculty?

Perhaps that isn't the intention at all? Perhaps it's good enough if the future engineers and company managers, taking different courses at the secondary stage, develop a critical, independent faculty?

The school's ability to realize the aims established in the educational plan is controlled by research, amongst other things. A researcher at the National Teaching College in Uppsala has been given the job of investigating how the technical courses fulfil the objectives of the educational plan. He has sent out questionnaires to over eight thousand former students.

But not one of these questions touches upon the "decorative" aims. The researcher himself has no idea what these aims refer to — this was obvious when I rang up and talked to him. So how could he check whether they were fulfilled?

One might ask what those who created the educational plan really had in mind, concretely, when they formulated these aims. Did they think that literature and art would teach the students to "observe their place of work"? That sociology and psychology would help them "analyse the social conditions" there? Did they imagine that the students would contact their predecessors in the job and their unknown workmates in foreign countries to find out about the "changeability of the place of work"? That they would learn to explore the history of their place of work in order to develop an "independent and critical faculty" vis-à-vis the company?

At this stage I was longing to see how the teaching was actually done in practice. The simplest thing, I thought, ought to be to go there and ask teachers and students directly.

But that was easier said than done. In reality no such course is offered. The training of future workers for the building materials industry so far only exists in theory.

- How does the *Educational Plan for the Secondary Stage* describe the training for your job? What aims are established, what directions are given, how is the realization checked? Does the training exist in reality?

Aids: Educational plans can be ordered by the county library. Old plans can demonstrate changes within certain jobs and give a picture of their history since 1918, when vocational

---

schools were introduced, or, in some cases, even earlier. The Education Authority (106 42 Stockholm, tel: 08/14 06 60) will send on request, free of cost, *Swedish Educational Research*, a catalogue of present research projects, which has been published annually since 1964.

- People today are trained for tomorrow's society. How does the educational plan for your job tally with the political aims of the workers' movement? Is it a suitable education for workers who are to take over the power of the companies? How should the training be planned?

Aids: This book.

9. VOCATIONAL GUIDANCE

The Swedish school system offers no vocational training for cement workers. But each pupil is given vocational guidance. The basis of this is partly recruiting brochures from companies and organizations, partly material from the Labour Market Board, such as the following encyclopaedia:

NORDIC
Occupational Classification. Systematic list of occupational areas, occupational groups, occupational "families" and individual occupations with code numbers and definitions. Published by the Labour Market Board. 3rd ed. Hälsingborg 1974.

At the end of this book there is an alphabetical occupational index, where you can look up different occupations, such as "company manager" (code number 111.10) or your own job, such as "cement burner" (code number 832.25).

The code number will help you find that your job belongs to a certain occupational area, such as "manufacturing work" (8) occupational group, "chemical processing work" (83) and the occupational family "boiler and kiln operators" (832). Your job is described like this:

832,25 *Cement burner* Operates the kiln for producing cement by burning different types of stone, clay and other materials; controls the heating and surveys the material deliveries; checks that the process runs normally; surveys the disposal of cement and slag.

If you want a more comprehensive description you can go on to another encyclopaedia:

SWEDISH
Professional index. Published by the Labour Market Board, Vocational Guidance Bureau. Part 1-2. Hälsingborg 1967-69. 3rd ed. 1972.

This book gives the following description:

Production worker in chemical industry (prof, group 83). Type of work. The production in chemical industry is mainly done by chemical procedures in closed plants, supervised by *process workers...*

As solid matter is being crushed, screened, sorted and separated, the worker surveys each machine and makes sure that the feeding is even and that there is no congestion. The deliveries are usually made continuously with transporters of different kinds. When liquid matter is being separated or filtrated, centrifuged, evaporated, distilled etc., the worker surveys and checks with instruments that the machines are working properly. He regularly reads the controls and writes operational reports. He tours the plant to check on the machinery. He also takes samples, which he occasionally checks with gauges, but usually sends to the laboratory for analysis. The process worker is sometimes assisted by an assistant. In a modern plant the worker can usually follow the procedures for which he is responsible from a manoeuvre room. With signalling lamps, pressure gauges, ampere hour and temperature meters, the worker can discover any disturbance in the normal production flow.

These disturbances are usually eliminated automatically by the controls of the machine, but if necessary, the worker must be able to intervene himself and control the procedure by various measures, such as changing the flow, the concentration, the temperature or pressure.

In most cases the process worker should be able to tell whether an operational disturbance is caused by mechanical, electrical or chemical process faults. He should be able to locate purely mechanical faults and at the same time make simple adjustments and repairs...

The index also tells us what organizations represent the process worker and his opposite number on the labour market. It also states the number of process workers in Sweden at the last census. Further, it judges future possibilities for the job and refers to literature that will tell you more about it. The only literature recommended on process work is the journal *The Factory Worker*.

How much does a process worker earn? The information on this point is very unsatisfactory. All it says is: "Regarding average hourly wages, see chapter headed Industrial wages." But the information in the chapter on industrial wages is, for one thing not very detailed, secondly, not comparable to the salary information given for other professions, such as engineers and company managers.

Why can't they give the maximum, minimum and average annual wages for each occupation? It would also be possible to express the wage level of each job as X times the minimum of subsistence. Or the process workers' wages could be expressed as X% of the average company manager's salary.

There is cause for a much more comprehensive picture than the one given by the index. So why not give it? Is that because it would, together with the description of the jobs, give a much too embarrassing picture of unfair social conditions in Sweden?

Occupational Hazards

The information on disadvantages and hazards connected with different jobs is also very incomplete. The word "disadvantage" is not even used. Instead they talk about "occupational requirements". The 1969 edition, for example, requires the following from a welder:

Good eyesight. The light when welding is strongly blinding, and negligence with protective eye-glasses could lead to damaged sight.

Strong back, legs and feet. Much of the work is done standing up.

Muscular strength. The welder often works with heavy workpieces and equipment.

Agility. There are many uncomfortable work positions.

Good balance. When working on wharfs and bridges, the welder may have to work on scaffolding, where there is risk of falling.

Miscellaneous. Splashes from the welding charge can give burns. Gasses developing when welding can be a strain on the lungs.

The blinding light is, in other words, presented as a demand for good eyesight. Risks for falling as a demand for balance, gasses as a demand for strong lungs. Who are making the demands? According to the index, not the employer but the job itself.

In the 1972 edition the words "occupational requirements" which might raise the question "required by whom", have been replaced by the abstract expression "conditions to consider". But the question is still there: *Who* expects the workers to accept these conditions?

The description of occupational hazards has been even more reduced in the 1979 edition. The gasses are no longer referred to as being "a strain" but are just "uncomfortable". No risk for eye injuries is referred to, but the strong welding light can be "a strain on the eyes". The risk for falling or getting burnt aren't even mentioned.

Are these changes of the occupational description due to the fact that the welder's work situation has been improved accordingly between 1969 and 1972? Definitely not. It is only the smoothing over of his reality that has been taken a step further.

The person using this index wants to know the following: *What* are the gasses developing with welding? *How* much of a strain are they to the lungs? *What* can be done to avoid them?

In order to get material for a more comprehensive occupational description, the editors of the *Swedish Occupational Index* can go to other encyclopaedias, such as:

HANSSON: Sven Ove
Working Environment from A to Z: Topical Encyclopaedia on Occupational Hazards
and Workers' Protection.
Lund 1975.

In this book, health hazards connected with welding are presented under the following headings: work positions, climate, noise, electrical injuries, light, fire risk and chemical risks.

The book points out the unexplored areas of chemical risks. For example, very little is known about the decomposition products formed with the welding of grease, oils, plastic or glue. The combination effects of different components in welding smoke are poorly researched.

Some of the substances known to have chemical risks connected with welding are ozone, nitrous fumes, carbon oxide, iron oxide, manganese, zinc, copper, lead, chrome, cadmium, plus a dozen other substances. Each of these is in turn a word for the encyclopaedia. "Ozone" has the following description:

Ozone is a gas formed from the oxygen in the air if it is exposed to ultraviolet radiation... Even in low concentration, ozone is a strong irritant for eyes, mouth, nose and throat. The substance also has a damaging effect on the lungs. — Very high concentrations have been found in large cities in periods with strong pollutions, smog. In those circumstances the content went up to 0.1 ppm... The Swedish maximum limit, like the American, is 0.1ppm. In the Soviet Union it is 0.05 ppm. — The American commission on maximum limits writes: "The maximum value of 0.1 may not cause any obvious or tangible injury but this limit could result in early ageing in a fashion similar to people for a long period exposed to radioactive radiation."

Nitrogen dioxide is one of the nitrous fumes formed by the nitrogen and oxygen in the air when affected by ultraviolet light. The Swedish maximum limit is 5ppm. In the Soviet Union it is 2ppm. In a Russian industry with air content of less than 2.6 the workers showed certain blood changes, increased susceptibility to infections and damaged teeth and gums. They also had evidence of lung emphysema, i.e. a breakdown of the walls between the different air-cells. Other investigations have also been able to establish a connection between nitrous fumes and emphysema.

Nitrous fumes, together with ozone, in certain conditions, will form a new substance, *nitrogen pentoxide*, the effects of which can be compared to the gasses used in the First World War.

Both the *Swedish Occupational Index* and *Working Environment from A to Z* probably give a factually correct picture of the welder's occupation. But having seen some examples of the gasses which, according to the *Swedish Occupational Index* of 1969, can be "a strain on the lungs" but in 1975 were only "uncomfortable", it is plain that facts are seen from two entirely different points of view.

The official publication, published by the Labour Market Board, sees it as undisputable that the worker should risk his life and health. The risks are "occupational requirements" which the employer is entitled to make or "preconditions" which he expects the worker to accept.

In *Working Environment from A to Z*, however, it is the worker who considers and makes the requirements. He demands a working environment which does not expose him to hidden danger. He expects his occupation not to jeopardize his life and health.

Both encyclopaedias state that the risks exist — but one tells the worker what he has to subject himself to, the other what he ought to rebel against.

The least you can expect from the *Swedish Occupational Index* is to simply call the occupational hazards in the next edition "occupational hazards" and present them in a way to give the person choosing an occupation a clear idea of what he is embarking upon.

• What description is given of your occupation in the *Swedish Occupational Index*? Is it correct? Is it sufficient?

Aids: The *Swedish Occupational Index* should be available at the county library dept. Ex. (in Sweden). *Working Environment from A to Z* is under Ö (in Sweden) where there are other books, too, about occupational hazards. See Chapter 10.

10. THE FACTORY INSPECTORATE

The Stockholm offices of the Factory Inspectorate are at 61, Strandbergsgatan, just under the E4 highway passing over Kungsholmen. At first you enter a little waiting room, where a receptionist is answering the telephone and receiving visitors.

"Good morning, I'm a Swedish citizen and I've come to see some official documents."

The minute she hears me mention "official documents" she calls the legal expert of the factory inspectorate. I ask him to show me all official acts connected with Cementa's factory in Stora Vika. At first we go to the company directory and find Cementa. The Stora Vika factory has the reference number 1-24 796. Then we go to the records and he produces the document with this number, i.e., a file with papers, which he peruses before handing them to me.

These documents are official, unless they contain production or business secrets. The legal expert keeps some descriptions of an invention produced at Stora Vika associated with a process to purify waste water. Apart from that, I can inspect everything. The file contains:

1. The correspondence between the Factory Inspectorate and the company, e.g. a reply to their application for permission to employ a minor.
2. Protocols from the factory inspector's visits to the factory. They are hand-written little notes, which can be quite hard to read. If you suspect that the factory inspector has not listened to the demands you've made, you can go and check the Factory Inspectorate's records to see if he has even taken note of the demands.
3. Orders. The factory inspector's visit often results in orders for the employer to "take certain measures". In that case

there is a typed copy, often with hand-written notes from follow-up visits.

4. Remittance letters. E.g., to the Nynäshamn County planning department, when Cementa asked to be exempted from applying for planning permission to extend their factory.

5. Printed letters from the security department of Cementa's headquarters, including instructions on how to perform certain dangerous jobs — such as lowering a worker into a cement silo to break congestion.

6. Protocols from the protection committee's meetings at Stora Vika, three or four times a year. Such protocols are usually accessible to the worker at the company. But to a worker applying for a job or an outsider who wants to investigate a company, the records of the Factory Inspectorate is a good place to find these protocols. Their information includes the following:

a) Accidents and narrow escapes. Brief, concrete descriptions. The following minor accidents and narrow escapes happened e.g., at Stora Vika the last week in January 1976.

21.1 When loading logs onto a lorry, the crane turned to the side and S. was hit on the head. He was not wearing a helmet. He was wounded.

24.1 When transporting parts to the no. 4 slurry mill which is in the process of being repaired, a "sack truck" was used. When S. loaded the first clamping ring, it came too far forward (i.e., in front of the wheels) and the shafts then came up to hit his nose. He was wounded.

25.1 When mounting a chain lock, K. slipped with the screwdriver, so that the screwdriver went in under his left thumbnail.

25.1 When a tractor was being repaired, the workmates dropped the sledge, so that X's big toe was hit. It bled.

26.1 While the three-wheel barrow was being lowered, T. was receiving it, but when the barrow hit the ground, the handle twisted itself and hit T. at the temple.

b) Accident statistics and comparison with other cement factories. This shows that 1967 after all was a year extraordinarily free from accidents at Stora Vika. In the whole year only one incident, officially considered an accident, occurred.

c) A list of the measures taken to reduce risks and discomfort in the working environment. In earlier protocols these measures are mainly distribution of brochures, cautionary notices etc. In later protocols some real changes are actually accounted for.

d) Results of measuring values in the working environment and health examinations. Example: At the fine crushing works, in 1974, 73 milligrams per cubic metre, at the crushing pocket 30 mg/m and by the sliding drills in the lime pit 19.5 mg/m. The maximum limit is 10 mg/m. The measuring was made by the Cementa section for working environment issues.

e) Demands for new measures. Example: At the first meeting of the Cementa protection committee in 1967, the senior protection officer I. Steen made the following demands: speed limit within the factory area, radio connection between crane driver and door manager when unloading, supervision of the locking devices for the crane, another spotlight at the harbour and measures against the dust at the burning site. The safety representative B. Ulfves inquired whether the gas formed with welding the new plastic coating in the mills could be poisonous.

As you can see, the records of the Factory Inspectorate contain a lot of concrete information about conditions at a factory. There is only one problem — all documents are disposed of after about ten years. Before 1964, there were no documents on Stora Vika among its records. Yet it is a question of few documents, which shouldn't be too difficult to keep. Every little note from national and local government departments is kept for centuries. But the evidence of the condition of our places of work are systematically destroyed every ten years!

- Go to the Factory Inspection office and ask to see the documents on your place of work.

Aids: The Factory Inspection has nineteen different branches. The address is in the telephone directory. Bring this book along if you like and refer to it if you run into trouble.

The Case of Asbestos

Why is it important that the documents of the Factory Inspectorate are kept? Because, generally, it takes a long time before the effects of a certain working environment are known. And even longer before the discovery leads to measures.

In 1900, a young worker died at the Charing Cross Hospital in London. A postmortem showed that there were strange changes in his lungs, caused by microscopic asbestos fibres that had been embedded in the lung tissue. The man had been working in the carding room of an asbestos textile mill. They found that he was the last of ten people of the same age who had all worked in the same room and all died from "pulmonary trouble".

The case was described by the British scientist Murray in 1907 but did not attract any attention. The disease *asbestosis* was not taken seriously in England until the early 1920s and was officially recognized only in 1930. In Sweden it was not until 1964 that the Labour Safety Committee formulated the first instructions for "preventing occupational injury through asbestos".

The connection between asbestos and lung cancer was suggested for the first time in an official British report in 1947. Doll's investigations in 1955 confirmed it. The connection between the cancer type mesothelioma and asbestos was described by Selikoff in 1964.

In Sweden these investigations were noticed in connection with a conference in 1969. The then Labour Medicine Institute started an investigation of thirty-five factories where asbestos was part of the operation. The final result of the investigation was given in 1974. In the meantime stricter instructions considering the risk for cancer, were being issued.

The asbestos industry would not hear of a restriction of regulations. Industrial AB Euroc took part through its subsidiary Scandinavian Eternite in Lomma, which had manufactured asbestos cement since 1906. The company wrote their own proposal for new regulations, maintaining categorically that there was no dust from asbestos cement and so it was harmless. Because of the resistance of the industry and especially Euroc, the new regulations had to be rewritten at least twelve times before they were finally approved by the Labour Safety Committee in 1975.

Later the same year, the alarm was raised. The LO (TUC) doctor Anders Englund found that eight workers at Nohab in Trollhättan had died of mesothelioma. They had all worked with asbestos insulation. The discovery lead to further restrictions of regulations, which was one reason — a welcome reason, according to some — why Euroc had to close down its daughter company at Lomma.

Note that the deaths which were the cause of the asbestos alarm had occurred between 1959 and 1969 — i.e., the workers had died from asbestos fibres they had breathed in long before the Labour Safety Committee had published their first asbestos instructions in 1964. In other words, it is important that the documents of the Factory Inspectorate are kept. Even tomorrow, people will die due to working conditions which were prevalent in factories twenty, thirty, or even fifty years ago.

Even in the late 1960s, people died of lung cancer caused by asbestos fibre because they had worked in the gas mask factories of the First World War.

One forty-seven-year-old woman died of asbestos cancer. When she was between two and six, she had been exposed to the dust from her parents' working clothes when they came home from their work in an asbestos factory. This is one of several examples of children who have contracted lung cancer through contact with their parents' working clothes.

A foreman at an asbestos pit sometimes brought home asbestos pieces for his little girl to play with. As an adult she died of mesothelioma. Another little girl would take a lunch basket to her father at the asbestos factory every day for one year. More than forty years later, she died of mesothelioma.

Thus history lives on in living people's bodies. It lurks there and finally it kills. When the dead body is opened up, history can be found in the shape of silvery fibres — the last remnants of the air these people breathed in the factories and workers' homes of the 1910s and 20s.

And when the votes are counted at the Board meetings, the same history is still there — the profits from those days still endow some people with power and dividends. Just as the workers' children inherited the fibres, other children inherited the shares. History is not dead. Even tomorrow it will do its utmost to influence the instructions issued by the Labour Safety Committee.

- What are the risks at your place of work, in your occupation? When were they discovered? When was something first done about them?

Aids: The asbestos issue is discussed by Arne Stråby in *Risky Environment* (Sthlm 1977) and in the report from the Labour Safety Committee AMT 102/74 *Asbestos in Our Factories* by Nils Boman e.a. The history of the discovery of occupational diseases is described comprehensively in *The Diseases of Occupations*, 5th ed. London 1975, by Donald Hunter.

The best Swedish encyclopaedia on occupational hazards is Sven Ove Hansson's already mentioned *Work Environment from A to Z* (Lund 1975). In English there are *Encyclopaedia of Occupational Health and safety*, 1-2, International Labour Office, Geneva, 1971, and N. Irving Sax, *Dangerous Properties of Industrial Materials*, 4th ed. New York 1975.

The factory workers' environment at work was investigated by the LO inquiry *Risks at Work: Factories* by Erik Bolinder e.a. (Lund 1971). Corresponding enquiries have been carried out for many other trade unions. Bolinder considered the work environment of cement workers to be relatively risk-free. Quite a different opinion is expressed in *Chemical Risk in Factories* (Report on enquiry to the Congress of Swedish Factory Workers 1976) Sthlm 1976, which strongly emphasizes the dangers of cement dust.

Dust

The first Swedish labour safety act, *The Occupational Hazard Act of 1889*, set up the Factory Inspectorate. In his book *The State and Workers' Safety 1850-1919* (Uppsala 1950), Hjalmar Stenberg describes how this law came about.

The resistance of the employers was not so much against the law but against the idea that special factory inspectors would be commissioned to make sure the rules were applied in practice. Before the law was approved by the employers' representatives in Parliament, it had to be given the following addition: the factory inspector could not visit a factory without first announcing his arrival. This was to "maintain discipline amongst workers". The law was reduced further by this demand:

when carrying out their job, the inspectors must show tact and care, they must not make excessive demands on working premises and equipment that make the work unnecessarily difficult or expensive or cause unnecessary expenditure. If there is no imminent danger, necessary improvements can be made successively, considering the employer's ability to apply them, and the inspectors should always keep in mind the fact that work under less favourable conditions is preferable to unemployment.

Equipped with these words, the first three factory inspectors started their activities. We can follow them in:

SUMMARY
of factory inspectors' reports from 1890-94. (The Home Office. Publication 13, 14, 19, 23.) Sthlm 1891-95.

And then yearly in:

THE FACTORY INSPECTION
Activities 1895-1948.
Published by the Institute of Commerce 1895-1912.
By the Department of Social Affairs 1913-1938.
By the National Insurance Institute 1939-1948.

And then yearly in:

THE LABOUR SAFETY COMMITTEE
and the activities of Factory Inspection. 1949 -

The dust in cement factories soon attracted the factory inspectors' attention. The inspector of the southern district toured Gotland in 1893 and reports that:

a special dust chamber with a suction fan should be installed in a cement factory in Visby County, to protect the workers from the dust developing in the factory when materials are mixed for producing cement, but the works manager explained that the setting up of such a chamber with a suction fan was impossible at this time due to lack of space. He was also of the opinion that the dust in question was not dangerous. After the medical officer of the County Council on request had judged conditions at the factory and thereafter voiced the same opinion, that there was no cause to suppose that the dust should be harmful to the workers' lungs, the District Council decided not to take any action in this matter at present.

The report of 1894 returns to the problem:

Experience shows, just like the previous year, that the inspection of factories and other working premises proves them to be highly unsatisfactory from a hygienic point of view... Because the inspector of the southern district on inspection of cement factories found the working premises full of dust, he has tried to gain some knowledge of measures taken to avoid the spreading of dust in similar factories in Denmark. However, these arrangements had not yielded fully satisfactory results. Still, the inspector had discussed with the managers of a cement factory in the southern district attempts to stop the cement dust from spreading on the work premises and according to messages sent to the inspector, these attempts have had some success.

The report of 1909 looks upon the dust problem as resolved in the new factory built outside Visby:

Here the manufacture is done by the wet method, which means you avoid a lot of dust, which was the worst problem of this and similar factories, from a hygienic point of view. When lime is being crushed, which is done in a chewer, no water needs to be flushed thanks to the dampness of the Gotland lime, but the grinding in the ball mill is done with so much water flushing and at the same time adding a suitable amount of marl, that the ground goods leaves it as a viscid semi-liquid. After this has been properly flushed, the water evaporates in a rotary tube-type furnace and only the grinding of the cement is done dry. In the factory 18 men are now employed, 9 on each shift, and of them only two work in the mill, which is completely separated from the rest of the factory where the dry grinding is done, but in this room ventilation is good.

By comparing the number of people busy in the factory itself, 18 men instead of 52, or in all 111 men instead of 172, whilst production has risen from 140,000 to 200,000 drums a year, one can state that this change of manufacturing method brings not only hygienic improvements but also a great financial advantage.

After this, nothing is said about the dust problem in the cement industry. But obviously the problem was not resolved, as they introduced the wet method. On the 18/7/1914, engineer H.O. Ödlund gave an account in the Technical Journal of a German investigation showing that cement factories offered the dustiest working environment of that time. In an ordinary living room the air contained about 1 milligram dust per cubic metre, in the cleaning shop of an ironworks 72 mg, in a felt shoe factory 175 mg. The cement factory topped the statistics with 224 milligram per cubic metre of air. A number of other investigations had given similar results.

SICKNESS
Statistics of the Leipzig Ideal Sick Fund: Twenty-Fourth Annual Report of the Commissioner Of Labour, 1909. Vol. 1, p. 1255. Government printing office. Washington 1911.

THOMPSON, L.R. e.a.
The Health of Workers in Dusty Trades. 1. Health of Workers in a Portland Cement Plant. (Public health bulletin, 176). Government printing office. Washington 1928.

VACAREZZA, Rodolfo A.
Higiene y salubridad en la industria del cemento Portland.
Buenos Aires 1950.

These investigations show on the one hand that the cement workers of the time were exposed to very high dust contents (up to 197 million particles per cubic foot or over four billion particles per cubic metre of air, according to the American investigation), and also that cement workers more often than other workers suffered from pulmonary diseases. The American investigation suggested a maximum limit of ten-twelve million particles per thirty-three cubic feet as a compromise between conflicting financial and medical opinions.

At the International Congress on Occupational Diseases in Brighton in 1975, a Yugoslav research group again showed that cement workers run a greater risk than others of contracting certain pulmonary diseases, such as chronic bronchitis, which manifests itself as a stubborn cough. Their pulmonary functions were also poorer than those of the average population. Greek researchers who have made a similar investigation came to the conclusion that the lungs of cement workers age prematurely. All persons experience poorer lung functions as they grow older. This manifests itself as shortness of breath. In workers in Greek and Yugoslav cement factories, this effect has been found to occur sooner than in the normal population.

In the report of the Factory Workers' Union to the congress of 1976, *Risks in Factories*, the cement dust is described as follows:

In Sweden mainly so called Portland cement is used. It consists mainly of quartz (risk for silicosis) and calcium oxide. There are also smaller amounts of aluminium oxide and iron oxide and other substances...

Calcium oxide (quick lime) has an irritant effect on eyes and mucous membranes. The substances can bring on nasty wounds, especially on the nose diaphragm, which can sometimes be perforated. Dust particles entering the eyes can cause permanent damage to eyesight. This risk is particularly great if the eyes are exposed to the substance repeatedly.

Calcium oxide can also cause inflammation of the pulmonary tracts, in bad cases pneumonia. Mental ailments have also been reported, such as headaches, fatigue, anorexia etc.

Together with the risk for silicosis, the calcium oxide in cement is a good reason why the dust content must be kept very low.

Today's Swedish maximum limit was recently lowered from ten to five milligrams per cubic metre. In the protocols from Stora Vika 1974 we could see that they had dust contents of up to seventy-three milligrams in the fine crusher works and thirty milligrams at the coarse crusher.

The main agent today to keep dust down in cement factories is the electrostatic filter. In principle it was invented as early as 1884 by Sir Oliver Joseph Lodge. A practically usable electrostatic filter was designed by F.G. Cottrell in 1906. One of the first filters was installed at the cement factory Riverside in California. The company had been given a court order to close the factory unless they managed to clean the exhaust fumes, which damaged surrounding orange groves. The electrostatic filter absorbed up to 98% of the dust, which equalled one hundred tons a day.

Cottrell's method was not unknown to Swedish cement companies. It was presented in, among other places, the Technical Journal in 1920 by technician Joh. Härdén and again in 1922 by Åke Esbjörnsson. The first Cottrell plant in Sweden was installed at Slite Cement in 1923. The intention was not to protect the health of workers or local inhabitants, but to extract potash from the fumes. The production proved unprofitable and was discontinued in 1926.

The first Swedish cement factory to be originally equipped with an — albeit insufficient — electrostatic filter was Köping in 1940. Limhamn did not get its first filters until 1951. Hällekis was last in 1969. By then the electrostatic filter had existed for sixty years. Two generations of cement workers had breathed in tons of cement dust, and millions of tons of dust had been spread over the environment. But for each year that Skånska Cement managed to avoid installing an electrostatic filter, the company could save some money at the expense of the workers and the local population.

This money has not disappeared. It is still there and today forms part of the capital of Industri AB Euroc.

Rectifier to the first electrostatic filter in Cottrell's laboratory.

11. DEATH

The first factory inspectors had to concentrate their efforts on the most obvious deficiencies. Above all they tried to prevent bad accidents in the factories. In the reports from the Malmöhus District several fatal accidents in the lime pits are described as being caused by the wrong work instructions. Finally, in 1901, one factory inspector had had enough and reacted like this:

5. Whilst shifting gear for a train in a lime pit, one shifter fell, as he tried to jump onto the running train. Both his legs were cut off by the wheels, which lead to his death later the same day.

The employer in his report of this accident writes that the accident was due to the carelessness of the shifter himself — employers generally claim that accidents are due to carelessness of the workers — and therefore I would like to give a more detailed description of this particular accident to show how unfounded this claim can be. The now dead worker was employed as a shifter for a lime train. His job was to operate the points by jumping off the train, running past it to change the point and then jump on to one of the wagons of the train, which was in motion all the time. He then travelled on to the next point to change that in the same manner. The lime wagons — ordinary tip-wagons — have neither steps nor handles, so the shifter has to run in between the moving wagons to jump onto the train, and stand on a buffer in the middle of the wagon, that is, between the rails. The slightest consideration on the part of the employer should have indicated that it was only a question of time before this shifter, who spent his time jumping off and onto trains, would slip and fall on the rails and subsequently be run over. Yet they are claiming that this man's death was caused by his own carelessness. I called for a police enquiry, and as a consequence of that, stationary point shifters have now been employed to operate the points.

As the years go by, the descriptions of accidents take up more and more room in the factory inspectors' reports. Page-by-page, working men die. Their heads are blown off in explosions, their feet are chopped off or their arms sawn off, they are dragged into machines, they are shut in containers whilst acid is being filled, they are found dead under debris. The fatal accidents in the cement industry are among the most trivial:

1902:
10. In a cement factory a machine greaser with the assistance of another worker was to apply a trace, while the machine was running, and for this reason had climbed a ladder. As the trace was applied, the man's clothes got stuck between the trace and the pulley. As a consequence, he was flung violently against a stone wall, crushing his head against it. Death was instantaneous.

In this case, as in the one before it, the trace was quarter-twisted and one axle set vertically, which makes the process of applying the trace with the machine running much more dangerous.

1904:
3. On August 8, the worker Gustaf Persson at the cement factory the Klaghamns Lime Quarry Ltd in Västra Klagtorp was pulled into a transmission line. Death was almost instantaneous.

1905:
5. While quarrying lime on June 20 at the Klagstorp lime pit, a lump of earth came loose and fell from a small height

onto the worker Mårten Jönsson, who was sitting down. His hypogastrium was split open.

7. At the brick works of Skånska Cement at Lomma, Nils Larsson-Hörlin on August 5 was busy transporting raw bricks in a lift, and was himself present in the lift, as is usual at some brick works. Hörlin then had the upper part of his body crushed between the lift and the floor of the upper storey, and because of this he died shortly afterwards.

1907:
5. At the Limhamn lime pit, belonging to Skånska Cement, the wharf carpenter Hans Jönsson on March 31 on his way towards the wharf workshop crossed the railway of the lime pit. He was then run over and killed by the train.

1911:
6. At the railway of Skånska Cement in Limhamn, the brakeman Otto Fredrik Persson was killed on July 18, as a wagon derailed.

1912:
8. At the Maltesholm cement factory, on August 18, the chief machine operator Svante Hjalmar Boström was killed by an electric current of 250 Volts. He was busy putting up a meter device on the large electric instrument panel in the engine room. He had not turned off the mains, which were close to the location of the meter, and probably by accident touched one of the mains, with the consequence that the killing electric current went through his body. When the factory inspector examined the case, the government inspector on electricity had already given protective instructions.

In 1912 came a new law for workers' protection making the board of Social Affairs chiefly responsible for the Factory Inspectorate. Accidents are thereafter described in

SOCIAL
notices published by the Board of Social Affairs. 1913-1927.
(Statistic notices. Series P.)

1913:
47. A worker in a cement factory, who happened to be working in a warehouse, was hit by falling debris and killed. The work is usually done like this: Cement is brought in through holes in the roof and stored at a height of 5 metres. When required it is taken out through channels made in the floor with shells, so that the cement runs through holes made in the roof of the channel. In the layer of cement above these holes there are often formations of conical holes, where the cement, when running down, is always loose, whilst between the holes it is firm enough to walk on. The workers sometimes must push down the firmer part of the cement, and when the now deceased man entered the conical hole to do this, the cement collapsed, and he suffocated. The Factory Inspectorate suggested that in the future at least two workers should be at the same spot. A belt with a rope should be used for entering the conical hole, doors on the roof should be kept open to remove cement dust, and there should be silos provided in the warehouse.

1917:
56. An electric fitter, G., employed by a cement factory, on one occasion was to put up a new cable from the carpenter shop adjoining the factory to a lamp-post at the factory. In spite of instructions from the foreman, he had not beforehand turned off the current in the cable, from which the new one was to come.

G. climbed a ladder raised against the wall, spliced the cables together and then descended with the new cable in his hand. As his feet touched the ground, the current (220 volts A/C) went through his body. Before he had been freed from the cable by his workmates, who rushed to assist him, he was unconscious and probably died shortly afterwards, as attempts to revive him were unsuccessful. The main contributory factor to the tragic accident would be the fact that G. had a heart condition.

89. In a cement factory there was a fatal accident. For storing coal cinder needed for the night, a 10 metre high concrete silo with a cross-section of 4 x 6 metres was used. At the vertical outlet at the bottom of the silo, there is a feeding roller conveying the coal cinder to an elevator. During the day, coal cinder is fed into the silo, which is eventually filled up to a level of 7 metres. Just before the accident, it had been noted that the cinder was deteriorating inasmuch as it was more fine-grained and moreover wet, which made it form vaults or bridges inside the silo, especially near the outlet. On the day of the accident, no one had noticed any delay in the feeding, but one worker, S., still went up to the top of the silo to push down the surface of the cinder. It is believed that he lost his balance and was pulled down and suffocated by the cinder. The electric lamp was lowered into the silo, which indicates that S. may have left the vertical pole with cross bars, which is used for support when the cinder collapses, and walked on the surface itself. The cinder must have collapsed right through to the bottom, since S. had 4-5 metres of cinder over him.

To prevent a repetition of such accidents, the Factory Inspectorate together with the company management ruled that no one is allowed to enter the silo without a safety rope around his body, and one man should be on the bridge holding this rope. Moreover, a bridge should be built at a height of four metres in the silo and be equipped with proper banisters. The cinder can then be pressed down from this bridge, if it has sunk below that height.

The accounts of activities also contain occasional descriptions of accidents:

1919:

An explosion in a *cement factory* in the 5th district. The factory inspectorate writes: "On February 13; 1919 quite a strange accident occurred in a cement factory."

A coal dust chamber of armed concrete, 18.5 m long, 1.6 m wide and 2.5 m high, placed between the 2nd and 3rd storeys of the factory, exploded after a 2 hours' rest as the conveyor worm running along the bottom of the chamber was started.

At the vehement explosion, the 100mm thick concrete walls of the chamber were fragmented and the thick external walls of the building were slightly expelled. Flames burst out in the factory, and two workers, standing about 15m from the chamber, were badly burnt.

It is considered likely that the coal dust gathered at the bottom of the chamber had become congested and started to glow, which may have lit the coal dust and gasses present, as the conveyor worm was started.

The coal dust chamber has now been replaced by a larger iron pipe with a conveyor worm inside.

As you can see, the accident reports have become more anonymous. It has become more difficult to find out where they happened. And as the number of fatal accidents increased, they became less and less worthy of description. After 1919 I have only found this description from 1936:

3. At a *cement factory* there is a conveyor device for loading cement, both loose and packed in sacks. This device consists of a *conveyor belt* of "rubber", 8mm thick and 600mm wide, enclosed to prevent it from weathering. Next to the conveyor belt, the load-carrying part of which runs 1m above the floor level of the building, there is a path, along which workers can walk...

Especially when loose cement is being loaded, the supporting and breaking rolls are coated with a thin layer of cement. In bad weather, rain and snow enter the building, making the cement burn and stick to the supporting and breaking rolls. The deposits thus formed grow gradually, and finally the conveyor belt is affected: its path becomes unbalanced and hits the guide of the counterweight roll, risking damage to the conveyor belt. To avoid this, the foreman should check early on that the rolls are scraped clean of any cement deposits. This work need, however, be done only a few times annually.

The shift foreman K. had been told to do this, i.e. scrape clean the rolls underneath the conveyor belt. For this he used an 80 cm long iron scraper, bent at a right angle, which could be kept in position by a wooden trestle, as he cleaned the rolls.

Suddenly a couple of loud screams were heard, and at the same time, the conveyor belt stopped, although the driving motor was still running. The current to the motor was immediately turned off. It turned out that K. had been pulled into the meshing between the conveyor belt and the breaking roll. To get him out, the conveyor belt had to be cut. K. who had been badly injured died later the same day.

To prevent more accidents in this machine, the breaking rolls have now been completely encased.

When in 1939 the Factory Inspectorate was transferred to the National Insurance Office, the publication of accident reports ceased temporarily. But in 1944, reports reappear in the journal *Labour Safety*, now called *Working Environment*, which still publishes regular summaries of factory inspectors' accident reports.

This material is never used when a company's history is written. Very few people know that it even exists. I think the material ought to be compiled and made accessible in a book. The descriptions of cases are often told with a laconic sense of drama — dark little pieces of prose about the monotonous reappearance of occupational death and its constant surprises.

But above all it presents a picture of the working environment and the working conditions of Swedish industry over almost one century.

The term "risk capital" is often used. But in the reports of the Factory Inspectorate, there is not one example indicating that the shareholders of the company have been hurt. It was not the shareholders who were pulled into the conveyor belt or were badly burnt when the coal chamber exploded. It was not the company managers who were buried by coal cinder, killed by electricity, suffocated by cement or run over by lime trains. The reports of the Factory Inspectorate show who took the real risks.

- What do the Factory Inspectorate reports have to tell about death in your occupation, at the company where you work? Is there any more material in the local press? In the records of the company?

Death in Figures

The published reports of occupational accidents have always been only a fraction of the number of accidents that actually occurred. The majority remain a statistical figure.

It was the so called Workers' Insurance Committee in 1884 that compiled the first information on accidents in Swedish factories. The replies of the employers are still kept in the National Archives. It is reported from the Lomma cement factory that the earth worker Nils Persson, on 11 October 1884, was unable to work for 120 days. Reason: "Two toes on his left foot were injured as he carelessly touched the piston rod of a steam engine." The miller Nils Bengtsson, on 13 November 1884, had two fingers injured against a running grindstone and could not work for thirty-six days.

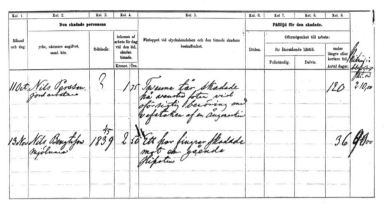

Accident in Lomma cement factory 1/9 1884-28/2 1885. According to the employer's information to the Workers' Insurance Committee. National Archives.

There was an account of a new investigation by Hjalmar Gullberg in *Accidents at Work* (Sthlm 1899). Regular statistics of accidents at work were published annually from 1906 by the Institute of Commerce in the series *Work Statistics*:

ACCIDENTS
at work. Swedish official statistics (SOS)
OCCUPATIONAL INJURIES 1955 -
Swedish official statistics (SOS).

These statistics have many shortcomings. Sometimes they do not apply to the indication in the title — cement factories are sometimes confused with cement goods factories. Accidents that have occurred in a side-line enterprise are also referred to the main company.

On the other hand, the statistics only list some of the accidents that really occur in industry. The employer's duty to report has been more or less obligatory at different times. Many work accidents have not been included in occupational injuries statistics because they were reported as ordinary sickness, and some haven't been reported at all. The occupational diseases are particularly underrated, because only a small number of diseases are regarded as occupational from the insurance point of view. Before 1936 there is no such thing in statistics as occupational diseases.

If you keep this in mind and attach due criticism to each separate figure, the following tables still give a rough idea of the number of people injured in Swedish cement industry over the-years:

Accidents and Days of Sick Leave Caused by These in the Swedish Cement Industry, 1913-1954

Period	Accidents	Disabled	Deaths	Days of sick leave	Per annual worker
1913-14	212	14	2	7,250	3.2
1915-19	1000	29	12	-	
1920-24	1214	23	13	-	
1925-29	1589	36	8	-	
1930-34	1471	34	1	34,800	3.8
1935-39	1595	23	12	33,200	3.2
1940-44	956	18	11	19,300	2.4
1945-49	1441	22	10	30,200	3.2
1950-54	1660	25	11	33,300	3.1
1913-54	**11138**	**224**	**80**		

As you can see, the accident frequency is about the same at the end of the period as at the beginning. With the odd improvement and the odd deterioration, about the same number of people are killed or disabled in each five-year-period, and accidents cause about the same number of days of sick leave per annual worker.

After 1955, figures are no longer comparable to the earlier ones. A new more abstract frequency measure has been introduced — "occupational injuries per one million working hours". The employers' obligation to report accidents at work has been restricted, and less than half of the earlier reported cases are now included in the statistics. But improvements have been made which is proved by the figures on disablement and death, which have been strongly reduced.

Accidents and Days of Sick Leave Caused by These in the Swedish Cement Industry, 1955-1974

Period	Occ. injuries	Disabled	Deaths	Days of sick leave	Occ. injuries per million working hours	Occ. injuries per million working hours, average of all occ. injuries
1955-59	596	12	4	18,600	23.1	24.9
1960-64	504	16	3	15,900	18.2	23.8
1965-69	374	7	3	13,500	15.8	23.6
1970-74	382	13	6	11,400	18.4	22.0
1955-1974	**1856**	**48**	**16**	**59,400**	**18.9**	**23.6**

- What do the statistics on occupational injuries tell about the risks in your profession? How have the risks changed over the years? Is your company above or below average in its branch? Above or below average for Swedish industries?

- The insurance companies will classify occupations into different risk groups, based on occupational injury statistics. Which group does your job come under?

Aids: The insurance company Folksam will on request send you free of cost Tariff 11: 1 *Occupational List: Individual Insurance for Illness or Accidents.* The occupations are divided into four different risk groups. The risk in group 4 is considered to be 60% greater than the risk in group 1. Workers in cement factories come under group 4, technical managers group 2 and office staff who don't travel group 1. Shareholders are not included in the list.

Behind the Statistics

The material, on which a statistical table is based, is usually called *primary information.* The primary information contains the separate cases behind the statistics. Primary information for Swedish official statistics is usually secret for twenty years and then becomes official.

The primary information for occupational injury statistics is reports to the *National Insurance Office,* and its department for occupational injuries at Krossvägen 8 in Vinsta (near Vällingby, tube Johannelund).

But if you go there to find the people and factories behind the statistical figures, you run into the same problem as in the archive of the Factory Inspectorate — the reports are systematically burnt after fifteen years.

Just think of all the other little notes that are kept — and this enormous testimony to conditions and mal-conditions in Swedish Industries is regarded as too insignificant to be preserved. Why?

The odd accident in the past fifteen years can be shown to you in spite of being secret, according to the records official at the National Insurance Office. But the so called employers' acts, giving information about the companies, are strictly secret. "They don't want anyone to poke into them." To be sure that no one does, they are burnt five years before they become public.

The only files that remain of the basis of the occupational injury statistics refer to *life annuities*. For each life annuity paid out by the National Insurance Office to a disabled worker or to the family of a dead worker, the file has been kept.

Some files are kept in a basement room beneath the proper archive. They have been cleaned up and contain very little of interest. But thousands of files from 1903 onwards have been kept intact.

These generally contain police reports describing conditions at the factory and circumstances surrounding the accident. There is also correspondence with the recipients of the annuity — widows should send in regular assurances that they have not remarried. The files of those who became the victim of occupational diseases can be full of doctors' certificates, assuring you year after year, that their case is not one of silicosis, until one day the worker collapses and his disease is properly confirmed so that he can get his annuity — which won't cost much, since he will soon be dead.

It is important that this material does not go the same way as so many other files handled by the National Insurance Office. The evidence still remaining must not be destroyed.

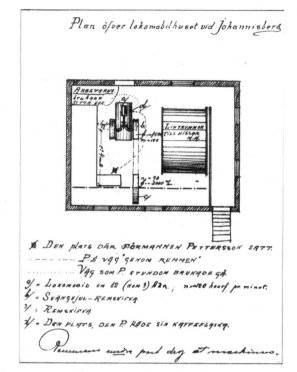

Plan öfver lokomobilhuset vid Johannisberg

Life annuity number one, the first distributed by the National
Insurance Office, went to Matilda Pettersson (120 SEK per year)
and her children Anna, Elvira, Leander and Ester (60 SEK each). The
drawing is an appendix to the police protocol and shows the engine
house where their father died the 27/1/1903. To fetch the coffee pot
that was standing on the steam engine by d/ August Pettersson went
through the conveyor belt between b/ and c/). He got stuck in the
belt, was drawn along up into the flywheel and thrown to the ground,
whereby his forehead and back where crushed. Matilda Pettersson
received life annuity number one until her death in 1927.

Aids: The files are more or less chronologically arranged in several different series and it is difficult to find a particular case or company. If you still want to try, it helps to know the name and birth date of the dead man and the date of the accident. There is a card index but this is regularly cleared of cases where the annuity is no longer paid. John Nordin's *Occupational Diseases 1-2* (Uppsala 1947) describes hundreds of cases of seemingly obvious occupational injuries which were not legally classified as "occupational disease".

12. GENEALOGY

When I was reading about occupational injuries in the records of the National Insurance Office, it was assumed that I was looking up some relation of mine. Researching the history of your own family is a common hobby. Less common is to research the history of your own company.

Who were my ancestors? Who came after them? These are the two main questions of genealogy.

They are of interest to many people. At the time this is being written, in Stockholm alone there are ten study groups working on genealogy. It is the only course in research technology for non-professional researchers at present being offered in this city. Genealogy is also one of the few areas where a good popular research handbook is available:

FURTENBACH, Börje
Genealogy for All.
Motala 1971.

This is a practical handbook based on great experience in guiding beginners. It describes how to interview old people, how to research records, how to arrange your results. It advises you of shortcuts and shows how to avoid pitfalls. It gives concrete, stimulating examples of the author's own research. *Why are there no handbooks like that for other areas of research?*

The conditions for genealogy in Sweden are better than in most other countries. We have *census registers* dating from 1625. We have *parish registers* dating back to 1686 that are fairly complete from 1749, when they became the basis of our census registration.

Birth and death registers are among the most important parish registers. *The birth books* contain dates for birth and christening, the name of the child and the names and address of the parents. *The death books* contain the name of the dead person, date of death and funeral and cause of death. *The registers of altered residence* contain the names of people moving into or out of a parish and states from where they came or where they are going.

If you know when someone was born or died, or when he or she moved from one place to another, one of these three parish registers can give you the complementary information you need to find a person in the most complete *parish register,* which is now called the *parish book.* Its original aim was to check the parishioners' ability to read and understand the Bible. In the old parish books, you can find a person's name, date of birth (year, month, day and place), ability to read, when he moved in (year, date and place), when he took communion, attended hearings of catechism, when he moved out, as well as other "circumstances and conditions".

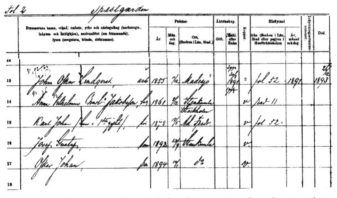

An excerpt from an old parish book from Stenkumla Parish in Gotland with notes on my grandfather, the worker Johan Oskar Lindqvist.

The old parish register is quite unusual. Often in other countries only the nobility can trace their origins — in Sweden everyone has the same chances of tracing their forebears. I can see why it fascinates so many. Especially with the great migration we've had in this country and with the lack of roots experienced by many people in large anonymous estates. It's natural to want to know where you come from.

But genealogy, I think, is too limited. All you find are more and more relatives. One example is my grandfather — why should I regard him only as an intermediary link to tracing as many generations as possible? I could also try to find out more about my grandfather himself, about the world in which he lived and the work he did.

He worked at the Visby Cement Factory in the 1890s. What were his wages? What about his working conditions? How was cement manufactured in those days? What part in the process did my grandfather play? What were the occupational hazards? Why did he die so early? To whom did the profits go? Where is that money today?

Genealogists seldom ask these questions. But someone ought to.

- What was your grandfather's occupation? Where did he work? Under what conditions?

Aids: This book. If he is still alive you should naturally start by asking him.

The Community

Another limitation of genealogy is the focus on your own family. But blood relationships are not the only path leading into the maze of history. There are other types of relationships.

What happened to that nice bloke you worked with in the late Fifties? You can trace him with the parish registers. It could be just as worthwhile as looking for some distant relation you've never even seen.

Who were the people working at the Limhamn lime pit in the 1890s? If you work there today it might be worthwhile to know. Who operated the kilns at Slite when they were first lit in 1917? No company history will tell you this, but they were the people producing the cement. From where did the workers come when the Stora Vika factory opened in 1949? Who were they, how long did they stay, where did they go, how long did they live, why did they die, what happened to their children?

All this is recorded in the parish registers. They can be used to explore the history of the industrial community.

- You have a job. Who were your predecessors in this job? You work in a factory. Who worked there before you?

Aids: You'll get the names from the membership lists of the trade union or via the union from the company records. The parish registers are kept at your parish registry office for a hundred years, and then at the National Archives. Filmed copies of all old parish books of each district are usually kept at the district library. Excerpts from the parish books of the whole country for the period 1860-1949 are with the Central Office of Statistics in Stockholm (see Chapter 26). The excerpts are arranged by year and then by district, and within the district by parish, with towns first.

Parish books older than seventy years are official documents. To gain access to more recent parish books, you may sometimes have to sign a form "not to abuse them with the intention to harm or denigrate the individual or his family". One exciting attempt to employ the people of the census register as a basis of history, rather than kings or politicians, is *The Biography of a People: Population and Society in Sweden from Past to Present*. Uddevalla 1975. Using the same methods, you could explore a company, a factory or even a single work team.

The Wehtje Family

A company is owned by people. It is managed by people. The work is done by people. Often genealogical conditions decide who own it, who manage it, who do the work. Genealogical aids could therefore be used as keys to the history of the capital.

The Swedish *Calendar of the Nobility*, is the bible of genealogists. It is still, over a century after aristocratic titles were abolished, a useful encyclopaedia, where you can find the explanation of many shareholdings and Board appointments. A middle-class equivalent is the *Swedish Family Calendar*, published since 1912 and accounting for a total of two thousand families, including the large financier families.

The 1967 edition of the *Swedish Family Calendar* for example, gives comprehensive information about the Wehtje family. It was founded by an immigrant, Ernst Ludwig Hermann, farmer and merchant, born in 1825, and died in 1911.

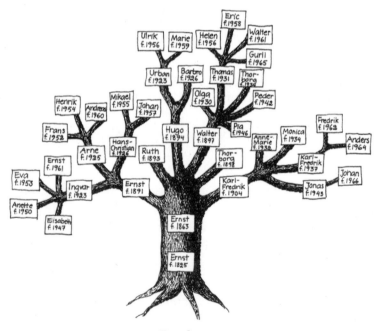

Family tree.

His son, Ernst Fredrik, born in 1863, deputy district judge, Managing Director of Skånska Cement AB, died in 1936, had the following children:

1. Ernst Jonas, b. 1891. MD of AB Ifö-verken and Skånska Cement AB. Married to Britta Elfverson.
2. Ruth, b. 1893, married to General Helge Ljung.
3. Hugo, b. 1894, MD of the Limhamn wood industry AB.
4. Walter, b. 1897, MD of AB Investor.
5. Thorborg Cecilia Dorothea, b. 1898, married to Herbert Dieden, MD of AB Herbert Dieden A Co.Walter, b. 1897, MD of AB Ivestor.
6. Karl-Fredrik, b. 1904, MD of Rörstrands China Factories AB.

It appears that out of the four sons, three were placed as managing directors of companies where the father had a dominant influence. The family calendar does not list the women's children, but on the male side there are the following grandchildren:

1.1 Ernst Ingvar, b. 1923. MD of Scandinavian Eternite AB.
1.2 Arne Henrik, b. 1926. MD of AB Scania Stone Industry.
1.3 Hans-Christian, b.1920, owner of the Ellinge estate at Eslöv.
3.1 Claes Hugo, b. 1922, dead 1923.
3.2 Urban Hugo, b. 1923, MD of the Limhamn Wood industry AB.
3.3 Barbro, b. 1926, married to Hans Söderlund, deputy MD of The Limhamn Wood Industry AB.
4.1 Ingegerd Anita Maria, b. 1927, married to Doctor Lars Wadström.
4.2 Gerda Olga Maria, b. 1930, married to Marc Wallenberg, MD. Stockholms Enskilda Bank.
4.3 Thomas Walter, b. 1931, a director of Atlas Copco AB (Vienna).

4.4 Thorborg Eva Maria, b. 1934, married to Adolf Lundin, mining engineer.

4.5 Peder Walter, b. 1942, student of economics (USA).

4.6 Margit Pia Maria, b. 1946, married to Erik Anderlin, student of economics. (Switzerland).

6.1 Anne-Marie, b. 1932, MD of the Svea-Line Agency (Hamburg).

6.2 Monica Cecilia Dorothea Louise, b. 1934, married to Lars Wohlfahrt, architect.

6.3 Karl Fredrik, b. 1937, owner of Pilegård, Tygelsjö.

6.4 Jonas Ernst Fredrik, b. 1943, student of economics (Zurich).

It appears that out of the five sons who have reached professional age, three have been placed as managing directors in companies where the father had a dominant influence. Even two sons-in-law have been in such positions. Two sons own large properties that form part of the family fortune. Ignoring the seven female grandchildren, the calendar records the male line with the following great-grandchildren:

1.1.1 Maria Elisabeth, b. 1947

1.1.2 Britta Anette, b. 1950

1.1.3 Eva Ingrid, b. 1953

1.1.4 Björn Ernst, b. 1961

1.2.1 Frans Göran Ernst, b. 1952

1.2.2 Sven Jones Henrik, b. 1954

1.2.3 Arbe Staffan Andreas, b. 1960

1.3.1 Hans Mikael, b. 1955

1.3.2 Ernst Johan, b. 1957

3.2.1 Ulrik Hugo, b. 1956

3.2.2 Marie, b. 1959

4.3.1 Helen, b. 1956

4.3.2 Eric Walter, b. 1958

4.3.3 Walter Gustaf Rickard, b. 1961

4.3.4 Viveka Tiu Gurli, b. 1965

6.3.1 Karl Fredrik Axel, b. 1962
6.3.2 Andreas Fredrik Axel, b. 1964
6.4.1 Johan Fredrik Ernst, b. 1966

All this according to the *Swedish Family Calendar* of 1967. It explains a lot of things which would otherwise be incomprehensible. It shows *why* little Anette at the age of fifteen had an income of 86,000 kr, while her twelve-year-old sister Ingrid took home 80,000 kr and their four-year-old brother Ernst earned 26,000 kr. The calendar also explains *why* Frans, Henrik, Andreas, Mikael and Johan, without even lifting a finger, were among the main private shareholders of Euroc.

• What have family conditions meant to the power over your place of work? What do they mean today?

Aids: *The Swedish Family Calendar* should be available at the county library. A number of other aids are listed in Sven Ågren's *Swedish Biographical Encyclopaedic Literature*, Uppsala 1929, which has a special section for people seeking information about industrialists. Local aids include Otto Brenner's *Personal History Sources for Skåne, Halland and Blekinge*, Malmö 1967, and Emil Nyberg's, *Gotland Family Book*, Ekenäs 1938. Similar books exist for most provinces.

The genealogists have their own journals. *Personal History Journal* has been published since 1898 and *Family and History* since 1950. Pontus Möller, *Swedish Genealogists' List 1970*, Sthlm 1971, records almost five hundred active amateur genealogists with addresses and information on the families they are investigating. *The Genealogical Society*, Arkivgatan 3, 111 28 Stockholm, tel. 08/21 34 54, gives the individual genealogist support and contacts to about two thousand people sharing this interest. When will the person trying to research a place of work or an industry get equally good support?

Birgitta and Olof Forsgren, *Who Owns What in Swedish Industry?* (1st ed. Sthlm 1968, 3rd ed. Sthlm 1977) informs you of the major shareholders of all large Swedish companies. If the company is listed by the Document of Value Centre (VPC) you can obtain a more comprehensive list of the owners with their addresses and personal identification codes by writing to or phoning the VPC (Malmskillnadsgatan 42, PO Box 7077, 103 32 Stockholm, tel: 08/ 23 82 30). Ask for a copy of the 'last list' for the company in question.

The list of Euroc's shareholders contains many names from the history of the Swedish cement industry. Shareholding by the Wehtje family is now insignificant.

One interesting example of genealogical methods applied to the exploration of a whole industry is S.J. Francis, *The Cement Industry 1796-1914* (Newton Abbot 1977).

13. THE TAXATION CALENDAR

During 1912-1974, *The Swedish Taxation Calendar* was published annually with information on the income of all Swedish high-income citizens. Finding out the incomes of owners and managers before 1912 is not impossible, only much more complicated.

Let's say that we start in 1900. Ernst Wehtje was then thirty-seven years old. He is listed in the *State Calendar* as District Bailiff for the Oxie and Skytt District, but even then, his main income came from work done for Skånska Cement AB, situated within the same district. He lives in Malmö. *The Address Directory of Malmö City* gives his address as 14, Skomakaregatan. The attached property registry lists this property as 61, Gyllenstjerna, in the city between the bridges.

Equipped with this information, you go to the City Archive in Malmö and ask to see the *Malmö City Tax Register* for 1900. This is a thick volume, as heavy and dusty as a sack of cement. In it, you find the property and the man and thus his taxable income: 13,950 kr. The total tax on that income was 515.67 kr. In other words, Ernst Wehtje paid less than 4% of his income in tax.

Then you simply continue with 1901, 1902, 1903... but it stops in 1904. Ernst Wehtje must have moved. Where? Well, as shown in Chapter 12, that can easily be established. *The Change of Residence Register* at the Parish Office states that he moved to Limhamn. And sure enough, he is listed in the *Limhamn Tax Register*, kept at the City Archive. He lives in the property denoted as 54, Sälen, and in 1906 had a taxable income of 31,830 kr.

That is quite a lot of money, compared to people living around him. Fisherman Johan Magnus Jönsson, no income, "old". Iron-monger Matsson, 10,000 kr. Worker Hans Kristensson, 1,100 kr. Worker Kristian Hansson, no income, "infirm".

In 1907, Ernst Wehtje is appointed Managing Director of Skånska Cement AB. This year, the first taxation calendar is published, one for Stockholm and one for fifty-two other cities. But Ernst Wehtje, because he lived in the country, is not included. As from 1912, however, it is easy and simple to follow his and similar people's income in the *Swedish Taxation Calendar*.

Amounts, as always with taxation, must of course be taken with a pinch of salt. The figures refer to the income after deductions in accordance with current legislation. Persons with high incomes can employ the best legal experts to avoid unnecessarily high taxation. The taxation calendar lists the portion of their incomes that they were obliged to declare, no more.

Noting these reservations, we can thus compile the incomes of Ernst Wehtje for the period between the turn of the century and the First World War:

1900	13900
1901	15000
1902	16200
1903	26114
1904	No information
1905	No information
1906	31830
1907	32070
1908	39710
1909	40350
1910	45100
1911	43980
1912	53510
1913	64590

Skånska Cement was not his only source of income. But his position as Managing Director there led to other appointments. A handy summary is the *List of Board Members of Swedish Companies 1912* (Stockholm 1912). In it, Ernst Wehtje is listed as a board member of the following companies:

AB C.J. Hommerberg & Son, Malmö
AB United Lime Quarries, Malmö
AB Gotland Lime works, Stockholm
AB Ifö Charmotte and Caolin Works, Bromölla
AB Limau Mani's Caotchouc Plantation, Malmö
AB Malmö Joinery Mill, Limhamn
AB Skånska Cement Foundry, Malmö
Property Co Triangeln, Malmö
Property Co Granen, Malmö
Ifö Cement Factory AB, Bromölla
Limhamn Port AB, Limhamn
Limhamn Shipping, Limhamn
Malmö-Limhamn Rail Co. Malmö
Malmö New Steam Kitchen AB, Malmö
Nordic Oxygen Co, Stockholm
Skånska Cement AB, Malmö
Skånska Brick Sales, AB, Malmö
Swedish Binding Thread Factory, AB, Lund
Swedish Rubber Factory AB, Gislaved
Sydsvenska Gjuteri AB, Limhamn

These companies in turn can be examined. You don't have to go further than the Company List in the address directory of Malmö City to satisfy some of your curiosity regarding e.g. "AB Limau Mani's Caotchouc Plantation":

The articles of association accepted in 1907, 1910 and 1911. Aim: After acquiring the plantation Limau Manis, situated on the East Coast of Sumatra and now belonging to Oscar Richter, to grow caotchouc and engage in the activities therewith associated. Joint capital: SKr 814,000.

In 1915, the first edition of the *Swedish Wealth Calendar* was first published. It is based on the taxation of the national-defence levy introduced during the First World War. Ernst Wehtje's capital is taxed at 462,000 kr, i.e. more than his total income in the preceding ten years.

In 1914, 462,000 kr was naturally worth more than it is today. But how much more? 1914 is the initial year of a living costs index published in the *Statistical Yearbook*. An index that has been running for so many years is no doubt slightly vague, but it can still be used to give an idea of the difference of monetary value then and now.

This index assesses 1914 as 100. 1975 was 887. To find the present-day value of Wehtje's capital we should therefore multiply 462,000 with 8.87. In other words, his capital was in excess of 4 million kr.

In a similar manner, the information of the taxation calendar on E.W.'s income can be converted into today's monetary value with the *Living Costs Index*. One example: 1915 has the index number 115. Divide the index number in 1975, 887, by the number in 1915, 115. That gives 7.71, and means that one krona in 1915 was worth 7.71 times more than one krona in 1975. Or in other words: 7.71 is the figure to be used to convert Wehtje's incomes in 1915 to a figure valid for 1975.

Year	Taxable income		Conversion figure		Income in 1975 monetary value
1914	84000	x	8.87	=	748000
1915	101000	x	7.71	=	779000
1916	107000	x	6.82	=	730000
1917	132000	x	5.41	=	714000
1918	140000	x	3.82	=	535000
1919	152000	x	3.31	=	503000
1920	226000	x	3.30	=	746000

Year	Taxable income		Conversion figure		Income in 1975 monetary value
1921	338000	x	3.84	=	1298000
1922	204000	x	4.74	=	967000
1923	150000	x	5.10	=	765000
1924	189000	x	4.95	=	936000
1925	251000	x	5.13	=	1288000
1926	332000	x	5.19	=	1723000
1927	360000	x	5.19	=	1723000
1928	324000	x	5.22	=	1691000

In 1927-29, *The New Swedish Wealth Calendar* was published. In it, Ernst Wehtje's capital was estimated at 2.1 million kr or, by the 1975 monetary value, 11 million. His four sons are also included, together worth 1.4 million or, in today's monetary value, over 7 million.

Ernst Wehtje continued to have a good income

1930	360000	x	5.38	=	1,937,000
1931	467000	x	5.56	=	2,597,000
1932	340000	x	5.72	=	1,945,000
1933	302000	x	5.87	=	1773000
1934	292000	x	5.84	=	1705000
1935	230000	x	5.72	=	1316000
1936	327000	x	5.65	=	1848000
1937	350000	x	5.59	=	1873000

That marks the end. The estate of Ernst Wehtje did have an income up until 1961, in total 779,000 kr, but he himself was dead. During his lifetime, he had earned a taxable income of over 7 million kronor or, in today's monetary value, about 40 million.

The figures above do not include the portion of Ernst Wehtje's capital that consisted of the appreciation of real estate shares or other property. This increased value was not declared for tax. Generally, Ernst Wehtje was not very troubled by taxes and other duties in all these years. Local tax was still very low, and has already been deducted in the above figures, which only refer to national tax. The national tax rate in Ernst Wehtje's lifetime never exceeded 15% of the taxable income. A taxable income of 1.9 million kr, in the monetary value of 1975, means a net income, after tax, of at least 1.6 million.

How much remained after Ernst Wehtje's death? Anyone can demand to see the inventory at the City Archive in Malmö. Its reference number is 1937: 262. The proceeds are 3.6 million kr or more than 20 million in the 1975 monetary value.

Inventories of dead Swedes have been kept since the seventeenth century. As all genealogists know, they give a clear picture of the standard and style of living. First gold items are listed — E.W. left behind a watch, his wedding ring and cuff links. Then comes a list of silver items: thirty-six pairs of fish knives and forks, thirty-six dessert spoons, thirty-six oyster forks, thirty-six fruit forks, thirty-six stew forks, thirty-six lobster forks, thirty-six butter knives, thirty-six crayfish knives, etc., in all 1,626 items or 107 kg of silver. Then the furniture is listed, room by room. This is the dining room:

Item	Value
1 dining-table	40
1 cupboard	200
1 large and 2 small chests	500
2 serving tables	75
1 screen	5
12 dining chairs	240
4 easy-chairs	200
1 silver casket	125

Item	Value
1 metal box	30
1 wall clock	50
1 divan mat	200
4 lengths of curtains with rods and blinds	240
1 chandelier and 4 brackets	450
2 candlesticks	100
Various porcelain ornaments	750
1 Buddha	125

It continues like this, page after page, through the whole huge house. The linen is counted: 109 sheets, seventy-two pillowcases... "The wardrobe of the dead man" is valued at 350 kr. Then the works of art are listed, room by room, and picture by picture.

The proceeds also include various loans to sons and sons-in-law. Herbert Dieden had borrowed 375,000 kr, his son Ernst over half a million. Then shares in Swedish companies: 743,000 in Wilhelm Becker AB, 462,000 in Skånska Cement, etc., in all about fifty companies. Furthermore there are foreign shares, bonds and eighteen different properties, all carefully listed. Finally the will deciding who gets what.

Inventory of One of Ernst Wehtje's Dead Workers
1937:167
In 1937, on 16 February, in Malmö, the following inventory was set up after the cement worker Louis Rickard Nicanor Falck, born 9 July 1899, and married on 4 April 1931, to surviving wife Helga Eleonora Falck, nee Häggblom, He died in the Västra Skrävlinge parish on 30 December 1936, leaving behind as his only heir his wife. It was noted that the dead man also left behind his parents, the cement worker Karl Falck and his wife Hulda Falck in Limhamn.

Gold items	
One wedding ring	10

Silver-plated items	
12 tablespoons	6
12 coffee spoons	3
6 dessert spoons	3
1 soup ladle	2
1 sauce ladle	1
3 jam spoons	1
1 cake slice	1
12 pairs of eating forks and knives	12

Furniture	
1 cupboard, 1 combined cupboard, 1 dining table, four chairs	250
2 easy chairs	40
1 smoking table with a set	20
1 cupboard	30
1 table clock	5
1 radio set with table	50
1 chest of drawers	10
1 wicker table and 2 stools	15
1 divan bed with cover and cushions	40
1 mirror	4
1 sofa	5
1 table and 2 chairs	5
Various books	35
Electric light fittings	45
Pictures and adornments	40
Curtains and carpets	100
Working clothes	40

Furniture	
Wardrobe	50
2 pocket watches	40
Linen	15
Kitchen utensils	45
Glass and china	5
Cutlery	10

Cash at time of death	6
Funeral aid from sick and funeral fund	200
"Strength from Unity" Union funeral aid	100
Funeral aid from National Insurance Office	150
1 flat in the block Aspen	6,185
Claims	
Swedish Postal Bank, book nr. 10614 series V, with interest	26
Same bank, book nr. 207423, series D, with interest	1.16
Total	**7624.42**

Debts	
Funeral costs	518.35
Block Aspen, mortgage	5432.19
Malmö Poor Relief Authority	144.25
Rates for 1933	127.71
Rates for 1934	147.98
Rates for 1935	151.59
Income tax for 1936	111.23
Future taxes	300
Total	**6933.30**
Balance after commission	**684.21**

Hans Falck
Member of Magristrates' Court

The most valuable inheritance left by Ernst Wehtje Senior was, however, the position as Managing Director of Skånska Cement. It was taken over by his eldest son Ernst. He can be traced through the Taxation Calendar, just like his father.

In 1919, he appears with an income which, translated into the monetary value of 1975, equals 52,000 kr. His father appoints him director of the Ifö Works and his income increases to 222,000 kr. In 1925, he moves to Malmö, and in 1927 his income has reached 543,000 kr. The year before his father died, it was 943,000 kr, the year after his father died, it had increased.

His annual income stayed on that level during the 1930s and 40s. It went down (at least apparently) in the early 1950s, but in the late 1960s, Ernst Wehtje again earned his steady one and a half million per year. As of the Second World War, the tax on such incomes became considerable. In the 1950s and 1960s, the Inland Revenue claimed about 60% of Ernst Jonas Wehtje's taxable income. After rates, about one and a half million remained; after tax, about 600,000 kr.

The above figures do not include the part of Ernst Wehtje's income that consisted of the appreciation of real estate, shares or other property. This appreciation is still, even today, free of income tax. *The Swedish Property List* (Sthlm 1958) records Ernst Jonas Wehtje with a capital of only 2.3 million kr in today's monetary value, most of it having already been transferred to his sons — Ingvar 7 million, Arne 8 million and Hans-Christian 8.6 million. The total taxable capital of the Wehtje family now amounted to 92 million kr in the 1975 monetary value.

As from 1965, the *Swedish Taxation Calendar* also contains information on capital. It appears that Ernst Jonas Wehtje, even in his old age, was quite successful. His taxable capital, which in 1958 was only 2.3 million, in 1965 had increased to 12 million and in 1967 to 24 million. The total taxable capital of the members of the Wehtje family had increased to 132 million in the 1975 monetary value.

*Application to the Bank of Sweden for permission to take more than
ordinary tourist currency out of the country.*

In the 1970s it becomes more difficult to follow the family,
partly because so many of them emigrate. Hugo Wehtje's
widow, Hellvi, who in 1970 declared an income of 363,000 and
a capital of 7.4 million, in 1970/1 immigrated to Switzerland.
Wakter Wehtje, who in 1969 declared an income of nearly
one million and a capital of five million, immigrated to France
the same year. His and his wife's total declared life income
at the time of their emigration was 45 million kronor, in the
1975 monetary value. But southern latitudes were now more
tempting.

- What are the incomes over the years of the owners and directors in the company where you work? What capital have they collected? What appointments have they given their children? What are the grandchildren's incomes before they can even walk? Where do they go with the money after they've earned enough in Sweden?

Aids: *The Swedish Taxation Calendar* and the *Swedish Land Registry* are available at the county library or can be ordered there. Taxation information after 1974 can be found in the *Debit Registers*, which are official documents and available from the local Inland Revenue offices. The address is in the telephone directory. For examining the wages of workers, see Chapter 26.

We need a handy little book about the history of the Swedish taxation system, to show how the taxation has changed proportionally for different levels of income since the First World War. It is quite difficult now to establish how much people paid in tax in the old days. The rates can be found in the Statistical Yearbook for the year in question. Figures for local taxation can be found in the *Swedish Statute-Book* for the year in question, but the regulations are often difficult to interpret. One shortcut may be to read the tax investigations, among them *Official State Investigations* (SOU) 1936:13.

Inventories for Arboga, Borås, Jönköping, Malmö, Nyköping and Strängnäs are kept in the Town Archive for each town. Other inventories are kept among the local Assize Court records for a hundred years and then transferred to the District Archive. There are about one hundred Assize Courts in Sweden. They are listed in the telephone directory.

In order to take more than ordinary tourist currency out of the country, you must have special permission from the Bank of Sweden. The applications are kept for ten-fifteen years and are official documents. You can phone or write to *Bank of Sweden* (Brunkebergstorg 11, PO Box 16283, 103 25

Stockholm, tel. 08/ 22 82 00) and ask to see all applications from a certain named person. Applications from companies are, however, not available.

14. WHO'S WHO

1912, the year when the *Swedish Taxation Calendar* was first published, also the first Swedish edition of *Who's Who*. It is now being published for the thirty-second time. It is an important publication for people who want to keep track of the Swedish Establishment.

It naturally contains information about all the managing directors of Skånska Cement, from Ernst Wehtje Senior to Sten Lindh. This is an example:

> **Lindh, Sten,** ambassadör, Malmö, f l Kalmar 24/10/22 av dir Ernst L o Elisabeth Larsson.
> Jur kand Sthlm 45, civ:ekonom 46, attaché UD 45, tjg Washington, Paris, London; hdlsråd 59, byråch UD 59, ministers ställn 63, ambassadör EEC o Euratom Bryssel samt kol- o stålunionen Luxemburg ävensom ständ ombud Europarådet Strasbourg 64, i disponibilitet 68; verkst dir Industri ab Euroc sed 68.
> Sekr deleg OEEC 48-50, 50 års besparingsutredn, 50 års ekon långtidsutredn; omb hdlsförhandl m Storbritannien 54-58; sakk förhandl europ frihdlsområdet Paris 56-58; omb förhandl om upprättande av EFTA 59, organisatör o ch EFTA:s sekr Genève 60; UD:s förhandl:grupp 63; styr:-led Lamco, Liberian Iron Ore Ltd Canada sed 68, Skand ensk bkn sed 69, ab Skånska cementgjuteriet sed 69, Gränges ab sed 70, ab Cardo sed 72.
> LVSL.
> Gm 45 jur kand Maikki Velander, f 21, dtr av prof Edy V o Maj Halle.

The abbreviations are often difficult to interpret and only a few are explained in the book. But if you manage to solve these riddles, these lines contain a lot of concentrated information.

It is arranged like this: surname, Christian or given names, occupation, address, place of birth, date of birth (which provides half of the Swedish personal identification code), father's occupation and name, mother's name. Education, career. Other appointments. Published works. Titles and honours. Year of marriage, spouse's occupation, name, year of birth, occupation, name and occupation of father-in-law, name of mother-in-law.

The long sequence of annual editions of *Who's Who* provides a chance to examine changes — and, even more, the lack of changes — in Swedish society. How many women were included in the first edition? How has the proportion of women changed over the years? What proportion of the people listed in 1912 came from workers' homes? How has this proportion changed over the years?

What have been the most common career paths in the various occupations at different points in time? How many of the people listed in the first edition of *Who's Who* have been able to see their children in it? How many of the people listed in later editions of *Who's Who* had their fathers in it?

Briefly: To what extent is the Swedish Establishment as recorded in *Who's Who* a closed circle? I am asking this question in the hope that someone will find the time to answer it.

Information about company directors and shareholders can also be found in several other biographical encyclopaedias:

BIOGRAPHICAL
Directory of Famous Swedish Men, 1835-57, new ed. 1374-76.

SWEDISH
Biographical Directory. 1857-1907.

MEN
of Swedish Industry, series 1-2.
Sthlm 1874-80.

HOFBERG, Herman
Swedish Biographical Hand Directory.
Sthlm 1876.

SWEDISH
Biographical Directory.
Sthlm 1917 (Very comprehensive, still far from completed.)

SWEDISH
Biographical Calendar.
Sthlm 1919. (Only for Malmöhus District).

SWEDISH
Men and Women.
Sthlm 1942-1955.

These directories contain the same type of facts — parents, education, career, appointments, and publications by and about — like *Who's Who.* They also often give appraisals like this one:

R.P. Berg: "B's main characteristic is his extraordinary enthusiasm, which could not be absorbed entirely by his demanding tasks at Skånska Cement AB. He founded or participated as the leading initiator of about thirty different companies and his activities were noted for a rare, noble dedication to Swedish industry..."
(Swedish Biographical Directory).

Ernst Wehtje Senior: "Led by the firm and sound judgement of W. Skånska Cement continued its great expansion..."

Ernst Wehtje Junior: "Lead by the enterprising W., Skånska Cement has expanded to become one of Sweden's major large companies..."
(Swedish Men and Women)

No critical appraisal of the contributions of company directors is ever ventured in biographical handbooks. Embarrassing facts are avoided, whilst flattering judgements abound, together with conventional statements and meaningless phrases. Industrialists, like statues, are intended to be seen from underneath.

• How are the owners and directors of your company described in biographical encyclopaedias? Have they left anything out?

Aids: *Who's Who* and other biographical directories are available at the county library. The general encyclopaedias, such as the *Nordic Encyclopaedia* contain similar personal notices. They even find their way into scientific reports. Listen to this:

Ernst Wehtje's death means that a remarkable man in Swedish Industry has left us... Ernst Wehtje's main contribution is no doubt to the Skånska Cement concern, which after a modest start in his time developed into a large modern industry. Behind this development was a lot of hard and intense work, mainly by Ernst Wehtje himself, but also by his assistants at all levels, whom he managed to stimulate for their tasks. Ernst Wehtje had an ability for co-operation and the talent to choose the right assistants. He was also a man of a rare charm, natural and unaffected, with great factual knowledge. Ernst Wehtje, the industrialist, was noted for his strong will together with tough endurance, imagination and inventiveness, guided by an unusually sound judgement and efficiency together with great calm. Ernst Wehtje leaves behind a complete contribution and a bright memory.

(Director Elan Tunhammar in *Yearbook of 1973 for the Science Society in Lund*.)

Facts rarely included in this type of context are to be found in this book, for example in chapters 10, 13 and 23.

The Workers

It is much more difficult to find out anything about a worker at Skånska Cement. Workers are not listed in *Who's Who*. But a small number of cement workers did get sufficiently important appointments within the workers' movement to be included in the Swedish directory *Swedish Popular Movements*, Sthlm 1936. One example:

SAMUELSSON: GUSTAF Ernst Eugen, cement worker, Visby. 3. Visby 5.11.90, son of builder Johan and Amanda Samuelsson. Bricklayer '08-18, cement worker since '18. Member of the Labourers' and Factory Workers' Union, Chairman of Union dept. 327 Visby since '25, Board member local dept of Workers' Educational Committee '25-29, member Visby Town Council '30-34, member Visby Workers' Community 24-31. Married '16 Maria Bohm, b.19.8.34.

As you can see, the Swedish popular movements give exactly the same type of information as the Establishment directories.

The appointments and positions are listed. But what kind of work did Gustaf Samuelsson do at the cement factory? What strikes did he take part in? What was his political affiliation? What issues did he promote? What was he like, as a man and a friend?

The employer had his own reply to these questions. In November 1935, Gustaf Samulsson was a member of the workers' delegation in the negotiations with the Building Materials Federation. The employers' organization wrote to the Visby Cement Factory asking for more detailed information about him. The reply is kept in the Visby Archive:

Visby, Nov. 22nd, 1935 The Building Materials Federation, Malmö.

Re: The worker Gustaf Stauelsson.

This worker was born on November 5th, 1890, and he has been employed at this factory since August 13th, 1919. More or less all the time he has worked in the cement works as a cement miller.... His economy used to be badly strained but seems to have improved lately, judging by the fact that he does not apply for loans so often. It is however well-known that he has considerable debts.

During the first years of his employment here, his manner with foremen was coarse and loud-mouthed. It has improved over the years and is now more insinuating; anyway, no objection can be made against his behaviour and he is regarded and respected as a good worker. Samuelsson likes to talk and it is not difficult to get him to reveal matters which are internal to his organisation. In 1934, his total income was 1..578.35 kronor (work did not start until April 6th) and for the first three quarters of this year 1.713.85 kr. We hope that this information will prove helpful to you.

Yours faithfully

This is the earliest portrait of an individual Swedish cement worker that I've been able to find. The employer's view is the only one preserved. The workers' view of the truth was never documented and therefore is lost forever. Gustaf Samuelsson lives on only in the eyes of his opponent.

Portraits of individual workers are sometimes published in connection with anniversaries and the like. They are kept in the collection of small prints of the Royal Library (see Chapter 6). *Skånska Cement's Memorial of the Medal Giving Celebration on December 5th, 1940*, for example, holds names and photographs of a large number of Swedish cement workers. But not a word about their personalities or contributions.

The house journal *Around the Rotary Kiln* was first published in 1950. The first issues contained brief biographies of workers, entitled "After long and faithful service". The following are among the people you meet there:

LIME PIT WORKER ALFRED THOMASSON, LIMHAMN. From birth Thomasson had a strong connection with the cement company — his father worked there too. He was born on July 6th, 1879, and devoted his first working years to farming, as a labourer. His first job at the cement company, dating back to 1900, was of short duration due to lack of work. From 1906 onwards, or in all 44 years, he has, however, been busy at the lime pit. Amongst his hobbies are first of all farming, and on his own acre of land, Thomasson has a well-tended vegetable plot.

FACTORY WORKER KARL ANDERSSON, LIMHAMN. Andersson, b. December 18th, 1880, after leaving school became a bricklayer's apprentice. At the age of 32, he began working at the Klagshamn lime pit, and eight years later transferred to the Limhamn pit. He stayed there for 16 years and in 1937 moved to the cement factory itself. At the end of this year he retired after a total of almost 28 years in the service of the cement company.

OLGA SJÖBERG, LIMHAMN. b. December 1st, 1886. Employed May 8th, 1906. Retired September 1951. Mrs Sjöberg started as a leather seamstress at Fougstedts in Malmö at the age of 17. In 1906, her mother took over the canteen at the Limhamn cement factory and she assisted her mother until 1914 when she started as a sack seamstress at the factory. Mrs Sjöberg was employed as a sack-counter for a while before being transferred to the factory baths as a bath-mistress in 1946.

The staff journal in this way preserved some fragments of a few workers' lives for their successors at the factory. But they are seen through the eyes of the personnel officer. He knows nothing about their real contribution at the lime pit, in the factory or at the sack-sewing room. No one has ever made a serious attempt to find out what contributed the real contribution of the lives of Alfred Thomasson, Karl Andersson or Olga Sjöberg.

- What would you like to know about Alfred Thomasson? What would you like to know about your predecessors in your job at your factory? Are there any old photos, letters, minutes from associations, newspaper cuttings, technical descriptions or memories of living people that could provide the answers?

- What will your successors in your job know about you? Will only the judgement of the personnel department remain? Or will you and your workmates leave behind some material describing your work and your experiences?

Aids: See chapters 15,17,19 and 21.

---

15. LETTERS AND DIARIES

It's not every day that you can read the love letters of a Swedish industrialist. But you have the occasion in:

WÄSTBERG, Per
Ernst and Miami
Lund 1964.

When you read these letters, you find it easy to agree with Per Wästberg's characterization of Ernst Wehtje: A very sober person, he is seldom seized by great passion. He does not want change and adventure, he lacks intellectual curiosity. He never undertakes anything unexpected. He seeks to limit his existence rather than expand it.

He strives doggedly to attain a social position, and once he has reached it, he adapts to its established conservative comforts. Decade after decade, family letters are written in the same tone. Business is going well. Maids walk in and out. Packs of cards are worn out and renewed. Delight in food and drink leads to increasing obesity.

Every morning at half past seven, Ernst Wehtje lies down on the Board table at Skånska Cement for a massage. He is a member of two hundred boards and cartels. He does not have time for books — his library consists of the *Nordic Encyclopaedia* and the collected works of Albert Engström. But in all rooms, expensive clocks are ticking away, and every Sunday morning, Ernst Wehtje himself walks round the rooms to wind them.

The book also gives a concrete, vivid picture of the family in which Ernst Wehtje grew up. His father was a German immigrant, an unsuccessful tenant farmer at different farms in Scania, an unsuccessful store-keeper in Helsingborg, an unsuccessful agent of agricultural equipment in Lund. The family set their hopes on the son's education. The mother managed to keep things going by taking in paying guests. They were a poor middle-class family without much education and with only one major ambition: not to sink to the level of the working class.

Per Wästberg has chosen to emphasize one aspect of Ernst Wehtje's life:

The purpose of this description is to give a picture of the man who created a memorable home, with empty hands and great debts, but also with a good heart and common sense.

His letters will show the awareness and perception with which, from the very start, he attempts to make the home the centre of his life, a concrete manifestation of love. That's all he dreams about, and once he succeeds in this effort, he remains faithful to it till the end.

My purpose is different. I intend to compare Ernst Wehtje to one of his workers, the engine operator Jöns Nilsson of Lomma. When the latter died, he left behind a notebook, which is now kept by the historian Sven Nordengren in Lund.

Week by week Jöns Nilsson took down careful notes of his earnings between 1880 and 1917. He too started with two empty hands, he too had a good heart and common sense. Yet their lives developed along very different lines:

Jöns Nilsson and Ernst Wehtje
1880
Jöns: "I have worked for my food and lodgings for the smith Ericksson from January 7th to July 26th." — Ernst is the fourth last in his graduation exams. He buys tails for 22 kr, a graduation cap for 2.75. He commences law studies in Lund.

1881
Jöns: "From May 22nd to August 6th and in September and October 3 weeks at 1.50 weekly." — Ernst as a tutor earns 20 kr monthly.

1882
Jöns: "Did the national service which cost me in all 60 kr. From January 30th to May 20th 2 kr weekly. From September 25th to November 12th and from November 20th to December 23rd 2 kr weekly." — While studying, Ernst works as a tutor earning 400 kr annually plus food and lodgings.

1883
Jöns: "I began work at Lomma cement factory on April 2nd 1883. Earning 1.25 daily until May 23rd... In 1883 my annual earnings were 436.45." — Ernst is a tutor at Dala. On November 20th he gets engaged to Mimmi Ahlfeldt.

1885
Jöns: "On October 21st I had the misfortune to lose three fingers. Had to be hospitalised for 36 days, then I was off work until I started again as assistant to Ahlstrand. In 1885 my annual earnings were 586 kr 45 öre." — Ernst is doing his national service.

1889

Jöns: "On March 15ᵗʰ 1889 at 12 noon the cement factory and all brick works in Lomma closed, because a Socialist workers' Union had been formed."

The same day Ernst wrote to Mimmi: "What's the progress of your theatre? It is almost embarrassing to hear people talk about it so much, as if it was something more than a joke to amuse yourselves and possibly some other people. Father had heard a whole crowd talking about it the other day. I could tell that Mother was annoyed by all the talk but I did not bother to ask exactly what it was..."

Jöns: "Wednesday March 26ᵗʰ the smiths left their programmes and cards and went back to work."
"Friday evening March 28ᵗʰ 18 riding hussars came to maintain law and order."
"Saturday the 29ᵗʰ, the red flag of the union was torn down and the union scattered."
"Friday April 5ᵗʰ the number of new and old together was 250 men."
"On Monday the 8ᵗʰ the factory opened again, the whistle sounded and the lockout was over. The workers amounted to 350 men, the time of work 10 hours and the union was dissolved so that only the 34 dismissed workers and some odd members remained."

Ernst to Mimmi: "Your assurance that you would like to devote your life to my happiness is something I remind myself of again and again... Please dismiss your occasionally flaring suspicions and trust me more and give up your various reservations. My dear little girl, if that's what you really think, you should never entertain this notion of being in the wrong place in life etcetera, as you can rest assured that you have found the right one..."

Jöns: "November 2nd was the first time I saw my betrothed Maria. We promised each other to be faithful for life on December 26th. In 1889 my annual earnings were 789 kr 55 öre."

Ernst is employed at the Malmö Chancery-Office. Annual income 2,700 kr. He is looking round for extra income: "Today I visited Mr Berg here, the engineer, the so called 'Cement Berg' who handles the Limhamn affairs. Aurell suggested that I should handle the conveyance of Limhamn residents. That may prove useful in my spare time and could give some extra income."

1890
Jöns: "We bought a house on March 24th and were photographed on March 25th. In 1890 my annual earnings were 800 kr 11 öre." — Ernst becomes Deputy District Judge and Secretary of the Town Council. Annual income 5,164 kr.
He furnishes a flat in oak and walnut for 5,000 kr and gets married on October 10th.

1893
Jöns: "December 16th I jammed my finger in a pulley and it healed so that I was discharged on January 3rd 1894 and went back to work on Jan 8th. On Jan 19th I was paid damages for my accident for 16 days, 16 kr."

In 1897, Ernst notes that his shares are worth 197,997 kr. He expects their value to rise by 40,000 during 1898. Jöns as usual notes his annual earnings: 846 kr and 83 öre. His total life income has now gone up to 11,280 kr plus a few kronor he earned as an apprentice with the smith Eriksson. That is the payment for forty-seven years of labour — a quarter of the amount Ernst expected his shares to increase by in one single year.

We have examined Ernst Wehtje's taxable income from 1900 (see Chapter 13) and we can compare it to Jöns' yearly notes:

Year	Jöns Nilsson's yearly income	Ernst Wehtje's yearly income	Jöns income in percentage of Ernst's
1900	1010.42	13900	7.3
1901	953.79	15000	6.4
1902	913.70	16200	5.6
1903	895.67	26114	3.2
1904	991.82	-	-
1905	1577.84	-	-
1906	1092	31830	3.4
1907	1096.48	32070	3.4
1908	1134.06	39710	2.9
1909	1021.52	40350	2.5
1910	1169.88	45100	2.6
1911	1292.07	43980	2.9
1912	1298.24	53510	2.4
1913	1298.21	64590	2.0
1914	1283.13	84300	1.5
1915	1260.34	101000	1.2
1916	1254.91	107000	1.2
1917	1542.83	132000	1.2

In these eighteen years, Jöns Nilsson's annual income goes down steadily in relation to that of Ernst Wehtje — towards the end of the period he earns only a little more than 1% of what Wehtje earns. If we convert the incomes to the monetary value of 1975, using the method applied in Chapter 13, we find that Jöns' buying power was strongly reduced during the First World War, whereas Wehtje could defend his:

Year	Conversion figure	Jöns Nilsson's yearly income	Ernst Wehtje's yearly income
1914	8.84	11381	748000
1915	7.17	9717	779000
1916	6.82	8558	730000
1917	5.41	8346	714000

Throughout his life, Jöns Nilsson takes note of important events. But Ernst Wehtje's letters to Minimi become fewer and fewer as years go by:

1904
Jöns: "21.3 All factory workers were told that when the slurry ran out, the factory would close down."
"27.9 I started work at the lime sandstone factory." — Ernst Wehtje is appointed financial director of Skånska Cement.

1907
Jöns: "On December 8th at five-thirty, the engineer R.F. Berg died." — Wehtje succeeded Berg as Managing Director of Skånska Cement.

1918
Jöns: "On Sunday December 29th at 3.55, my wife Maria died. The funeral was in Lomma Church Saturday January 4th at 1 o'clock." — Wehtje was appointed Chairman of Malmö Town Council.

1933
Jöns: "On June 14th I was told take four days paid holiday and then I would be given leave for an indefinite period or until the brick works open. What will happen? Will the brick works ever open again? At the same time the engineer Mr Hansson said that he would get me a pension when I retire." — Wehtje celebrates his 70th birthday at Latorp Manor, awakened by the song "Thunder ye brothers". The

grandchildren perform in his honour "The Golden Heart", a tableau. — Jöns: "On August 14th I was told to start working with the steam engine and boiler and be ready to start operating on August 17th."

1935
Jöns: "1833, on April 1st, I started work at C.B. On February 20th 1935 it was all over. My work has thus lasted for 51 years and 11 months." — The following year, Ernst Wehtje died.

1940
Jöns: "On December 5th, a statue was uncovered in Limhamn and then medals were given out to 392 workers and foremen."

Two human lives, two working lives. They began working the same year, Jöns as a smith apprentice, Ernst as a tutor. They got married the same year. They both left their jobs at Skånska Cement during the course of a few months — one with a promise from the engineer, Mr Hansson, that he might get a small pension from the company, the other being one of the richest men in Sweden. Between them the class society is clearly defined.

Even the sparse notes made by Jöns Nilsson gives us the outline of a worker's life. What if he had told us more about his life at the cement factory and the brick works, what if he had also included the everyday details, the insignificant events, the gradual change. What a unique, irreplaceable document it would have been now! Diaries like that are extremely rare and valuable. The only one I know is this one:

WAHLBERG, Lambert
The View from a Traverse: Diary from Sickla Works.
Sthlm 1973.

Lambert Wahlberg started working for Atlas Copco in 1928. His diary consists of fourteen volumes and in all two thousand pages. The printed version is much abbreviated without justifying how and published by the company as a memorial publication — naturally an unsuitable form of publishing if you want to know the whole truth of working life.

Even so, it is a book well worth reading, because it shows how all these little things, which when seen apart seem too insignificant to even notice, together form a huge picture of people at work. It shows how each worker can make a permanent contribution to research simply by observing what goes on at his place of work and writing down his observations.

- Has any predecessor of yours, on your job, at your factory, left behind any letters, diaries or other documents of their working life?

Aids: Ask the pensioners, ask the children. If you are lucky enough to find an old diary from your factory, it will be a natural starting-point for your future research. Each chapter in this book indicates questions to ask the diary and methods to use to find out more about the man who wrote the diary and his work.

- Does anyone at your place of work keep a diary? Why don't you?

Aids: You can start on your own, quite secretly. You can also form a group who meet every other week to discuss their notes from the factory.

• The capital which today controls Swedish industries has often been created as Wehtje created his. It has been formed through incredible appreciation, and through high, almost untaxed incomes in a past class society. How was the capital formed in the company where you work?

Aids: See chapters 12-13.

16. THE HOME

To Ernst Wehtje, the home was "the centre of life, the concrete manifestation of love", according to Per Wästberg. His home was a dream to which he remained faithful throughout life. He had greater possibilities than others to realize it. It found its final form at 11, Fridhemsvägen in Malmö:

> If you drive from the centre along the beautiful Promenade, past Ribersborg with the busy Sound on your right, and approach Wehtje's villa, slightly up from the waterfront, you will find the exterior not particularly impressive. Your eye is tempted by the row of huge villas, or rather, little palaces, built along the Promenade. Wehtje's house behind its high stone wall is more like the villas along the slopes at Saint Cloud outside Paris. There is something remote, reserved, about the building and the surrounding garden, similar to a French private chateaux. If an outsider was told that this considerable house holds no more than three rooms on the first floor and four on the second, including bedrooms and a small sitting-room, he would probably be very surprised and quite rightly presume that the rooms must be of a considerable size. If you add that these four walls house the most beautiful and valuable art collection in Malmö, the astonishment would probably be even greater. Let us enter!

This is arts journalist Harald Schiller talking in the journal *Swedish Homes in Words and Pictures* (1933:1). He enters. He examines one room after another with the care of an antique dealer. This is a corner of the dining-room which we recognize from the inventory (see Chapter 13):

From the hall we catch a glimpse of the dining-room — one of the high windows, framed by maroon curtains, and a Renaissance chest, with a huge piece (terrine) of silver, made in Paris in 1774. The furniture is generally Renaissance-style, and the colours of the room are red and white. No less than three beautifully carved Renaissance chests have been placed here, all of them used for displaying pieces of art. Except for the one already mentioned with the French silver terrine, there is a similar chest by one of the long walls with a chair on either side, forming a group with a pair of crystal light brackets and a still life by Adrian von Utrecht (1599-1652).

On the chest there is a collection of East India china and two church candlesticks of tin. On the third chest between the windows on the end wall is a collection of modern silver and on the wall above the time-piece of the room, a Louis XIV clock framed by porcelain. The pattern of the gilt leather of the chairs was drawn by Mrs L. Ouchterlony and made by one of the daughters of the house, Mrs Ruth Jung. A keepsake from the former home is a tea table from Rörstrand with a picture of Strandbo on the china table top. It is placed in front of the window.

Ernst Wehtje's home: the lower hall with a glimpse of the dining-room. From Swedish Homes 1933:1.

The tour is finished in the servants' quarters:

Finally, for the sake of being inclusive, a couple of words about the attic and kitchen. The attic holds a number of box-rooms and closets and two beautiful spare bedrooms with a view of the Sound. There is also a bathroom here, which is hardly surprising, considering the fact that even the servants in the basement have one. The kitchen is in the basement, as large as in a manor house, tiled, like all the store-rooms and scullery. Dumb-waiters and internal telephones make the staff's work easier, along with the newly installed oil central heating. The servants' quarters are also down below, with running water in each room, and another two large spare bedrooms. Even down here the windows are high enough to admit plenty of air and sunshine. In the summer, the rose beds outside offer a most attractive sight with roses climbing along the window-frames. The fittings, cupboards, fridge, larder and store-rooms are naturally of the most modern and practical kind in this Patrician villa, to serve this superior household, where possibilities and good taste have come together in a way quite unique to our country.

Ernst Jonas Wehtje's home: the dining-room at Ellinge House.

Yes — these possibilities were indeed unique. But the son of the District Judge, Ernst Jonas Wehtje, in due course got himself an even more splendid residence. In 1957, he handed it down to his son Hans Christian as a gift. Just like many other directors' residences, it has been described in *Swedish Stately Homes,* Malmö 1966.

ELLINGE
Paris: Västra Sallerup, District: Harjager, Scania. Area: 587 ha. value: 3569,500 kronor.

Ellinge is one of the oldest stately homes in Scania, dating back to the 13th century. — The noblemen who owned Ellinge in the Middle Ages were among the most powerful in the country. When they came here to take advantage of the yield of the estate, they needed plenty of space...

Since Ellinge became the property of Mr Ernst Wehtje, Tech. Dr., and his wife in the 1950s, the house has been the object of extensive restoration and renovation. Old architectural remains of the interior have thereby been preserved, whereas furniture and pieces of art have been added by the present owner.

The entrance hall leads directly into the lower hall, the floor of hexagonal tiles. The hall is furnished as a reception room with comfortable rococo chairs and oriental carpets...

The lower hall leads into the present dining-room, which still retains some of the Baroque character it probably assumed when the house was re-designed in the days of Governor Wilhelm Bennet. This is indicated by the panelling, the doors and the deeply fluted ceiling cornice. The dining-room runs along the width of the house and has two windows in either facade.

Above the white panel, the walls are covered with printed grisaille wallpaper, which used to cover the walls of the former dining-room on the first floor. The wall-covering depicts a hunting party in a river landscape with palaces and churches, and was probably drawn by the French lithographer and horse painter Carle Vernet (1759-1836) and printed in 1815 by Jacquemart et Benard in Paris. The furniture of the room is rococo chairs and a couple of long carved Baroque chests along the internal walls — one is Italian and has a display of old table silver, the other is Scandinavian and has pieces of Chinese export porcelain. The large Baroque-style chandelier is remarkable.

The homes which Ernst Wehtje, father and son, made available for workers were naturally not so grand. A summary is given in

CURMAN, Jöran
Industrial Workers´ Housing (Industrial Research Institute. Preface by Ernst Jonas Wehtje.)
Sthlm 1944.

This gives an account of company housing for 55000 workers in all different fields of industry. Over 16% of Swedish workers at this time had their employer as landlord. In the earth and stone industries, one worker out of four lived in company-owned housing.

The industrial workers' dwelling was generally cramped — 75% had just one room and a kitchen or even less. Almost half of the flats were in buildings erected before 1900, almost half were without running water and drainage. 81% were without a WC, 86 % without central heating, 96 % without a bath or shower room.

The rents were on average 20% below local rents, but some companies charged 480 kr (or at the 1975 monetary value, 1,820 kr) for a one-room-flat without any mod cons in the provinces. A low rent usually had certain terms attached to it, e.g., saving by wages deduction or demands to have children. The following rental agreement from Hällekis was held up as exemplary.

Hyreskontrakt

Skånska Cementaktiebolaget, Hällekis, nedan benämnt bolaget, upplåter och för-
hyr härmed till
nedan benämnd hyresgästen, lägenheten n:r   i radhuset n:r   inom Sjö-
säters egnahemssamhälle, vilken lägenhet innehåller 1 rum och kök med tillhörande
källare, ävensom potatisland om   ar på av bolaget anvisad plats.
    Hyran utgår med kr. 12: — (Tolv) per månad att erläggas i efterskott. För vatten
betalas efter 25 öre per m³ och för elektrisk energi efter 25 öre per kWt.
    Lägenheten får disponeras under maximum 5 (Fem) år räknat från den
        Hyresgästen förbinder sig att, under den tid han bor i lägen-
heten, månatligen avsätta minst kr. 30: — (Trettio) till ett grundkapital för byggande
av ett egethem, och medgiver han bolaget rätt att för varje månad genom avdrag
å arbetsförtjänst hos bolaget innehålla nämnda belopp. Ifrågavarande penningar
förbinder sig bolaget att förränta under fem år med 5 % ränta på ränta. Parterna
äro ense om, att på så sätt uppkommet kapital utbetalas till hyresgästen endast
för byggande av ett egethem, vid avflyttning ur lägenheten, i händelse av hyresgästens dödsfall eller om hyresgästen slutar att arbeta hos bolaget.
    Bolaget äger rätt att med en månads uppsägningstid skilja hyresgästen från lägen-
heten:
om hyran ej erlägges å bestämd tid av annan orsak än sjukdom,
om hyresgästen slutar att arbeta hos bolaget,
om kontraktet transporteras på annan utan bolagets medgivande,
om hyresgästen låter annan person nyttja lägenheten utan bolagets medgivande,
om hyresgästen ej iakttager, vad som erfordras för bevarandet av sundhet, ordning
    och skick eller han befinnes missfara eller skada den hyrda eller and:a delar av
    fastigheten,
om hyresgästen icke uppfyller kontraktets bestämmelser i övrigt eller fullgör sina
    skyldigheter enligt gällande lag.
    Då denna lägenhet är avsedd för familjer med barn, äger bolaget påfordra, att
hyresgästen avflyttar inom skälig uppsägningstid, om hyresgästens familj varaktigt
synes förbliva barnlös.
    Hällekis den
    Ovanstående hyreskontrakt antages i alla delar till efterrättelse och att noga
fullgöras av undertecknad.
    Hällekis den

- How have directors and owners of your company lived over the years? How do they live today?

Aids: The Journal *Swedish Homes in Words and Pictures* was first published in 1913. Like *Swedish Stately Homes* and many similar splendid books, it can be found under IC at a Swedish library.

- What housing has been offered to workers by your company over the years? On what terms?

Aids: A background is given by the architect John ÅkerLund in *Workers' Housing in Industry* (Swedish Industrial Federation,

Various publications 13), Sthlm 1917. Pictures and drawings are here shown from Linköping, Norrköping, Jönköping, Huskvarna, SKF Göteborg, AGA, ASEA and Holmens Bruk. Note that exemplary models have been selected. "The Industrial Housing Association" was formed in 1945 with the aim to coordinate the building of company housing after the war. In *Industrial Association Housing,* the association presents plans, drawings and pictures of the new housing estates of about 30 different companies, including those at Slite and Stora Vika. The ethnologist Rut Liedgren's book *How We Lived: Workers' Housing as a Type and Period Phenomenon.* Sthlm 1961, describes both models and reality. The examples are from Göteborg and Stockholm with the odd glimpse of other industrial areas. Conditions in your hometown can be found in the housing investigations.

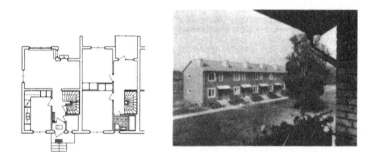

Two-storeyed terraced houses for workers at Stora Vika, about 1950. From Industrial Housing.

Local Housing Investigations

The first Swedish housing investigation was carried out by the so called "pauperism committee" in Göteborg in 1865. The committee summarized its impressions thus:

The housing generally inhabited by the working-class is often flats in old, dilapidated wooden buildings, either detached or in the courtyard of a newer, better building. The wind blows in through draughty windows, doors that do not close properly and rough decayed walls. The upper floors are over laundries, wood-sheds etc., draughty and cold, and on the ground floor rotten, often damp, since rain or melting snow will seep in through the joints between old planks in ceilings and walls, running down from the building and lingering underneath it.

The basement rooms are, almost without exception, dark, damp and unhealthy. The windows are level with, or slightly above, the street or courtyard. In many places, water runs from the courtyard or street down the stairs and into the room, or seeps in between the external wall and the possible panelling of the walls. The windows, covered in dirt from the street, face the courtyard, often against a wall, and so admit very little light, especially in winter. The air in these rooms is always musty...

The men who work outdoors suffer relatively less, the women are more plagued by rheumatism, chronic chest infections, green-sickness etc. But those who suffer most are the children. A wretched generation is growing up here in darkness, damp and dirty rags, bloated and scrofulous, with tuberculosis, rickets and chronic intestinal ailments.

This report did not lead to any measures.

The first attempt to describe the workers' housing in figures was also made in Göteborg:

WALLQVIST, Hjalmar
Housing for Poor People in Göteborg.
(Works published by the Lorén Foundation 5.) Sthlm 1899.

Wallqvist was not satisfied with general impressions but measured the flats assessing the floor space, the volume of air and number of windows available for each person. The same method was applied for investigating living conditions for mechanics and textile workers in Stockholm:

GEIJERSTAM, Gustaf Af
Notes on Workers' Conditions in Stockholm. (Works published by the Lorén
Foundation, 9.)
Sthlm 1894.

In the same series, Geijerstam described workers' housing in *Norberg, Dannemora, Grängesberg* and *Gällivare-Malmberget* (1897) and K. Key-Åberg described workers' housing in *Norrköping* (1896) and at *glass works* (1399).

In Stockholm, primitive assessments had been made of the housing in 1868, 1880, 1890, 1893 and 1894. But on the initiative of the Lorén Foundation, more complete housing investigations were carried out by the local councils:

Stockholm in 1896, 1900, 1902, 1907 and 1908
Göteborg in 1905, 1910 and 1912
Limhamn in 1905
Karlskrona in 1905-06
Vänersborg in 1906
Uppsala in 1907
Linköping in 1907-08
Nyköping in 1907-08
Örebro in 1909-1912

Let's take the Limhamn investigation as an example. It was reported in:

STJERNSTRÖM, Gustaf
Limhamn. Its industrial and social development, I, Social Journal 1906-07.

Stjernström investigated all inhabited buildings in Limhamn — 797 altogether. There were 1,510 flats with 4,940 inhabitants (two children under fifteen counted as one person). So there were 3.2 persons in each flat. 73% of the flats were of less than 15sq.m., but the standard was still considered very satisfactory, since 67% of the flats had more than twenty cubic metres air for each person.

The heating was usually by iron stoves, but there were also plenty of tiled stoves. Even central heating existed in a couple of cases. "In 88 kitchens the water in the kitchen comes directly through a pump, a convenience which probably is quite rare." The average rent was 5.50 kr/room, if the kitchen was regarded as half a room.

Like many other early housing investigations, Stjernström's essay also describes a number of other details as regards local conditions. He especially emphasizes R.F. Berg's contribution to Limhamn. Berg (both a socially involved employer and a company director interested in a stable work force and increased cement production) was an eager supporter of the scheme to provide workers with their own homes:

In 1888, to reduce the lack of housing and to give workers a chance to have their own homes, with the help of Mr R.F. Berg, a large portion of the property near 24 Hyllie, now called the Peacock estate, was bought. The site was divided into building-plots, and the cement company offered building material on credit terms at reduced prices.

Mr Berg supported the scheme personally with advice and assistance, resulting in the whole area soon yielding a number of 21 buildings, containing 49 flats with up to three rooms and a kitchen in each, plus some rooms without kitchens.

The homes are comfortable with plenty of space, which is obvious from the fact that each inhabitant has at his disposal on average a floor space of 10.8 sq.m and a volume of air of 28.4 cubic metres and 1.2 sq.m of window space.

The rent is on average SKr 5.90 per room and month...In the same way, 6 buildings were bought on the Stenskvättan site in 1891, nr 1 Hylltorp was bought, 13 of which were divided into plots and now have houses on them on both sides of Linnégatan, surrounded by well-tended gardens.

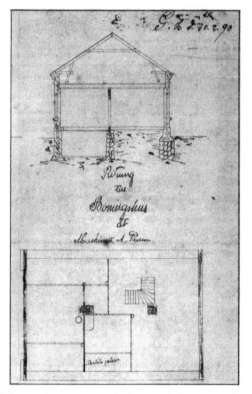

A plan of the engine operator A. Persson's house on the estate 24 Hyllie in Limhamn, allocated by the company for housing in 1888. Now in the archive of the Malmö Building Committee.

National Housing Surveys

The general housing survey attempts to give an idea of the housing situation in the whole country. The first was carried out in 1912-14 by the Ministry of Social Affairs and was published in *Swedish Official Statistics*, the series *Social Statistics Special*

Investigations, made in Vänersborg, Sundbyberg, Björkvik, Luleå, Karlstad, Jönköping, Uråsa, Brännkyrka, Norrköping, Eskilstuna, Sundsvall and Stora Tuna. Of particular interest are the concrete, often illustrated housing descriptions in:

INVESTIGATIONS
regarding the poorer people's housing in certain Swedish towns and cities.
1. Norrköping. 2. Jönköping. (SOS, Social Statistics.) Sthlm 1916-17.

The second general housing survey was carried out in 1920. It contains no concrete descriptions but gives the following information for all towns and places:

Limhamn	
Population	10654
Number of blocks of flats	1317
Number of state-owned buildings	-
Number of council-owned buildings	23
Building associations and public companies	1
Industrial and commercial companies	71
Others	1,222
Number of buildings with	
1 flat	733
2 flats	339
3-9 flats	226
10 or more flats	19
Average number of flats per building	2.0
Number of buildings with central heating	
For all flats	101
For some flats	28
Occupied after 25.5.1917	
Number of buildings	13

Number of flats	14
Number of buildings with	
3 or fewer occupiers	291
4-7 occupiers	563
8-29 occupiers	427
30 or more occupiers	36
Average number of occupiers per building	8
Number of rooms	8283
Proportion of living rooms/bedrooms	5797
Kitchens	2486
(Thus: living/bedroom per flat	2.2
occupier per living/bedroom)	1.8
Number of occupiers per 100 rooms	
In all flats	131
In small flats	161
In single rooms	156
In flats with shared kitchen	147
In one room and kitchen	199
In two rooms and kitchen	138
In larger flats	93
Average annual rent for flats with	
1 kitchen, no room	117
1 room without kitchen	132
2 or more rooms without kitchen	245
1 or more rooms with shared kitchen	228
1 room and kitchen	208
2 rooms and kitchen	321
3 rooms and kitchen	516
4 rooms and kitchen	786
5 rooms and kitchen	869
6 rooms and kitchen	600
7 rooms and kitchen	1,250

(To convert 1920 rents to the 1975 monetary value, multiply by 3.3. See Chapter 13.)

Malmö	
Number of rented households	
Less well-to-do	14592
More well-to-do	2622
Average annual rent for	
Less-well-to-do workers' households	294
Clerical staff households	465
Self-employed people's households	521
Old age pensioners' households, etc.	421
Average	350
Average for more well-to-do households	950
Average income for	
Less-well-to-do workers' households	3826
Clerical staff households	4207
Self-employed people's households	3778
Old age pensioners' households, etc.	3336
Average	3839
Average for more well-to-do households	15156
Average rent percentage for	
Less-well-to-do workers' households	7.7
Clerical staff households	11.1
Self-employed people's households	13.8
Old age pensioners' households, etc.	12.3
Average	9.1
Average for more well-to-do households	6.5

(Later housing surveys (1933, 1945 and 1960) give similar information. As from 1965, housing surveys are done with census counts.)

Brita Åkerman's investigations: one of the 214 families at their dining-table. Compare Wehtje's dining-room.

• How did your predecessors on the job, at the factory, live?

Aids: The housing surveys are available at the county library or can be ordered there. The County Councils' planning departments often have the answers of later investigations reported even for small areas — e.g., a block or two within one part a town.

In some towns, *housing inventories* have been carried out, describing the history of each building. Printed inventories are available at the county library; the unprinted are with the County Antiquarian. If no inventory has been made, you can go to the Archive of the Housing Authority, which generally keeps the plans of town houses built after 1784, when the Building Statute was established. After 1955 there are also technical descriptions with the planning applications. In some towns the Housing Authority keeps a *Local Buildings Register,* giving information on planning applications, taxation of real estate and different special inventories. Fire insurance documents often give extensive information about older houses — see Chapter 20. The census registers will tell you who lived in the house at different times — see Chapter 12. — These sources and others are described more closely in Fredric Bedoire e.a.

Records Guide for Building Researchers (l: Fataburen 1974) and
Ola Siksiö e.a. *To Select and Collect Housing Data* (Information
from the National Institute for Building Research 1976:14).

Sociological Housing Investigations

The housing surveys supply information about the physical
and financial conditions of housing. But they say nothing
about how people lived in their flats. How did they cope with
overcrowded dwellings, how did they eat, sleep, live with a large
family living in only one room? The first Swedish investigation
to attempt to answer this question is:

ÅKERMAN-JOHANSSON, Brita
The Family That Grew Out of Its Home.
Sthlm 1941.

This is an overlooked pioneering work of Swedish sociology
and at the same time a very readable book. It tells more of
Swedish family life in the 1930s than any other book I've
read. The investigation concerns two hundred and fourteen
Stockholm families, who were partly interviewed, partly asked
to keep a record of anything the family did and where in the
home they were during one week:

About half were working-class families with one or two children,
living in one room and a kitchen. The one-room flats typically
had one large table and a smaller one, two pieces for storage,
four chairs and one easy-chair. The divan was by far the most
common type of bed — there were only 40 beds to 326 divans
for adults. Half of the flats had a desk and one more bed, often
a child's cot or a chair bed. Parents and small children usually
slept in the room, older children in the kitchen. This could cause
problems, because the small children needed silence while the
parents wanted to talk, listen to the wireless, etc.

The one-room flat families ate in the kitchen. Cooking usually took up 13 hours a week for the housewife, washing up 7.5 hours, baking 2.3 hours. 94% of the housewives baked their own bread. The most common leisure activity outside the home was to go visiting. 82% of the families were also visited themselves during the week.

The families living in the smallest flats were most dissatisfied with their homes, especially if they had several children. The conclusions today seem obvious: "A one-room flat is unsuitable if you have children, 2 rooms should be the least available for families." "Families with children have such an extensive household that they need a proper kitchen." "For families with children a small cottage is much better than a flat at the same price."

After the Second World War, the authorities took more responsibility for housing, both by legislation, financing and directly through local council-owned housing companies. Brita Åkerman wanted to assist the planners of this development with information on the habits, needs and wishes of the people. With the same purpose, a large number of sociological housing investigations were carried out, from the beginning of the 1950s, concentrating on questions like: How are the different parts of the flat used? Why do people want to move? What shops and services are required on a housing estate? A survey of methods and results are given in:

BOALT, Gunnar e.a.
Housing Sociology.
Borås 1969.

The aim was to produce the type of housing people required at prices they could afford. But either the methods to establish their needs, or the methods of meeting their requirements failed for the intention never quite seems to have been realized. One attempt to systematically compare the aim with the result of a modern, well-planned housing estate is:

LANDELL, Nils-Erik
Hallonbergen — The Future Sweden?
Malmö 1974.

A comparison between a modern Stockholm suburb, Vårby, 1972, and an old workers' housing area, Reymersholm, at the beginning of the century, is made in:

DAUN, Åke
Suburban Life: An Ethnological Study of Cultural Changes.
Lund 1974.

Landell deals with not only the flats but above all the possibilities of children, old age pensioners and people with disabilities, the occupational health (*arbetsvården*), the cars, the energy consumption, etc. According to his thesis, the welfare state creates problems which cannot be solved only by more welfare. Daun writes about ways to spend weekday evenings, weekends and holidays, about contact with neighbours, relations and friends. Life in modern housing estates as described by him appears more human and understandable.

- What do you do at home? Several housing sociological methods can be applied to investigate your own ways of using your home.

Aids: Brita Åkerman's book is particularly useful. It would be interesting to repeat her investigation now, forty years later.

- What did the planners of your housing estate try to achieve? Did they succeed? What is your housing estate like compared to the housing of workers in the 1890s or 1930s?

Aids: Landell's and Daun's books can be used also where you live. At the end of Daun's book there is a detailed account of his methods. It contains many concrete tips, such as getting old people to remember and tell you about daily life of by-gone days.

17. MEMOIRS

One day at the beginning of the century, a young lad called Gustaf was employed at the Skånska Cement Head Office in Malmö. As Secretary to the Managing Director he gained some insight into various covert activities — such as the fraudulent sale of a patent and a secret agreement between Cementa and the Klagshamn cement factory. He concluded that "business life was apparently incompatible with ethical standards".

His employment with Skånska Cement did not last long. The company learnt that Gustaf was a member of the Socialist Youth Club in Malmö. He was given the choice of either leaving the club or being fired. "The idea was to leave me without a livelihood and a home." Preferring unemployment, Gustaf went on to work as a journalist at a newspaper called *The Worker*. In due course he became Minister of Social Affairs and in his old age wrote his memoirs:

MÖLLER, Gustaf
Remembrances. (The Workers' Movement's Yearbook 1971)
Lund 1971.

But most former secretaries never become Ministers of Social Affairs. Very rarely do they write their memoirs. How did Ernst Wehtje's secretary see his employer? What covert activities did Ernst Jonas Wehtje's secretary witness? What would Sten Lindh's secretary have been able to tell? We'll probably never know. The professional corps which has more personal insight into the functions of capitalism than any other, as a rule loyally take their secrets with them to the grave.

On the whole, it is unusual for ordinary people to write their memoirs. Check in the library under Lz (in Sweden) and you will find only politicians, actors and other celebrities. The people we can watch closely are generally the same as those in *Who's Who*. In their memoirs, the Swedish upper classes describe their contributions. We can also find the life experiences and social attitudes of the middle classes. But where are the memoirs of the Swedish working classes?

This is a huge gap in our knowledge of the past. Mats Rehnberg, the ethnologist, discovered it in the mid-1940s and began to cooperate with the trade union press to get old workers to write down their memoirs.

In the period 1945-60, Mats Rehnberg sent out a long series of calls to different occupations and unions. Thousands of workers wrote their memoirs. A small part of this material has been published in the series *Swedish Life and Work*. Above all, the following volumes record the memoirs of industrial workers:

SAWMILL MEMOIRS, Sthlm 1948.
IRONWORKS MEMOIRS, Sthlm 1952.
WORKSHOP MEMOIRS, Sthlm 1953.
CARBEHTHY MEMOIRS, Sthlm 1961.

This is a fantastic series. Every person working in wood or metal here has a human chance to see his own occupation in vivid human remembrance and trace it back to the late nineteenth century.

The contents of the workers' memoirs to a certain extent have been controlled by the directions given by Mats Rehnberg to the people who contributed. The formulation varies slightly for different occupations — this one comes from *Workshop Memoirs*:

1. The described person's year and place of birth. Parents' occupation, origin, living conditions.
2. Childhood and adolescence. Brothers and sisters. Work at home. The family's living conditions

3. The first home. Describe all the homes the family had, furnishings, beds, meals. Cooking, cleaning, and laundering. Every day and holiday life at home. Friends.

4. Describe the surroundings of the home, the building, the nearest buildings, or the industrial community in the area. Describe shops and service institutions, neighbours and life in the community in the different seasons.

5. First job outside home. Type of work, place, working hours, mates, bosses. How did the older workers treat the younger ones? Wages and their use. At what age did he leave his parents' home?

6. Adolescence. How he spent his time, what made him happy or sad, what were his interests in life, at leisure? Relationship between the sexes etc.

7. Marriage and family. How did the spouses meet? Describe engagement, wedding and marriage, family life, children, home, friends, leisure etc.

8. Work in industry or in other places. This is one of the most important parts. Give a comprehensive account of the workshops, metal workshops and other places where he has been working. The reason why he changed jobs. Describe the work itself in each place, the nature of work legislation, the organization of the different work stages. Describe the places of work and their various facilities, breaks and meals, mates and foremen. Working hours, wages in different periods. How were people employed and dismissed? Views on different conditions at work at different times during his life.

9. Tell us about spiritual and religious interests. What part was played by church and non-conformism? What people's movements did he come across, such as teetotallers, the workers' movement, the athletes' movement etc?

The trade union and the political battle should naturally have been more emphasized in these questions. The class conflicts should at least have been mentioned. Occupational hazards and working environment should have been in the foreground. But even these tame questions that were asked give a clear and merciless description of companies and places of work in the workers' memoirs.

- Is your company described in the workers' memoirs?

Aids: The published memoirs are available at the library, under M (in Sweden). The complete collected material, which is many times larger, is available at the archive of the Nordic Museum. There is a place index which makes searching easier. You can write to them and ask; address: Djurgårdsvägen 6, 115 21 Stockholm. Tel: 08/63 05 00.

Bo Gustafsson has examined the credibility of the workers' memoirs in *The Workers of Sawmill Industry in Northern Sweden 1890-1913: Working and Living Conditions.* (Socio-economic studies, 1) Uppsala 1965. Edvard Bull, on the basis of Norwegian workers' memoirs, published in the series *Workers Remember*, has written *Working Environment During the Industrial Revolution*, 3rd ed., Oslo 1975. This is a study of the conditions for the workers' movement's appearance in three Norwegian industrial areas. Bull's book shows a way to coordinate individual workers' biographies to a kind of working-class biography — in a particular company.

- The collection of workers' memoirs is still in progress. Would you like to write down your memoirs?

Aids: Write to the Cultural Historical Investigation, The Nordic Museum, 115 21 Stockholm, or phone 08/63 05 00 and tell them you are interested. You will then receive a friendly letter, a memorandum for writers of memoirs and a list with some questions on everyday life. For over fifty years, such questionnaires have been sent out regularly to volunteers all over the country. The answers are kept in the Nordic Museum archive. A list of earlier questionnaires are sent free on request. Some of the earlier contributors are introduced by Mats Rehnberg in *Researchers Among the People* (Fataburen 1947). At present the cultural-historical investigation is sending out three to five questionnaires yearly to about three hundred permanent contributors and are actively seeking new ones — especially younger people, industrial workers, people in service jobs and industrialists.

The Factory Remembered

This is the story of a deaf-and-dumb smith, Alfred Olsson, as interpreted by his daughter:

> As a child I would walk along the lake from Ivetofta to Bromölla and stand on the road looking down at the "factory". Then they had only one kiln, in which they burnt first lime and then bricks. This first lime kiln was roughly in the same place as the cement factory later. It was only like a white shed with a vaulted roof, like a round heap and nothing else.

The farmer Gottfrid Jönsson who would drive with horses for the company was present when they built the cement factory:

> The cement factory had concrete walls, more than a metre thick. They drove stone to it from all directions. I remember they took a lot of stones from the factory farm, and blasted it and used it for the construction down there. The factory farm was the farm they bought from Ola Nilsson. It has been pulled down now.
> They mixed cement and stone at the site and founded it in moulds to concrete which they then used for construction.

We only dealt with the boss of the building site, they had a boss there called Pelle Maja, a stonemason boss. He went to America later.

The raw material came from Ifön, where the crane driver Anders Nilsson worked. He writes:

In 1910 the first excavator came, but it was only used for clearing away topsoil and such... The cement lime was loaded with shovels into wooden boxes, each holding one cubic metre. The wooden boxes were taken away on rails to a hand-driven windlass. As one box went down, another went up.

There were two platforms and from one of them the box went down to the quay. There the box was lifted onto the barge with a hand-driven crane. For five years I operated that crane. For each barge I would note the number of boxes going into it and each Tuesday I gave the office the information.

It was a pile quay and only one barge could be loaded at any one time. The rails in the lime pit were hand-driven, there were no horses. The lime was quarried on two levels. One shaft was called the shaft of death, because two or three workers had been buried by falling rocks. One was a Galician and he had his head cut off by the rail.

"For five years I operated that crane." There are plenty of expressions of impressive factual knowledge in these accounts. "I myself drew out the kilns." Or: "There were three pools. I found them in 1918." Or: "The Galicians had many accidents. I know because I handled their insurances." Nils Mattsson also knows what he talks about when he describes the burning of cement:

I joined the Ifö works in the spring of 1914... I started as a worker at the cement factory, burning cement. My hourly wage was 33 öre. We worked for 10 1/2 hours, starting at 6, stopping for breakfast 8.30 — 9, dinner at 12 — 1 and finishing at 6 in the evening. The burners had their working hours changed in 1918. Before then we had had a shift of two, now it became a shift of three. The manager, Mr Kärfve, arranged this. The first shift was from 6AM to 2PM. The second shift (the following week) was from 2PM to 10PM, and the third shift (third week) was from 10PM to 6AM. When the shifts changed we were given 35 öre an hour.

The hourly wage can be converted to the 1975 monetary value, with the method used above to convert Wehtje's millions (see Chapter 13). 35 öre an hour equals 1 kr 34 öre. Nils Mattsson continues:

All work at the Cement was shift work. The first years there were about 30 men in each shift, but if the winter was severe (all raw material was transported on the lake) they had to cut down the number of workers or cease production.

In 1914, August Holmqvist was foreman at Cement, he had been there since Cement started in 1908. The other foreman was Aust. He was transferred to the slurry works in 1918, then Gustafsson came, and after him I became foreman. I was made foreman in 1920 in the department I had joined in 1914. The wages were 230 kr monthly, then in 1921 they went up to exactly 300 (759 and 1,152 kr respectively by the 1975 monetary value).

Jöns Strand originally worked at the brick kilns. He saw his transfer to the cement factory as a form of punishment:

We had thick sacks on our heads to cope with the heat, but sometimes my eyebrows were singed when I came home. I did not have one dry garment on when I came home at night, and I still had to go out into the cold to unload, and I soon had aches and pains everywhere. — From there I was sent to Cement as punishment. We had been given orders to take a kiln down but we said it was impossible, and I, being the oldest, did not want to start, because the heat was so bad it was impossible. As punishment I was sent to Cement. There I was in Nils Persson's shift. I was a clinker-weigher. When they stopped making cement I came to the outdoor team instead.

ACC. NR M. **14104**: /- /6.

Landskap: SKÅNE	Upptecknare: Ulla Andersson	
Härad: VILLANDS	Berättare: Jöns Strand	
Socken: IVETOFTA	Berättarens yrke: F.d. generatorbrännare	
Uppteckningsår: 1954	Född år 1873 i Näsum	

	Sid.1
Biografiska uppgifter	" "
Vaktepåg, diverse arbeten	" "
Anställning på Iföverken	" "
Kollastning, kolförlag	" 1-2
Järnvägen fabriken-stationen, den grå hästen	" 2
Lokomotiv	" 2-3
Ugnarna, arbetet där	" 3
Generatorbrännare, arbetstider	" 3-4
Arbete på cementfabriken m.m.	" 4
Avlöningen, avlöningskontoret m.m.	" 4-5
Ångvisslan	" 5
Arbetarnas sjukkassa	" "
Brandkåren	" 5-6
Nattvakter	" 6
När fackföreningen hade bildats	" "
Konkursen	" "
Fabriksområdet	" 6-7
Hamnen, s.7;	
Slammeriet, s.7.	forts.

Skriv endast på denna sida

Jöns Strand's memoirs are in the ethnological records in Lund. The first page has personal details and a list of contents.

Edvard Mårtensson, finally, was employed as a cooper:

An ad in the paper said the Ifö works wanted a cooper. It was in 1908 and I had a good job in Eslöv, but there was a bit of trouble between the boss and myself, so I rang the Ifö works, Mr Köster, an engineer, who managed the cement factory. In August of 1908 I came to Bromölla.

In the coopers' workshop we made cement containers.

When the work force was at its largest there were about 40 of us. The coopers had their own trade union and we were paid 42 öre an hour for a 10 hour working day.

The coopers' workshop was built along with the cement factory. The workshop is still there, but the building is used, partly as a warehouse for painters, partly as a cement foundry.

In 1949 Brita Åkerblad listened to these accounts and wrote them down. Ulla Andersson continued with the interviews in 1954. In all about forty accounts were taken down from the history of the Ifö works. They are now kept among the ethnological records at Finngatan 8 in Lund. You can go there yourself to read them.

Very few Swedish industries have had their story told by the workers. Even the Bromölla memoirs are very scant, probably due to a lack of knowledge in the interviewers. They themselves had never stood by a rotary kiln or in a lime pit. If a cement worker had handled the questioning, he would have had many more questions to ask about work and working conditions.

The worker, not the scientist, has the factual knowledge required by this particular research task. And the workers, not the scientists, need the results. Those who work in today's and will work in tomorrow's cement factories need to preserve the experience of yesterday's cement workers.

The cooper Edvard Mårtensson.

- Have any memories been written down from the company where you work?

Aids: The reports are kept at the ethnological archive in Lund, Göteborg or Uppsala or at the Nordic Museum in Stockholm. These archives have place indexes that make searching easier.

- The evidence of many workers together give a picture of the company. What would the history of your company look like if its workers told it?

Aids: You and your workmates have better possibilities than anyone else to collect the material for such a history. Instructions on interviewing methods can be found e.g., in Daun (Chapter 16) and Furtenbach (Chapter 12). Sven B. Ek has written about workers' living conditions in the Nöden area in Lund 1890-1920, based on interview material. It's called *Nöden in Lund: An Ethnological Town Study*, (publications of the ethnological records in Lund, 1l) Landskrona 1971. A factory can be investigated with the same method.

In literature about workers there are many autobiographical accounts with portraits of workmates. *Swedish Accounts of Workers 1945-74* is a useful survey (published by the association BHS) Borås 1977. It should be available at the library. If not, it can be ordered from Bibliotekshögskolan, Box 55067, 500 05 Borås.

18. THE VOCABULARY

I suggest, in other words, that you have knowledge that science has not.

Don't you believe me? Let's try that statement by checking what linguistic researchers know about your place of work.

Each occupation has its own characteristic vocabulary. *Clearing* for example. When the crane driver Anders Nilsson wanted to say that the first Ifö excavator in 1910 was used only for "clearing" he wasn't sure that this was clear to the person he was addressing. So he wrote: "clearing away topsoil and such" to clarify that "clearing" means to remove the topsoil covering the limestone.

Anyone who has worked in a lime pit knows the meaning of *clearing*. They also know the meaning of other characteristic words such as *cuttings, tamping, stool, stone bench, overloading*. Anyone working in a cement factory knows that the area in front of the kiln head where the burner stands is called a *burner's platform*. They know that the kiln is erected with *ball races* on *kiln rolls* and that it is cooled by a *rust cooler*. Or by a *planetary cooler* consisting of steel tubes placed around the kiln pipe like planets around the sun.

In a cement factory employing the wet method, everyone knows that there will be slurry rings forming inside the kiln when the water content of the slurry is reduced and it becomes viscous like treacle. They know that a certain amount of extra burning is required to protect the brick lining in the hottest parts of the kiln. But if there is too much extra burning, *gypsum rings* will form that dam up the flow of material and hamper the passage of the fumes through the kiln. And *ash rings* which can cause sudden unexpected flows of dammed-up material at the outlet of the kiln. The hot cement clinker is taken away by *trajectories* and the *skip car*. Next to the *skip car* is a little container that warns when the skip car is overfull. That is the *skip*. These words are common and familiar to anyone working in a cement factory. Now let's see what the linguists know about them.

Dictionaries

Words are collected in dictionaries. One of the most popular Swedish dictionaries is Olof Östergren's *Dictionary of Modern Swedish*, which was first published in 1919. It answers the question: In what forms and with what meanings is this word used? If for example you look under "cement", Östergren gives four different meanings of this word and some of its combinations, such as "cement factory". But Östergren's dictionary does not include any of the eighteen words we seek.

Elof Hellqvist's Swedish *Etymological Dictionary*, republished in a new edition in 1957, is almost equally famous. It answers the question: What is the origin of this word? We are told that "cement" is derived from the Latin word "caementum", cut stone, which in turn is derived from "caedere", cut. Explanation: "In the Middle Ages, mortar was usually prepared from crushed bricks, later the usage has become more specialised." In many cases, Hellqvist also tells us when the word first appeared in the Swedish language. But the eighteen words we are looking for are not included in his book.

Sture Allén´s Modern *Swedish Frequency Dictionary* based on newspaper text came out in 1970. It answers the question: How common is this word? The most common Swedish word is the equivalent of "and", which appeared over thirty thousand times in the examined newspaper text. "Cement" is not very common, it only appeared six times. The eighteen words we are looking for did not appear at all in the newspaper text examined by Allén — newspapers do not often write about work in a cement factory.

Except for the general dictionaries, there are slang dictionaries, dialect dictionaries, lists of the language of individual authors and many other specialized dictionaries. For technical language there are a number of dictionaries published by the Technical Nomenclature Centre (TNC) which comes under the Department of Industry.

These dictionaries do not describe the actual usage of the words but *the proper usage* of them. Therefore they are called *normative*. Wood enamel, plastic, pulp and paper, nuclear power, paints, rubber, water, forest and brewery technology are some of the areas covered by specialized technical dictionaries.

Cement is taken up by *Dictionary of Concrete Technology* (TCN publications 46), published in 1971. It answers the question: What is the technically correct meaning of the word "cement"? Answer: a "finely ground hydraulic binding agent":

A "binding agent" means a "substance which in appropriate use has the property of binding other materials by adhering". A "hydraulic binding agent" is a binding agent "which after the adding of water binds and hardens in both water and air", — "Portland cement" is a hydraulic binding agent "produced by the grounding of Portland clinker with the addition of a certain limited amount of gypsum and possibly some limited amounts of other additives produced for special purposes". If someone wants to know the meaning of "Portland clinker", the answer is: "an intermediate product in cement production, mainly consisting of calcium silicates, obtained by the sintering of a homogenous mixture of lime (CaO) and silicon dioxide $(SiO2)$ plus small amounts of iron oxide and aluminium oxide $(F202$ and $Al202)$."

All this about cement. But not one of the eighteen words we are looking for is listed in the *Dictionary of Concrete Technology*.

The major Swedish dictionary, the one supposedly comprising all the others, is the *Dictionary of the Swedish*

Language published by the Swedish Academy, usually referred to as the Swedish Academy Dictionary or the SAOB. The word "cement" is in the fifth volume, BLÅ — CZEK, published in 1925. It gives the answer to a lot of questions, such as:

How is the word pronounced? Cement is pronounced "seament".

What forms of the word are known? "Cement" has only one form. What is the origin of the word? This explanation is more comprehensive than that of Hellqvist.

When and where was the word used for the first time? The answers are given in abbreviations, which become comprehensible with the aid of a *Source List* (Lund 1939) which should unconditionally accompany the dictionary on the library shelf. The word "cement" (here spelt ciment") was found for the first time in J.J. Berzelius *Textbook on chemistry*, part 5, Sthim 1828, p. 1172.

What compounds have been formed with the word "cement"? As early as 1925, there were about a hundred such compounds such as "cement worker" and "cement factory".

When and where were these combinations used for the first time? These answers, too, are given in abbreviations explained in the source list.

The *Swedish Academy Dictionary* (for as far as it goes as yet they have only got to the letter S) is the most comprehensive Swedish dictionary. Does it have the eighteen words we are looking for?

Yes, it has four of them, i.e., *tamping*, *skip car*, *ball race* and *stool*. The other fourteen words are not listed.

One more possibility remains. If you have found a word not included in the *Swedish Academy Dictionary*, you can phone or write to their archive in Lund and ask for information about this word. So I wrote down these fourteen words together with an example of the usage of each one, like this:

CLEARING
Before the driller can start, the lime stone must be freed from topsoil, this is called clearing.

CUTTINGS
On its way up through the hole, the pressure air takes along
the drilled stone, which is called cuttings.

I immediately received an answer. Three of the words were
included in their records: *clearing, stone bench* and *overloading*.
They sent me their examples two from the 1880s and one
rather recent:

CLEARING
Excavating as it is also called, is these days always done by
excavator. Technical journal 1961, 1226 b.

The name of Anders Nilsson's activities with the first Ifö
excavator in 1910 was, in other words, unknown to scientists
for another fifty years! And eleven of the eighteen everyday
cement factory words were still completely unknown to
linguistics. The records of the *Swedish Academy Dictionary*
thanked me politely for the samples I had sent them and
for the first time ever included the words *cuttings, burner's
platform, kiln roll, rust cooler, planetary cooler, slurry ring, extra
burning, gypsum ring, ash ring, trajectory* and *small skip* in their
records.

If you make the same investigation with some typical words
from your own factory, you will probably get the same result;
linguists have never heard some of your words.

This is partly due to the fact that dictionaries only include
written words — and many factories have never been
described in writing. It is also due to the fact that linguistic
researchers have been relatively uninterested in investigating
the language of the factories. This is a survey of the modest
attempts that have been made:

BANNBERS, Ola
The Worker and the Language (I: The History of the Swedish
Working-Classes. Part 5.)
Sthlm 1943.

The most comprehensive linguistic investigations in factories are Erik Holmqvist, *The Mining language in Bergslagen*, Uppsala 1941, and *The Smelting Language in Bergslagen*, Uppsala 1945. Apart from these, linguists have mainly taken an interest in the so called secret language of the chimney sweeps, the fleecers and the pedlars.

The archives of dialects and ethnology in Lund, Göteborg and Uppsala have been given the task of collecting and preserving examples of the spoken Swedish language. The Uppsala archive has three to four persons busy recording these data during a few months each summer. They seek mainly old-fashioned and obsolete expressions in order to preserve them. They keep e.g., lists of the language of the following crafts: tile stove-makers, cobblers, potters, glass-blowers, coopers, smiths and masons. But they *have not got a single list of the language of an industrial site.*

"We simply never thought of industry," they say. But they add that they would be very pleased to come and investigate examples of industrial language if some workers invited them to do so.

- What are the characteristic words at your place of work? Are they included in the dictionaries? In the Swedish Academy Dictionary records?

Aids: The address to the archive of the *Swedish Academy Dictionary* is PO Box 1010, 221 03 Lund 1. Tel: 046/11 13 56.

If you are interested in collecting words at your place of work — get a ring file of the smaller format with lined, punched pages. Use one leaf for each word or expression. Arrange the leaves alphabetically.

Write the word as the headline. Describe its usage by giving an example including the word. The sentence should explain the meaning of the word as clearly as possible. Write down especially words that need explaining to people who have never seen your place of work.

One good way to think of these words is to go through the working day from beginning to end. What do you see — what is it called? What do you do — what is it called? What do you hear — what is it called? What do you smell — what is it called?

Also go through the building from one end to the other, chasing for words. What are the names of places, objects, events?

Further tips for word collectors in industry can be found at the end of Peter Wright's book *The Language of British Industry*, London 1974.

• What words were used by your predecessors? How do the words reflect the history of the job?

Aids: Your own memories, interviews, diaries, letters. An English example of how words can tell the history of the work is G.C. Greenwell's dictionary *A Glossary of Terms Used in the Coal Trade of Northumberland and Durham*, 1849. Reprinted Newcastle 1970. The brief, concrete and precise explanations to the specialized vocabulary of the coal mine gives a clear picture of the efforts and dangers involved with this job.

Words are only the building stones of language. The most interesting thing about them is how they can be put together and used by different people in different situations — e.g., to exert and resist power.

- How do the "power language" and the "resistance language" sound at your factory? What changes have you noticed in these languages in your working experience?

Aids: The concepts "power language" and "resistance language" have been taken from Göran Palm, *Balance Sheet from LM,* Uddevalla 1974, the chapter headed confounded language. He describes three forms of power language used by the company to the employees. A *technocratic language,* filled with technicians' and economists' terms. A *PR language* — smiling, friendly and insinuating. A *commanding language,* used for regulations and verbal instructions. The workers use different kinds of *resistance language.* Palm here indicates a research area which seems to be both exciting scientifically and practically important, but very little has been done about it by linguistic researchers.

19. THE MUSEUMS

"Where is the Working-Class Museum?"

"There isn't one."

"Perhaps it's called something else. Where is the Museum of the Workers' Movement?"

"There isn't one."

"There isn't one? But where is the Museum of Work?"

"There isn't one. Unless you're thinking of Skansen."

"Oh no, Skansen only depicts the crafts and farming communities. There isn't a single machine there..."

"If you want machines you should go to the Museum of Technology."

"But they have nothing but machines. Nothing on factories, on strikes, on occupational hazards, on unemployment, on the reality of the workers. It's a museum for technicians and industrialists."

"Then go to the Nordic Museum."

"But I´m not mainly interested the work of the gamekeepers, fishermen and farmers. Sweden is an industrial nation. We have had an industry, in the modern sense of the word, for over a hundred years. I am asking: Where is the museum depicting the history of industrial work, of the workers' movement, of the working classes?"

"There isn't one. We don't have political museums like that in Sweden."

"Oh? So farmers are not politics? But industrial workers are? And politics is something dirty which is not admitted into museums? What's wrong with politics? Why shouldn't we have a political museum?"

"I say there isn't one. That's enough."

The Nordic Museum

Cement could be said to be the complete opposite to the interests of the Nordic Museum.

It is a modern product, without any anchorage in the old Swedish farming community. It is an international product without regional or national characteristics. It is a standardized product showing no trace of the people who made it. Manufacture even at the beginning was done on an industrial scale without any significant crafts contributing. The cement has replaced older building materials such as wood and stone and thus has contributed to eliminating traditional methods of construction.

Ethnology began as a rescue action for old buildings which had been rendered obsolete because of cement. There was a wish to preserve at least the knowledge that there had once been houses that looked different in different parts of the country. In the same way they wanted to preserve the spinning wheel and traditional costumes from the advancing textile industry; the hammer and the sickle from the engineering industry and the rake from the combine harvester.

Having that as a chief objective, it was naturally difficult for the Nordic Museum to take an interest in industrial sites or modern building materials. They wanted to study the "culture of the people", people meaning the peasantry and culture meaning the preindustrial forms of culture.

In the meantime industrialization progressed. The people from rural areas moved to the towns and cities, farmers and craftsmen changed their occupations. The "people" studied by ethnologists, from being a huge majority, now turned into a few per cent of the population.

The Nordic Museum has made several attempts to wake up and adjust to the new conditions. In the late 1930s, the museum staff took part in a very ambitious project called "The History of the Swedish Working Classes". Their job was to investigate the homes, environment, food, clothes, wages and entertainment of the workers. They collected eighteen thousand pages of notes and questionnaires and over three thousand photographs and drawings.

But the investigation never reached the industrial workers proper. They did chart some workers' estates in industrial cities such as Västerås and Eskilstuna, they did study traditions and living conditions of textile workers around Alingsås and working conditions in the lime stone industry in Hellvi and Lärbro in Gotland. But the large majority of material applied to small farmers, crofters, farm-labourers and craftsmen. This bias also distinguishes the finished publication:

THE WORKER
On Holy Days and Weekdays. (The History of the Swedish Working Classes, 4.) Sthlm 1943.

It describes things like the history of the provision-bag. We learn all about the looks of the provision-bag at different points in time, for farm-workers, for smiths, for timber-floaters, fishermen and clearing-workers. The provision-bag of the industrial workers, however, is left unopened — and has so remained.

It also describes the history of home decor. We learn what the homes looked like for farmers, crofters, mill-hands and craftsmen of different kinds. There is a brief reference to the homes of industrial workers:

The boom of large industry brought various changes. Many people arrived from different directions, and even the despised peasants were accepted as industrial workers. Iron stoves were installed — the open hearth was now gone — and bright oil lamps were used for light. The bread-oven disappeared, open shelves were replaced by cupboards, chests by chests of drawers. The more well-to-do men got themselves a secretaire which was placed in the bed-chamber and adorned with all sorts of ornaments. Hard chairs, upholstered furniture, American wall-clocks and rocking-chairs were bought at relatively reasonable prices... Briefly: it gave rise to a type of home that exists even today and which is beginning to yield to the new type of home decor finding its form at the very present.

The same thing applies to the history of working clothes. We are given details on the way peasants and crofters, maids and coach-drivers, journeymen and apprentices, and above all smiths, were dressed at work. We learn that the worker's smock originally was the professional attire of the boat swains (sailors could buy ready-made working clothes while docking as early as the eighteenth century). The boiler-suit appeared in Germany in the 1880s but did not have its breakthrough in Sweden until well into this century, when dungarees also became common. Apart from this, the attire of industrial workers is considered irrelevant. This is even considered a decisive step forward:

> In the old days, the craftsman would mark his occupation and position by the costume he wore most of the time. His only chance of social vindication was by professional pride. Now this mediaeval tradition has been broken, it is of no consequence in a free society. The working clothes became purely working clothes and the most practical form is chosen, depending on the job. A working costume is no longer the proper clothes for a whole social group, it is only there to protect you while you're working.

I disagree with these conclusions. Is it really true that working clothes in a "free society" no longer have a social function? What change of the attitude to the work is implied if the working costume "is only there to protect you"? How does it affect a man if his leisure clothes become his 'proper' clothes? Is it better to vindicate oneself with a smart suit or a new car than by professional pride, symbolized by working clothes? *The Worker on Holy Days and Weekdays* neither asks nor answers such questions. It only grazes the industrial society by the fingertips.

The collections of exhibits show the same limitation. The Nordic Museum and Skanse since they were created have collected about 750,000 different exhibits depicting different aspects of the life of Swedish people. They do not look for odd, remarkable or exclusive objects, but real everyday objects. The intention is to collect things that are *typical* of life for different social classes in rural or urban areas in different periods.

When preparing its centenary, the museum staff again went through the collections to assess the success of this intention. It turned out that the majority of collected exhibits come from the pre-industrial society and that most of them come from the higher social classes.

For example, as they sat down to count *chairs,* they found that the Nordic Museum possessed 1,348 chairs of known origin. Only nineteen of these chairs came from working-class homes, seventeen of which came from provincial workers' homes. The working classes of towns and cities were represented by *two* chairs. Out of 1,348.

I went to the museum and asked to see these two chairs. But it appeared that no one knew any more where they were kept. They had disappeared once more in the profusion of upper- and middle-class chairs.

Since the Nordic Museum serves as an example for the many local museums throughout the country, it is important to adjust this bias of the collections. They are in fact trying. The museum is at present looking for exhibits from the past fifty years, especially from towns and cities. And especially from working-class environments.

- What objects were typical of your job in the old days? Have they been preserved? Where did they go?

- What objects are typical of your factory today? Where will they go? Does anyone collect them?

- What picture is given by the local museum of the life of your predecessors and of your place of work in the old days? How could the museum be renewed?

Aids: The programme of the Nordic museum is presented in *Exhibit. Picture. Data. Guidelines for the Collecting Activities of the Nordic Museum.* Sthlm 1973. (Stencil). There is also a long list of types of exhibits required by the museum, from toys after 1920 to tools and machines for furniture-making after 1950. On request the museum sends out free a topical list of requirements. And since the collections increase almost solely by voluntary donations, they are grateful for all suggestions. Get in touch with your local museum, your district museum — they probably have the same attitude.

The Museum of Technology

The Museum of technology in Malmö has a model of the cement factory in Limhamn in1960. There is also a gear for a rotary kiln. That's all.

The Museum of Technology in Stockholm has nothing on the Swedish cement industry. You can go through the exhibitions from floor to ceiling without finding as much as a grain of cement. But let's not give up so easily. Here as in most other places, most items are behind the scenes.

The heart of the Museum of Technology is the library and the archive. The entrance is immediately on your right as you enter by the main entrance. You go through a long corridor and enter the catalogue room. The staff there are friendly and helpful.

First have a look at the *Catalogue of Books*. That includes special prints of industrial history and small publications difficult to find elsewhere. The catalogue is arranged according to a unique system, and there are instructions on top of the card cupboard.

The *Catalogue of Drawings* is arranged alphabetically after place names. There are large collections of mechanical drawings and plans of industrial buildings from some Swedish plants. However, many branches of industry, including the cement industry, are not represented at all.

The Lomma cement factory around 1880. Photo of a model in the Museum of Technology, Stockholm.

Then ask the librarian to produce the catalogue of records for the branch of industry that interests you. Within each branch, the catalogue is arranged alphabetically after the names of companies. Example:

Cement industry, general 393
Cementa 944

Write down the numbers on an order form, and the librarian will collect the record boxes, which contain a lovely mixture of newspaper cuttings, advertising material price lists, photographs of companies, machines, workers and their homes, correspondence with the company in question and sometimes the transcript of interviews. For example, a former worker at the cement factory at Lomma, Per Åkesson, born in 1858, was interviewed in 1941:

Lomma harbour is formed by the outlet of Höje Ås. On the south side it is reinforced by a constructed pier. The *lime stone* was transported on barges from Limhamn to the harbour and to the lime and bar store on its northern bank. The lime stores were often "as high as houses".

Clay was taken from the clay pits near the factory. In the clay pit up to 80-100 men worked in winter and the clay was transported in barrows, partly to the cement factory, partly to a large store for the brick works. Later this transport was made with horses and tipping cars, which were then replaced by a double-tracked railway, where the wagons were pulled by an engine and a line 1,600m long. The clay was brought into the slurry works...

The slurry was left to settle and the water was drawn through several pipes inserted into it. It ran into the lake. It went on like that until the dam was full of firm slurry up to its full height. This was then left for almost one year, after which the slurry was taken up by spades and wheeled off in barrows to the swamps...

The swamps were then filled with slurry and dry grinding, enough of the latter in hand-moulds to stones (raw stones) of about the same size as bricks...

In the early days, there were only two kilns, later 6 conical shaft kilns. There were three inlet openings, one above the other, i.e. four storeys. On the coulter, there were first wood shavings and combustibles and 4-5 loads of black coal (English), plus about 20 pails of coke. On top of this were the raw stones on edge, then one layer of coke etc. until the kiln was full. We used less coke higher up. In due course the inlets were sealed off and the kiln left to burn for two days and nights. We alternated so that at least one kiln could be emptied each day, i.e. 7-8 kilns per six-day-week...

When in the 1880s we had reached a production result of 100000 barrels a year, they hoisted the flag.

This is only a small part of the interview, which gives a very detailed description of the production process at the first Swedish cement factory. Note, however — not a word is said about the factory as a place of work, not a word about working conditions or terms. The interviewer, Torsten Althin the director of the Museum of Technology, had no interest in that.

The catalogue cards of the records also include numbers referring to the collections of exhibits. Example:

CEMENTA
Exhibits: TM prod. 17.823. Ref. 18.569 19.515 19.516

Ask the librarian to produce the catalogue of the collection of exhibits, where you can find these numbers:

17.283 Samples of clinker from rotary kilns. From Skånska Cement AB, Limhamn, 1918.

18.569 A model in proportion. 1:300 of the Limhamn cement factory. 1941. From Skånska Cement, Limhamn. The model was repainted May 1941 and re-indexed under nr 19.516

19.515 A Model in proportion 1:300 of the Lomma cement factory, about 1880. Prom Cementa, Sv Försäljn AB Malmö. Designed by the TM model workshop in 1941.

The models were turned into an exhibition on cement and concrete in May 1941, which is also recorded by the museum.

Finally, ask to see a thick hardback book with typed pages, called *Guiding Catalogue for Carl Sahlin's Mining Historical*

Collections, donated to the Museum of Technology on 8 January 1933.

Carl Sahlin was a mining engineer and later a director of various ironworks. Throughout his life, with indefatigable curiosity, he collected all kinds of objects associated mainly with mines and metal industry but also lime and cement as well as many other branches of industry.

The collections are divided into different classes:

1. Books
2. Travelogues
3. Stamp books (from the iron industry)
4. Small publications on mining and ironworks
5. Works on personal history
6. Works of general mining historical interest
7. Hand-written material concerning mining and ironworks, etc.
8. Biographical notes (incl. notes on Swedish gold-diggers)

The catalogue ends with a comprehensive catchword index, the so called miscellaneous index.

The classes 4. and 7. are particularly comprehensive (1,100 capsules and about 4,000 names of places). In practice, both classes contain about the same type of material. Example:

CLASS 4. Limhamn.
Advertising prints and directions for use. Off-prints by engineer A.V. Lundberg's childhood memories. Postcards from 1904 with a caricature of the directors of the cement companies rolling barrels to the sales company Cementa, from which money is flowing.

CLASS 7. Klagshamn.
A plan of the factory site in 1922. A description of Sahlin's visit to the factory in 1933. Small prints and newspaper cuttings with comments by Sahlin.

Carl Sahlin's descriptions and comments refer not only to purely technical details but also the issues of ownership and power. Example:

The Klagshamn lime pit and cement factory
Notes from a visit 23/8 1933.
Owner: Klagshamn cement works AB, which due to massive loans is completely run and ruled by AB Göteborgs Bank (through engineer E. Olsson).
Manager: Axel Edgren. Chief engineer: Ragnar Nordensten (appointed by the Göteborgs Bank to assist — or rather control — the manager).

The company seems to have been founded as a lime pit in 1896. The cement works founded in 1902 or 1903 applied a pioneering method. Its first managing director after the transfer to cement production was Henry Mueller, former mining engineer at Höganäs. A Danish works superintendent, Mr Gedde, who had been employed before him, however, did everything to make Mueller's work difficult. A severe conflict developed between the two men, and in due course Mueller had to retire...

The manager, Mr Edgren was not at home. The engineer Nordensten and the local harbour master showed us the plant. Nordensten, born at Striberg, did not like living in Scania. He found the winters along this flat coast dreadful. But worst of all was the bad state of affairs, in spite of all improvements undertaken.

Then follows a newspaper cutting from May 1934: "The Klagshamn cement works will close down definitely this autumn. The number of employees amounts to 250 people. Investigations are in progress regarding measures to find work for at least some of the work force." Carl Sahlin's comment:

Since the owner, AB Göteborgs Bank, has sorted out its own position, the turn has now come to its various industrial companies. Klagshamn is the first to be hit by close-down, it seems.

In March 1935, according to a newspaper cutting, the government considers investing SKr 20,000 in a replacement industry. In July 1935, Carl Sahlin wrote: "The destruction of Klagshamn" above the following cutting from "The Planter":

The workers were busy with their own homes and intense studies. Then it was decided that the cement factory, on which the whole community depends, was to close down. Not because it was unprofitable, but because the Limhamn factory was to be extended. This factory owner bought the Klagshamn factory in order to transfer its production quota to his own factory.

This was a hard blow to the workers. Those who have their own houses can't sell them, as people are now leaving the place, and they can't stay there without any work. Thanks to government intervention, the closedown of the factory was deferred until 1937, but by then the modern industrial community of Klagshamn will be without an industry.

Some remains of the workers' reality are in other words kept by the Museum of Technology — if you dig deep enough into the records. But I don't think that's enough.

For example, where are the hand-driven rails used at the Ifö lime pit in 1910? Where are the thick sacks used by the burners as hats? Where are the little tins that were later replaced by modern wage envelopes? And who will have saved a wages envelope, once these are replaced by other methods of paying wages?

These rails, sacks and tins certainly add no glamour to Swedish industry. They do not testify to victories of any

Swedish technological genius. They are part of a reality that donators to the Museum of Technology would rather forget.

What exhibits are the most characteristic of industrial work? Neither the machines in the Museum of Technology nor the finished products in the Nordic Museum. It is the *components* of not yet finished objects, the *piecework* rated per thousand, or ten thousand, the *parts* of a complete system, seen only by some people. Who collects them? Who collects the semi-finished, not yet complete reality, which is the result of the efforts of most industrial workers?

No one. And in what museum will you find the history of the time studies? Of capital concentration and closedowns? Or... I could fill a book with examples. I'm still asking: *Where is the Museum of the Working Classes?*

• What material is available at the Museum of Technology on your job and your factory?

Aids: The address to the Museum of Technology is: 115 27 Stockholm. Tel: 08/ 61 41 56, 10AM — 4PM. Phone or write to them and ask the librarian to check in the catalogues whether it would be worth your while to travel to the museum. — There are Museums of Technology also in Göteborg and Malmö. The Teko Museum in Borås is shown by former workers in the textile industry. — Some companies have their own technological museums which present the company's picture of history. Go through the company museum and consider how it ought to be changed and completed to give the workers' picture. — The exhibition *Machine Power* (1977) describes the technological development in textile industry from the point of view of the workers. The comprehensive, profusely illustrated catalogue of the exhibition can be ordered from National Exhibitions (Sandhamnsgatan 63, 115 28 Stockholm. Tel: 08/53 51 80).

- What do you think ought to be exhibited in a Museum of the working-classes in the place where you live? How could you find such exhibits? Have you and your workmates any items that would be suitable?

Aids: Go through your day and place of work in the way you did when looking for words (see Chapter 18). Also, go through the different chapters of this book and think of ways to illustrate them with objects.

20. THE INSURANCE COMPANY

Objects or machines kept in museums inform us of places of work of the past. But objects destroyed by fire can inform us of the same thing. When there is a fire, during a few hours it will light up old jobs usually covered by darkness. One example:

Protocol of Police Investigation in Degerhamn on 6 March 1891.
After a report that fire had broken out at Degerhamn the night between February 28th and March 1st, and that two structures for Cement drying had burnt down, the undersigned Sheriff went to Degerhamn today in order to investigate how the fire started and what else happened.

I was told that the two structures in question were inside the same building, built of planks under a roof of shingles and sticks. On inspection I found that the whole of this building had burnt down. It was situated south of the proper cement factory building, quite close to it, about 15 metres above the level of the other factory buildings, and had two storeys with three drying kilns at the north end and the same at the south, under the floor, which was of iron plate. From these slate-fired kilns pipes ran under the floor throughout the building. The following persons were interviewed:

Mr O. Hillfors, engineer:
At about midnight on the night in question, the night watchman I. Rydberg came and woke him up, shouting that the upper drying structures were on fire. H. immediately hurried out and arranged for the fire extinguishers to be applied; even then the fire had taken such a hold that

the flames could be seen through the roof, lighting up the surrounding landscape, which made it necessary, since there was also some wind blowing, to concentrate all attention on the other factory buildings close by and although there is not the slightest suspicion that the fire was started deliberately, H. can't imagine how it could possibly have started or what might have caused it.

As a reply to a question, H. added that every night, also on this particular night, certain persons are present at the drying kilns to tend the fire and also remove the burnt-out slate. These persons were called and interviewed:

Carl Nordberg and Carl-Johan Bergman, who made a joint statement:

That night they were watching and firing the southern kilns. The fire started in the western external wall, quite close to the northern kilns. They had neither heard nor seen anything unusual, nor noticed any smoke or unusual smell, since the wind was southerly or south-westerly and quite strong.

Only at midnight were they told by the stoker, I. Kindberg, who tended the northern kilns, about the fire, which had by then already spread extensively and was so strong it was impossible to extinguish. It had already gone through the roof of the building and raged unchecked, even more violent because the building was highly situated towards the lake without any protection from the south-westerly wind. They couldn't even make a guess as to how the fire might have started or its cause.

The above mentioned I. Kindberg, stoker, and August Jaensson, stoker, who tended the northerly kilns this particular night were interviewed next and reported:

that they knew nothing until the night watchman Rydberg came and told them.

that Kindberg immediately rushed to the western wall, through which the fire had already gone from inside.

that Kindberg tried to put the fire out by shovelling soil onto it, but was unsuccessful and at the same time he warned the others

and in the meantime Jaensson went into the room where the fire had started and found it raging unchecked. It had already caught the roof-shingles which were "whirling through the air".

They replied to a question that no lamp or lantern had been used, neither this night nor any other night inside or close to this building.

The night watchman I. Rydberg stated:

that at eleven-thirty on the night of February 28th, he was down by the harbour and from there discovered the light of fire up by the kilns, as from a lantern or some such thing. Seeing the light change, he hurried there and found the fire having caught the western external wall, without being noticed by the stokers Kindberg and Jaensson, who were duly warned.

The fire, due to the strong south-westerly wind, was so strong and violent that it was impossible to check, especially since no people had had time to arrive and no fire extinguishers had been possible to apply in time

All the interviewed people are convinced that the fire started inside the building in the western wooden wall, quite near the drying kilns situated under the floor at the northern end. They are also fully convinced that the fire was *not* started deliberately.

The only explanation for the fire is that it appeared in the wooden wall due to the intense heat from the drying kilns situated close by underneath the floor.

With no further information available, the investigation was closed.

As above
Aug. Thornell

This police report was sent to the insurance company Skandia, who paid out 750 kr for the ruined kilns. It was then retained together with thousands of similar reports, valuations, investigations and newspaper cuttings and other *fire damage acts* amongst Skandia's records.

After 1912, you have to know the year of a fire to be able to find the files. But for the period 1855-1912, there is a catalogue listing all fires in a certain branch of industry or at a certain company, provided that the company was insured by Skandia. It only takes a moment or two to find out that there was a fire in the coal store of the Visby Cement Factory on 15 October 1892 and on 26 February 1902 and that the mill-house in Limhamn burnt down on 1 April 1896. Each time they also give you the bonus of a description of the place of work.

The archive of the Skandia Concern is in Norrköping. You can phone them or write to the manager, Lars Lindblad, and ask if there is anything on the factory of particular interest to you. Take a note of the district code for the company, and possible former names of the company — it may have changed its name many times. Lars Lindblad will send you a reasonable number of copies free of cost.

But if you have a chance, I think you ought to go to Norrköping yourself. The archive is well worth a visit. Its premises are light and airy on the top floor of a large industrial block (take tram no. 3, stop: "Business works").

On the table is a bowl with gingerbread and Lars Lindblad gives you a cup of coffee. He has a lot to tell you. He was the one who found all these documents in some old basements in Stockholm in the late Sixties and decided to save them. He knows his records inside out and is pleased to help you dig into this goldmine.

Not only the documents of the Skandia Concern can be found here, but also *the records of the Swedish Damages Insurance Association*, which is even more interesting. Most of the insurance companies that accepted industrial insurances in 1873 formed a cartel, the so called Tariff Association, later the Swedish Damages Insurance Association. It existed until 1967, when all the companies had merged to the Skandia Concern. The task of this association was to decide the size of the premiums. As a basis of that assessment, they needed detailed descriptions and plans of the insured industries. The records include 150,000 such *industrial descriptions*.

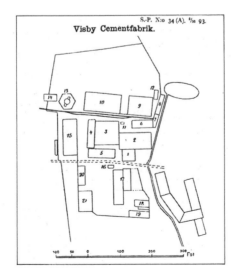

L. B.

Beskrifning
öfver
Visby Cementfabrik.

Belägenhet: vid Visby, fritt från staden.
Egare: Aktiebolag.
Disponent: Carl Ad. Carlson.
Byggnadsnadsätt och anordning:

N:o 1. Ångpanne- och maskinhus af sten under papptak. Stengolf. Inmurade pannor och fast maskin. Fristående, hög, murad skorsten.

N:o 2. Fabrikshus i flere våningar af sten under papptak. Sammanbyggdt med N:o 1, och med den gemensamma delen af väggen hel förutom öppning för drifremmen. Inrymmer cementqvarnar, stafsågar och tunnbinderi. Tunnorna svedjas uti ett litet rum, med stengolf och hvälfdt tak, som med stor dörröppning, utan dörr, står i förbindelse med tunnbindarverkstaden. Uti stafsågrummet finnes en murad ugn för torkning af staf på jernhåll med käpa af plåt och plåtskorsten. Hela husets inre är belamradt med en mängd pelare och strifvor af trä samt yttterst trångt och mörkt. Mellanbottnar af trä. Trätrappor.

N:o 3. Byggnad af resvirke och bräder under papptak. Uti 3 bottnar, hvilka alla medelst dörröppningar stå i förbindelse med N:o 2. Inrymmer upplag af råsten samt på nedra botten utrakningsmassan från ugnarna.

N:o 4. Fyra stycken schaktugnar för cementbränning. Sammanbyggda af sten, utan öfverbyggnad.

N:o 5. Träskjul under tak af dels bräder, dels plåt. Inrymmer en murad ugn för torkning af lera. Förbränningsprodukterna bortgå genom den höga, murade fabriksskorstenen.

N:o 6. Jernsvarfhus af trä under brädtak. Eldstad fanns ej nu, men brukar sådan uppsättas för vintern.

N:o 7. Gjuteri af sten och trä under dels plåttak på jernspant dels brädtak. Jordgolf. Gjutugn af jern med skorsten af plåt. Utan snickeri.

N:o 8. Reparationsverkstad af sten under tegeltak. Väggen mot N:o 7 hel förutom en dörröppning försedd med på ena sidan plåtslagen trädörr. Inrymmer smedja, plåtslagareverkstad, snickeriverkstäder och ett rum der påfylning af fotogen på lampor sker. För uppvärmning och limkokning 2:ne murade ugnar, den ena med murad skorsten den andra med plåtskorsten. Uti källaren, icke hvälfd, upplag af fotogen, hvaraf högst 2 fat, och maskinoljor.

N:o 9. Magasinsbyggnad af sten med gafvelspetsar af trä under papptak. Inrymmer upplag af cement.

N:o 10. Magasinsbyggnad af trä under dels papptak, dels brädtak. För upplag af koks.

N:o 11. Våghus af trä under papptak. Uppvärmning medelst kamin med plåtrör.

N:o 12. Magasinsbyggnad af trä under papptak. För upplag af förrådsartiklar.

N:o 13. Kalkugn med kringbyggnad af trä under papptak. För närvarande ingen bränning.

N:o 14. Träskjul under brädtak. För staf, virke och förrådsartiklar.

N:o 15. Magasinsbyggnad af trä under papptak. För upplag af cement samt för inpackning deraf på tunnor.

N:o 16. Förmanskontor af trä under spåntak. Uppvärmning medelst kamin med plåtrör.

N:o 17. Magasinsbyggnad af trä under spåntak. Utan eldstad. Upplag af hel- och halffabrikat. Inrymmer torkugn, nu slopad.

N:o 18. Mergelskjul af trä under brädtak.

N:o 19. Mergelskjul af trä under brädtak.

N:o 20. Cementgjuteri af trä under brädtak. För uppvärmning en kamin med plåtrör. Jordgolf.

N:o 21. Kontors- och laboratoriibyggnad af sten under papptak. Trätrappor. Inrymmer äfven bostadslägenheter.

N:o 22. Maskinhus af trä under brädtak, hvilket oförtöfvadt skulle utbytas mot tak af papp. Inrymmer lokomobilpanna med fast maskin. Skorsten af plåt utan vederbörlig gnistersläckare. Eldas med stenkol eller torf.

N:o 23. Hisshus af trä under papptak.

N:o 24. Mergelskjul under brädtak. Fribeläget.

N:o 25. Magasinsbyggnad af trä under papptak. För upplag af cement samt för inpackning deraf på tunnor. Fribeläget.

Drifkraft: ånga och fast maskin.

Belysning: fotogen.

Uppvärmning: med murade eldstäder och med kaminer.

Brandsläckningsredskap: assuranssprutor.

Inspekteradt i September 1893.

Brandförsäkrings-Aktiebolaget Fenix
P. BRANDELL.

Plan and description of Visby Cement Factory.

A card index makes searching easier. The index is arranged after the district code and the name of the company. One example: District letter I and company name of "Visby Cement Factory" leads you to two cards.

One refers to the association's printed protocol for the period 1887-98. The Visby Cement factory is described in May 1889 (16 buildings), in September 1893 (twenty-five buildings) in April 1895 (four-five buildings) and in November 1895 (extension). The description of 1893 also has a plan of the factory.

The other index card refers to corresponding descriptions for the period 1899-1950. It appears that there are no less than fourteen different descriptions of the Visby Cement Factory, most with plans printed in several colours by Lithografiska AB, who, incidentally, have their premises in the same house as the present archive. The latest description is dated 19 June 1940, just before cement production ceased.

The records also include industrial descriptions from the period 1951-1967. These are stencilled and kept in boxes. They are not catalogued, but it is quite easy to find what you're looking for, because there are only a few boxes for each district. There are some more descriptions of the premises of the closed-down factory that was used for hemp dressing.

I chose the Visby Cement Factory as an example, because there are so many different descriptions of it. But the records include at least one and often many different descriptions of all those *fourteen cement factories that ever existed in Sweden.*

Based on these descriptions, the association made decisions on so called special tariffs for each plant. These special tariffs are printed and arranged by district in special files, but they are not catalogued. The tariffs include a list of buildings on the factory site and gives the insurance premium for each one of them.

Each special tariff refers partly to the industrial description on which it has been based (such as S No 5717), partly to the association protocols recording the decision on the special tariff (such as S.P. No 18/1919, 26/1920). These protocols are available at the archive as bound volumes. They often include further material, such as investigations on risky conditions in the factory and arguments to increase or reduce the premium.

Getting in touch with the archive of the Skandia Concern in Norrköping is both the safest and easiest way to produce basic information about the former appearance of your place of work. Even if you don't do any of the other things I've suggested in this book, you ought to try that.

- What descriptions of your factory are there among the records of the Skandia concern? What picture is given in the fire damage acts of your predecessors' working conditions?

Aids: The address is: The archive of the Skandia Concern, Östra Promenaden 2, 602 27 Norrköping. Tel: 011/10 65 00. Ask for Lars Lindblad. He will also on request send you free a *Records list* and an offprint from *Nordic Insurance Journal* 4/71, describing the archive. Phone or write to him in advance if you're planning a visit.

Here are some other important insurance archives:

- The General Fire Insurance Office for Rural Buildings, now the Fire Insurance Office, has extensive records, including many descriptions of provincial industries from 1782 and about a hundred years on. To find them you must know district and parish. Reception quick, but slightly brusque. Address: Strandvägen 19, PO Box 14061, 104 40 Stockholm. Tel: 08/67 05 30. A list of described ironworks, mining buildings, smelting works and fabricators are included in *Hammer and Torch V*, Sthlm 1934.

- Buildings in towns and cities since 1828 have been insured by Town and City, General Fire Insurance Brokers, records of which are in the City Archive in Stockholm. Kungsklippan 6, PO Box 22063, 104 22 Stockholm. Tel: 08/54 17 20.

- Since 1740, many Stockholm buildings have been insured by Stockholm City Fire Insurance Company, records of which are kept at Mynttorget 4, PO Box 1233, 111 82 Stockholm. Tel: 08/23 41 60.

21. MONUMENTS

Institutions like the Royal Palace in Stockholm, the Uppsala Cathedral or the Hällekis Cement Factory can't be taken to museums for preservation. They are too bulky. They are better off where they are.

The Royal Palace in Stockholm is the main Swedish monument to the monarchy. It was built as a symbol of the king's view of himself and his position. It's still there — one of the most beautiful buildings in Europe — and keeps influencing the younger generations' idea of monarchy. In the same way, the churches are the monuments to the Church of Sweden (to such an extent that the same word is used to express both building and establishment). The stately homes are monuments to landowners and nobility. Law courts and other administrative buildings are monuments to bureaucracy. The bank palaces to big finance.

You are already guessing my question: Where are the monuments to the Swedish working classes?

Is it the environment around Norra Bantorget in Stockholm with the LO (TUC) castle and the buildings that housed the discontinued newspapers *MT* and *AT*? Are they the provincial civic halls with posters announcing "Sex shows" and "The Bone Cracking Gang"? Or is it the modern Co-op store that dominates the centre of most Swedish communities? If so, what do the almost identical private supermarkets across the road signify?

And the factories — the industries — whose monuments are they? Are they even worth preserving?

Industrial Archaeology

During the last two decades, this question has given rise to a popular movement in England, with a national organization and local branches, engaging amateurs and professionals, study groups and university courses, museums and collections, specialized publications and journals. All under the umbrella of "industrial archaeology".

"*To me the steam engine is a time machine. A way to enter history, knock off the rust, take it to pieces, clean it, polish it, oil it and start it again... You see how history works — that's what's so fantastic.*"

It all started in the Black Country of coal mines and ironworks between Birmingham and Wolverhampton — a smoky, grimy, polluted landscape, ruined by centuries of industrial progress. In the early 1950s, this area entered a new industrial era. The old should be obliterated. Hardly a day went by without a factory being pulled down or a workers' estate being demolished.

People were wondering. What will happen to the environment of the industrial revolution? Now that modern England has finally emerged out of low wages, tough working conditions, miserable housing and effective exploitation — should the testimony to this be allowed to disappear? Should the capital thus amassed really be permitted to sweep away all vestige of its accumulation?

Other people saw the aesthetic aspect of it. They saw obsolete machines as complete works of art. They claimed that an old brewery or an old textile mill would be worth preserving, just as well as a cathedral. Should the most valuable monuments not be protected? Should others not be at least recorded and described before being destroyed?

Rescue actions started, groups were formed to investigate things that had existed, still existed and ought to be preserved.

One such rescue action saved the five huge steam engines at the Kew Bridge Pumping Station (near Kew Gardens in south-west London). They had been in a scrap-yard for thirty years when they were re-discovered by Tony Cundick, Ivan Fear and Ron Plaster, who thought they were worth preserving. An association was formed in 1973, voluntary contributions were collected, a few dozen people started to spend their weekends at the pumping station, and a couple of years later, the first steam engine was working again.

The group consists of people who don't really enjoy libraries and archives but prefer to approach history with a spanner and a scaling hammer.

"To me the steam engine is a time machine," says Ron Plaster. "When I work on one of them, I feel it's a way to enter history, knock off the rust, take it to pieces, clean it, polish it, oil it and start it again. You can sense the odour of history, you hear it hissing and puffing when the steam is admitted. You can feel history tremble under the pressure, see it start slowly and begin to move, you see how history *works* — that's what's so fantastic."

To reconstruct an old text — that's research. To restore old murals in a church — that's culture. But to get one of the largest and oldest steam engines of the world to move again, after having been in a scrap-yard for thirty years — what is that?

Yet it's not the machines that Ron and his friends are most keen to preserve, remarkable as they may be, but the ability to operate and run them. This idea reappears constantly with them. Thirty years ago, these engines pumped out the drinking water of London. The last man to operate them died a few years back at the age of eighty-eight. With him died a professional skill, rendered obsolete by oil and petrol. Such *professional skills* can't be marked "culture" and exhibited in museums. They must be kept alive by human bodies.

"We are the ones to look after them now, and we'll make sure that they are carried on. Who knows when they will be required again?"

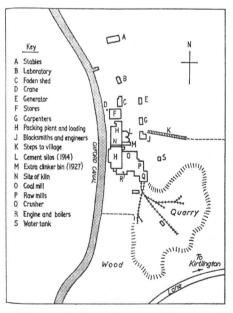

A plan from Charles Dodswirth's essay "The Early Years of the Oxford Cement Industry" in the journal Industrial Archaeology, 1973:3.

The term "industrial archaeology" was first used by a history teacher, Michael Rix, in an article in *The Amateur Historian* in 1955. It was taken up by the then industrial reporter of the BBC, Kenneth Hudson, in a series of television programmes and in his book *Industrial Archaeology: An introduction* (London 1963, 3rd ed. London 1976).

Kenneth Hudson is the central figure of the movement of industrial archaeology in England. In 1964, he founded the journal *Industrial Archaeology*, which became the focal point of the movement in England, until it was replaced in 1976 by the *Industrial Archaeology Review*. He wrote one of the first research handbooks, *Handbook for Industrial Archaeologists* (London 1967), which is already outdated. He helped start two large series of books, one regionally divided and one branch divided, published by David and Charles and Longman's publishing respectively. They now include fifteen to twenty volumes each. His contribution to the regional series is entitled *The Industrial Archaeology of Southern England* (Newton Abbot 1965). In the branch series he has written *Building Materials* (London 1972). (The chapter on lime and cement is not based on any industrial archaeological work of his own and so is rather scant.)

In the early 1970s, when the movement had grown to such an extent that its various branches had problems keeping in touch, Hudson together with Neil Cossons published the *Industrial Archaeologists Guide 1971-75* (Newton Abbot 1971). This book gives an account of British legislation regarding the preservation of industrial monuments, describing about thirty preservation projects, and giving the names and addresses of 169 industrial historical collections and museums and the names and addresses of about seventy societies and groups working with industrial archaeology, plus their main objectives and publications. A later, abbreviated version is *A Pocket Book for Industrial Archaeologists* (London 1976).

I myself find Kenneth Hudson most stimulating when he describes his own discoveries in handbook form, e.g. in *Exploring our Industrial Past* (Teach Yourself Series, Norwich

1975). This is a popular introduction to the subject with many concrete examples and clever suggestions for investigation. Hudson above all emphasizes the importance of talks with old people who can tell us about working methods and conditions of the past.

• What have the English industrial archaeologists found out about the equivalent of your job? How could you take advantage of their experience?

Aids: The address of the Kew Bridge Pumping Station is: Kew Bridge Road, Brentford, Middlesex, England. Open Saturdays and Sundays 11AM to 1PM, 2PM to 5PM. — One of the largest associations is the "Greater London industrial archaeological society" (GLIAS) which publishes, amongst other things, a stencilled newsletter. Address: Vere Glass, 69 St. Peter's Road, Croydon, England.

The best handbooks are J.P.M. Pannell, *The Techniques of Industrial Archaeology* (2nd ed. edited by J.K. Major, Newton Abbot 1974) and J.K. Major *Fieldwork in Industrial Archaeology* (London 1975). Pannell was a technician and a technology historian. Major is an architect. Both concentrate on the art of measuring buildings and machinery and making up plans. In addition, Pannell shows how to complement fieldwork by investigating records, maps, pictures and printed material. Many methods are directly applicable to Swedish conditions.

Industrial Archaeology for Schools (Project technology handbook 10, Heinemann Educational Books) London 1973, shows how local industrial investigations can be referred to different subjects taught in schools, such as history, sociology, chemistry, technology and art.

R.A. Buchanan *Industrial Archaeology in Britain* (Pelican 1972) is based on the experience of the author as the director of the "National Survey of Industrial Monuments", the official industrial archive in Bath, where both amateurs and professionals all over the country send descriptions of their finds. Arthur Raistrick is a technician and a geologist, specialising in the technology of the Roman era and the Middle Ages. His *Industrial Archaeology: An Historical Survey* (Methuen 1972) emphasizes mainly remains from the period before the industrial revolution.

Brian Bracegirdle *The Archaeology of the Industrial Revolution* (Heinemann 1973) is a full-colour photographic picture chronicle. Neil Gossons is a geographer and the director of the industrial historical open air museum in Ironbridge. His *BP Book of Industrial Archaeology* (Newton Abbot 1975) is mainly aimed at motorists who want to visit industrial monuments, with useful lists of places of interest, museums and societies. Many of these books are available in Swedish libraries. If not, they can be ordered from The Bookshop, Ironbridge Museum Trust, Ironbridge, Salop TP8 7RE, England.

Industrial Archaeology in Sweden

Kenneth Hudson's book *A Guide to the Industrial Archaeology of Europe* (Bath 1971) points out Sweden as an extraordinarily rich field for future industrial archaeological work. The book gives a brief description of about forty industrial monuments, mainly from the mining and iron industries.

Hudson visited Sweden in 1968. The same year his Swedish disciples, the Art Historian Marie Nisser and the architect Gunnar Sillén called for volunteers who might be interested in making an inventory of Swedish industrial monuments. Following the English example, they had index cards printed, to be filled in and returned to the National Antiquarian Dept. of Cultural History, Storgatan 41, 114 84 Stockholm.

However, those who knew better advised that one should steer clear of 'amateurs'. This was a matter for industry, not the general public. One should apply for state subsidies, not rely on volunteers. The initiators listened to this advice and the cards were never sent out. But by coincidence one card was found by a young man called Eric Juhlin in Karlsborg, and thanks to him, the industrial environments of the Skaraborg District are now among the best researched in the whole country. He is a Swedish one-man equivalent to the British popular movement.

MINNESMÄRKEN: Kvarn, gruva, fabrik, kanal, bro, o.s.v.			LÄNSBOKSTAV/KOMMUN	UTM-nr
BRANSCH	NUVARANDE ÄGARE	BYGGNADS-eller TILLVERKNINGSÅR	SOCKEN	REFERENSNUMMER
LOKALISERING: I stad, på landet, vid vattendrag, på slätt o.s.v.			FASTIGHETSNUMMER	DATUM FÖR RAPPORT
BESKRIVNING: 1. Om byggnaden (mått, byggnadsteknik, arkitektonisk utformning, nuvarande skick o.s.v.). 2. Om maskiner eller annan utrustning.				
(Ytterligare uppgifter kan antecknas på kortets baksida. Där kan även skiss eller foto bifogas.)				
NUVARANDE ANVÄNDNING: Fara för rivning, eller ödeläggelse. Har monumentet varit utsatt för skadegörelse.				
KÄLLMATERIAL: Tryckt litteratur, otryckta handlingar, kartor, ritningar eller fotografier.				
UPPGIFTSLÄMNARENS NAMN OCH ADRESS		BILAGOR		KORTET RETURNERAS TILL:
Teknikhistoriska Inventeringen				

One of the registry cards that were never sent out.

In Sweden instead, an expert committee was formed, the industrial monuments group, with representatives from museums, universities and the buildings conservation authority. They applied to the Labour Market Board for subsidies for unemployed academics to make an inventory of industrial buildings in the Stockholm and Kristianstad districts. The Architectural Museum published the first survey of Swedish industrial monuments:

NISSER, Marie e.a.
Industrial Monuments.
Sthlm 1974.

This is mainly a book describing ruined factories in different fields of Swedish industry, such as the following description of the cement factory at Valleviken in Gotland:

> The Valleviken Cement Factory in Bute, Gotland, was closed shortly after the Second World War. It's a ruin — a number of rusty kilns, dilapidated buildings and quays. Not far away is the village, a working-class area with wooden barracks, small houses with gardens and a civic hall in a romantic setting from the period just after the First World War.

This description is quite innocent — to anyone who has read Clas Engström's novel *Letter to the Editor* (Sthlm 1960), about the inhabitants of the wooden barracks at Valleviken. Significant of all descriptions of factories by Swedish industrial archaeologists is their skill to interweave production technical and art historical facts but completely disregard any social and political viewpoints. One example from the Visby Cement Factory:

> The rotary kiln at Visby was at first fired by peat, and a huge long building for it was erected, naturally of concrete and chalky sandstone, with large buttresses and window arcades. Soon another kiln was built, and rails and a rope railway connected the factory with the harbour and railway. The Visby Cement Factory operated like this for 30 years but was closed down during the Second World War.

A photograph from 1973 shows the Visby Cement Factory, "the only one of the city's monumental ruins today threatened by destruction". Soon after this was written it was demolished.

The Valleviken factory has also been demolished. So have Lomma, Maltesholm and Ifö. Only two factories remain of those bought up by Skånska Cement: Klagshamn, which is still on its headland south of Malmö, waiting for the price of land to go up even more; it's easy to imagine' the terraces and supermarkets of the 1980s. The Lanna cement factory is the best preserved. The old shaft kiln, outdated even at the time of installation in 1932, is still intact — but for how much longer?

These factories should at least be described and recorded before they disappear. The same goes for the cement factories that are now facing closedown: Hällekis, Köping, Limhamn, Stora Vika. How much of them will be preserved? And how will it be done? Will they be left as monuments of the companies — or of the workers?

Monuments of What?

Gunnar Sillén wrote in *Dagens Nyheter* on 22 March 1972:

> The care of cultural monuments, just like art and other expressions of culture, is a means used by groups, classes and nations to attain a higher degree of self-awareness, i.e. strength vis-a-vis other groups, classes and nations.

The way the care of cultural monuments has worked so far in Sweden, (controlled by experts, slow to form decisions, hampered by mighty financial interests) is only an expression of the values of the establishment. To make it meaningful, it must be decentralized, according to Sillén. It must become a way to counteract man's alienation in our technocratic society.

Sillén refers to the socialist states, where care and operation of industrial historical plants in many places have played an important part in strengthening the morale of the working people. They try to preserve both plants showing the industrial work of bygone days and plants with memories from the history of the workers' movement.

In Sweden we have mainly paid homage to the memory of the Swedish genius of technology or devoted ourselves to nostalgic daydreams about discontinued railways and steam boats. But it does happen that people go to see old industrial plants just to get a sense of the historical continuity of their own work contribution.

Even here in Sweden we should take care of industrial environments that carry the memories of the history of the working class. The plants should be preserved in such a way that they become the ideological property of the working class:

> At present (writes Sillén) there is a great risk for industrial monuments together with the palaces and churches to be pulled into the academic sphere of interest and so lose the deeper anchorage in the minds of the general public, which makes the preservation of them defendable. Another risk is for the industrial monuments to become the ideological property of the companies, as monuments to their own activities. Most industrial monuments kept in Sweden today have that function.
>
> If the industrial monuments are to be given the ideological significance to the working-class culture that I hope for, they must be put at the workers' disposal more immediately, for example by giving local trade unions their own money and their own executive rights to restore their own historical working environments and monuments.

A sound proposal. But we have a long way to go.

When, in the year of architectural heritage of 1975, Sweden was to select an industrial monument as the leading project, it was owned by the Johnson Concern. The Johnson Concern received subsidies from the Labour Market Board to realize it. The foundation of Axel and Margret Axson Johnson pays for the smart publication in English — *Swedish Industrial Archaeology The Engelsberg Ironworks* (Sthlm 1975) — the most advanced description ever made of a Swedish industrial monument. And when a tourist like myself arrives, when school classes and study groups are shown around as expected — then they are shown the monument to a major Swedish industry.

But where in Sweden is the monument to the working-classes?

The first rotary kiln at Slite, dating back to 1917, is cut up for scrap in 1977. Was that a wise thing to do?

- What places of work have there been in your county, in your town, in your area: What happened there? What remains of them today?

Aids: The best Swedish handbook is Gunnar Sillén, *We Go Towards the Light: On the Documentation of Industrial Monuments and Workers' Memories* (Malmö 1977). It includes many practical tips and suggestions and tries to consciously expand the perspective to include also the social and political facts as seen from the point of view of the workers.

Industrial Monuments Documentation: Handbook (Sthlm, without a year) can be ordered from the industrial historical committee of the Swedish Cellulose and Paperworks Federation, Villagatan 1, 114 32 Stockholm. It includes useful photographing advice and a pattern for interviews, but is written completely from the view of the employers. "Industrial monuments", it says, "constitute a part of the identity of the company that cannot be given away or left to be looked after by others."

Examples of industrial inventories made from this point of view are Marie Nisser and Helene Sjunnesson, *Pulp Factories and Paperworks in Värmland and Dalsland,* (Swedish pulp and cellulose engineers' association, Memorandum nr 19, Sthlm 1973) and Marie Nisser, *Foundries in Örebro District.* (The Iron office research department, series H, nr 10. 1974).

Eric Juhlin's industrial inventories from Hjo and Vara (1976) and Mullsjö (1977) can be ordered from the author, Järnvägsgatan 12A, 546 00 Karlsborg.

In 1974, in Denmark, the research project "Industrial Buildings and Housing" started. The researchers publish a journal with the same name. A four-year subscription to the journal including issues published so far costs 30 kr, by post giro nr 126 69 69, Norre Gade 7C, 1165 Copenhagen K. One of the researchers, Per Boje, has published *The Industrial Environment 1840-1940* (Copenhagen 1976), a handbook of sources and literature for investigations into Danish industrial social history.

- What monuments remain of your predecessors on the job? If you were to preserve the history of the workers rather than that of the owners and directors — what would you then chose to preserve of your place of work?

22. ON STRIKE

When you start to look for monuments to the working classes, you keep running into the difference between two so called production factors: capital and labour.

The capital's contribution to production takes the shape of buildings and machinery, which are tangible, permanent and possible to keep. They are very suitable monuments.

The work itself — the workers' contribution — on the other hand, is as volatile as gas. The work you do at the cement factory only shows while in progress. It is gone the minute it's completed.

What remains is a product sold by the company, distributed all over the country and, via the volatile labour of other workers, soon turned into buildings, which in turn form somebody else's capital: tangible, permanent and possible to keep.

The labour disappears, the capital remains — isn't it strange? Under those circumstances, how could you ever find any monuments to the working classes? The minute the result of their labour becomes tangible, permanent and possible to keep, it becomes somebody else's capital!

Only on one occasion is labour as a production factor tangible. That's when work stops. Perhaps that's where we should look for monument to the workers'?

Swedish Strike Dictionary

Strike is an ancient weapon. The first known Swedish strike occurred in 1665, at Stora Kopparberget. Eight mining-hands stopped work, demanding an adjustment of their wages "in new currency" to the value of their former wages. About a hundred early conflicts are recorded in:

KARLBOM, Rolf
Hunger Revolts and Strikes 1793-1867: A Study of the Appearance of the Swedish Workers' Movement.
(Lund 1967.)

A great deal of hunger revolts and strikes occurred around the year 1800 and in the summer and autumn of 1855, when the conflicts involved towns and communities all over the South of Sweden. These conflicts were very important, Karlbom says. "The Swedish workers' movement basically grew out of the fighting traditions of the common people."

Later strikes are recorded in:

RAPHAEL, Axel
Index of Strikes 1859-1900.
(Appendix to the parliament protocol 1903, colle., II:2)

This strike index is based on newspaper articles and far from complete. As of 1903, the information is slightly more reliable, since government authorities then started to record industrial conflicts systematically:

STRIKES
in Sweden During 1903-07. (Work statistics E:1. Publ. by the Royal Institute of Commerce, Dept. of Work Statistics.) Sthlm 1909.

"Strikes" was then published annually by the Institute of Commerce until 1911 and then by the Ministry of Social Affairs until 1938, when publication ceased. After 1938 the Government Industrial Tribunal went on recording strikes. A survey of the number of conflicts and "lost working days" is given annually in *Statistical Yearbook.*

These are some examples of the information given in the early strike statistics:

Year	1908	1917
Number	42	463
Beginning	17/2	12/12
Ending	8/3	15/12
Duration (days)	21	4
Type	Strike	Strike
Field	Cement factory workers	Cement and lime factory workers
Place	Visby	Slite
Conflict	Reinstatement of sacked workers	Increased pay
Number of employees involved	1	1
Number of workers on strike	190 (195)	200
Organised employees	Yes	Swedish Emply. Fed.
Organised workers	Yes	Labourers' u.
Result	Compromise mainly acc. to workers' demands	Workers received some of the increase they asked for plus an allowance
Information exists from	Both parties	Both parties
Notes	20 workers were made redundant	-

With this material, a very useful book could be written: *Swedish Strike Index 1793 to 1977*. The index would give immediate information on the strikes that occurred one certain year at a certain place or in a certain field.

Unfortunately, this book hasn't been written, since no one has taken the trouble to do so, you will have to search through Karlbom, Raphael, the thirty-two annual editions of "Strikes" and the primary details for the strike statistics after 1938, before you can find your own job, your own place or your own company.

It's time-consuming, but up to 1933 it's all right. I found the following industrial conflicts in Swedish cement industry:

1883
Lomma. Two days' strike in April for shorter working hours.

1889
Lomma. The first lockout in Sweden, involving about five hundred workers, lasting 15/3 to 8/4. The workers were told to dissolve the newly formed trade union. The conflict ended as those who left the union had a pay increase and the others, about forty, were sacked. (See Chapter 15.)

1899.
Klagshamn. Strike at the lime pit.

1900.
Klagshamn. Sixty trade union activists were sacked during negotiations. The others stopped work but returned after a couple of months of conflict. The trade union went underground.

1902.
Klagshamn. While work was in progress for building the cement factory, forty-seven organised helpers were sacked. The lime pit workers were told to replace them but refused. They too were sacked. The conflict lasted for over ten months but ended as the unionisation right was accepted on 27/11.

1908
Visby. Twenty-one days' strike for the reinstatement of a sacked worker. See above.
1909

The building materials industry. Lockout 17/5 to 14/6, during negotiations about a national agreement. The general strike.

1914
The building materials industry. Lockout 2/1 to 22/4.

1917
Strike. Four days' strike for pay increase. See above.

1919
Rute. Two days' strike to avoid handling blocked goods.

1922
Limhamn. Strike 12/1 to 22/3. against pay reduction.
Hällekis. Strike 22/2 to 23/3 to reinstate sacked worker.

1926
Rute. Strike 29/1 to 1/4 to raise hourly way from 88 öre to 1.15.

1927
Slite. Strike 12/5 to 13/10 about piecework rates when a crane had been bought for unloading coal.

1930
Hällekis. The construction work at a new cement factory stopped 14/2 to 2/8 and then from 26/10 to the end of the year. The employer refused to pay building trade wages for the building work.

1936.
Skövde. Short strike for pay increase.

1944
Limhamn. The staff at the cement company laboratory were

paid 290 kr/month and wanted more. The conflict led to the first strike caution in the history of SIF.

The data given by the cement workers at Valleviken to the Ministry of Social Affairs regarding the 1926 strike are kept in the National Archives. (The Government Industrial Tribunal. Strikes 1926, vol. 89, doc. 43.)

> • What strikes and other industrial conflicts have taken place in your occupation at your place, at your factory? What was the conflict about? What significance did it have?

Aids: Karlbom, Raphael and "Strikes" can be ordered by the county library. The primary data for strike statistics after 1938 should be at the Government Industrial Tribunal Office (Munkbron 9, 103 10 Stockholm, tel: 08/ 10 21 85). When you visit this sleepy and god-forsaken little institution in an attic in the Old City, it turns out that the statistics of wild strikes are usually based on lump sums from the Employers' Federation, who refuse to tell you where and when the strikes took place! It's scandalous that official Swedish statistics should have to be based on such primary material.

The Government Industrial Tribunal papers from 1907-1960 are in the National Archives. There is no list of the records, a lot of the papers are unsorted. There are "Tribunal files" 1907-1960 for eight different districts, including letters from the parties and newspaper cuttings about strikes. Further: "Strikes" 1913-1938, including forms with data on the conflict from both parties. Other series are e.g., "Special rulings" 1923-1938, "Newspaper cuttings" 1909-1939 and 785 editions of "Collective agreements".

The trade union archives often include correspondence with the local branch about the strike, information about strike allowances paid out ,etc. The local branch archive may include strike meeting protocols and other information. Old people's memories are often particularly detailed regarding experiences such as strikes.

Sometimes the army intervened in strikes. Troops were then commanded by the District Governor and there may be some material on this in the District Archive. The command should be reported to the Provincial Defence Command Committee. For example, on the 14/4, there was a report that in 1889 the Crown Prince's hussars had completed their command at Lomma. "The troops book" for the first squadron of the regiment gives daily details on officers, non-commissioned officers and privates who were at Lomma, but says nothing else. These papers are among the Military Archives, kept at

Banérgatan 64, 104 50 Stockholm. Tel: 08/67 08 05. Quick and friendly reception.

The liveliest descriptions of strikes are often found in the local press. Many strikes have also become the basis of novels, plays and films. The Archive of Popular History has published *Strike! Strikes and Strike songs 1873-1900* (Borås 1974). The odd major conflict has been investigated by professional historians, such as Bernt Schiller: *The General Strike in 1909: Prehistory and Causes*, (studia historica Gothoburgensia, 9.) Gbg 1967.

Wildcat Strikes

Is the role of strikes as a powerful tool over? In Sweden, official strikes have been very rare since the late 1930s. Usually this is pointed out as a contributory factor to the increase of pay capacity of the companies and as a condition for a solidarity as regards pay policy. But other arguments are in favour of the strike weapon. Some of them are described in:

ANDERSSON, Sven O.
Wildcat Strikes: An Investigation within the Swedish Metal Workers Union. Sthlm 1969. The book is based on the investigations carried out by the sociologists Walter Korpi and Bengt Abrahamsson of 350 wildcat strikes in the period 1948-1967.

These strikes were often a result of dissatisfaction with working environment, work organization or employers. Such dissatisfaction usually finds individual expressions. Workers stay at home for a couple of days when it gets too bad or simply resign from their job. The result is called "high sick leave" or "high turnover of personnel".

But if there is solidarity amongst the workers, the dissatisfaction can be given collective expression — a wildcat strike. These are often of short duration — 83 % of them lasted for less than four hours. In many cases the number of lost working hours is less with the collective action than if the workers individually stay at home.

After these investigations were carried out, miners, forest workers and cleaners have shown that wildcat strikes can work as an effective warning signal both to employers and unions, and to society as a whole.

The workers' legal right to participate (in Sweden called MBL) can be seen partly as a result of these wildcat strikes. The idea is that this system should legalize certain strikes which used to be termed wildcat and prevent others, mainly those that threaten the solidarity of pay policy or the negotiating position of the union. We do not know yet what the practical result will be.

I personally think it would be very unfortunate if strikes disappeared completely from Swedish industry. Whoever lives in a capitalist society in due course gets used to the fact that all work that isn't consumed is converted into capital for someone else. We get used to seeing work disappear and capital remain. Our eyes get used to seeing the world as the property of other people, not as a result of the work done by ourselves and our comrades.

But when the buildings are emptied and the machinery stops, another truth appears: *all capital consists of work.* Every grain of cement in these buildings has been made by workers and wouldn't have been there, unless they had worked. Each piece of metal in these machines has been made by workers and wouldn't have existed without them.

Only when work stops, does it become obvious. Out of the buildings and machinery of the capital, the work reappears to say: If we hadn't created the capital, it wouldn't have been there.

When the Swedish working classes reclaim the work hidden in the capital, it will no longer have to search for its monuments. They are there already, disguised as capital. The monuments to the working class exist — all you have to do is conquer them.

23. THE LAW

Cement worker Alfred Leonard Norling was drunk at 10pm on Saturday 22 June 1901.

It was the day before Midsummer's Eve. Police Constable Dahl found Norling in Västra Hamngatan in Limhamn. Dahl considered him to be under the influence of alcohol and offensive as he insulted passers-by. The policeman thus intervened and was then abused by Norling who is said to have uttered, amongst other things, the following: "Don't kill me, you devil!"

The whole thing was taken to the Assizes. Norling, who had never been in court before, had to pay a fine of 15 kr for failing to appear, 10 kr for being drunk, 15 kr for being disorderly in the street, 15 kr for abuse, He was then ordered to reimburse police constable Dahl 10 kr and the witness, police constable Larsson, 9 kr 22 öre.

The most common type of criminal offence among the working class in Limhamn at this time was, however, not drunkenness, but crime against lottery regulations. On 19 January 1904, for example, the cement worker Lars Strandqvist was ordered to appear in the Assizes for having kept a lottery of a coffee set, consisting of a coffee pot with a cream jug and a sugar bowl of nickel, together valued at 16 kr. Strandqvist had sold 95 lots, number one payable at 1öre, number two at 2 öre, and so on, up to number 95, which cost 95 öre. Number three won the set. Strandqvist confessed to his crime and was fined 15 kr.

Along with him, engine driver Berndt Lindegard, lime pit worker Anders Olsson, lime pit worker Per Olsson, braker Emil Andersson and nine other workers were convicted. The crimes had been committed at different places of work in Limhamn, such as the engine sheds and the Anneberg lime pit. Most of them had kept a lottery of their pocket watch, others of their bicycle or some piece of furniture. They all explained that they had been unaware of committing a crime, because lotteries like these were common and had never been prosecuted before. They were all fined 15 kr.

At the next session it continued. Worker Gustav Alm was convicted for having kept a lottery of a ladies' watch worth 8 kr, cooper Lorens Persson of a flute worth 12 kr, worker Albert Holmström of an alarm clock worth 5 kr, lime pit worker Johan Olsson of two canaries and a cage, together worth 10 kr. And so on — altogether about forty workers were each fined 15 kr on one occasion for having kept an American lottery.

Summons against cement worker Lars Strandqvist for having kept a lottery of a coffee pot with a cream jug and a sugar bowl of nickel. Excerpt from the 1904 Assize Court register of the Oxie and Skytt District, now with the Trelleborg Assize Court.

All this can be read in the *Oxie and Skytt District Court Register*, a series of thick, handwritten books kept by the Trelleborg Assize-Court, under which comes the Oxie and Skytt District. All sentences passed in this county are described and motivated in such court registers. They provide very interesting reading for someone investigating a place of work.

In this case the court register suggests what seems to have been a very common thing at the Limhamn cement factory at the turn of the century: the American lottery. What was that? Was it a business activity for smart alecs to rip off their workmates? Or was it a primitive form of social security — the mates loyally helping a man in trouble by buying some lots from his lottery?

The court register also gives a clear picture of the class-society. Different crimes were punished with varying degrees of severity and meant different things to people of different social strata. Leonard Norling's Saturday celebration in all cost him 74 kr and 22öre, which was a lot of money for a labourer in the cement industry who only made 22öre an hour. The fines were more than a tenth of his annual income.

Crime against lottery regulations cost 15 kr — between a third and a half of the proceeds of an American lottery. If the lottery was arranged to help a friend who was in trouble, it was a noticeable loss.

The employer Ernst Fredrik Wehtje did not take the risk of being hit by legislation. He could afford a cab when he was drunk. He did not have to arrange American lotteries to get money.

But occasionally the fingertips of the long arm of law managed to reach him as well. On 6 September 1904, as a board member of the Swedish Binding Thread Factory AB, Limhamn, he was served a summons for having failed to report an accident which had occurred on 22 March 1904, at 7.30am, when worker Mathilda Sjölin was hurt and subsequently unable to work for thirty-three days. Ernst Wehtje was fined 10 kr for having failed to report an accident at work.

That equalled 0.4 pro mille of Ernst Wehtje's taxable income in 1904. A negligible amount, both to him personally and to the company where the accident occurred.

Note that Wehtje was sentenced not for having failed to provide proper protection at the factory but only for having failed to report the accident.

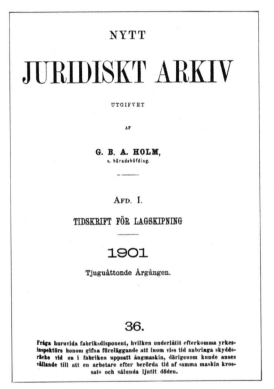

Caption: *The Journal New Legal Records has been published since 1873. It contains the court records of the Supreme Court. Year 1901, sentence 36, and describes the death of engine operator J.L. Lundin.*

NEW LEGAL RECORDS
published by G.B.A. Holm dep. District Judge
Part I: Journal for legislation
1901
25th edition: 36

The case: Whether a factory manager, after having failed to follow the orders of a factory inspector within a given period to erect a guard rail around a steam engine in the factory, could be considered responsible for a worker being crushed to death by this engine after the stated period.

Then, as now, it was extremely rare that employers were regarded as responsible for accidents occurring in their factories. But it did happen occasionally: One example:

In October 1896, the Factory Inspection ordered that guard rails be set up around the steam engines in the Lund Sugar Factory AB at Staffanstorp. The company was given one year to erect the rails. On 6 December 1899 the rails still hadn't been erected. That is when engine operator J.L. Lundin was killed after working at the factory for eight years "in which he always worked satisfactorily and was always sober and orderly in all regards".

It was thought the accident happened when Lundin was to pour oil into the grease cups of a pump and then was careless enough to put his head too near the driving kneel of the pump, so that the shafts of the wheel crushed his head and pulled both his head and most of his body into the wheel pit, after the driving wheel stopped. Death was said to have been instantaneous.

The Factory Inspection reported the employer, Mr G. Roman, works manager, and he was prosecuted for causing Lundin's death. He was acquitted by the Assize-court. The prosecutor appealed to the Appeal Court of Scania and Blekinge, where Roman was sentenced according to Chapter 14 paragraph 9, and fined 500 kr. Roman appealed to the Supreme Court, where the sentence of the appeal court was confirmed on 8 February 1901.

So it cost him 500 kronor. What proportion was that of the profit of the Lund Sugar Factory AB that year? What proportion of Mr Roman's taxable annual income? I haven't looked into the matter, but it is obvious that the justice of the class society punished the cement worker much more severely for being drunk one Saturday evening than the works manager for causing the death of one of his workers.

- What's today's price for causing the death of a worker? How often does it happen that an employer is sentenced for that crime?

Aids: *Swedish Law* is available at the county library. Statistics of crimes and sentences were published annually 1913-1966 in the series *Crime* and *Activities of Law Courts and Executive Authorities*; hence annually in the series *Criminal Statistics 1-2* and *The Law Courts*. All these form part of the Official Swedish Statistics (SOS) and can be ordered by the county library.

- What do the court registers tell about your predecessors in your job, about conditions at your place of work? What picture is given by the court records of the past and present class society?

Aids: All offences came under either District Court (in the provinces) or a Magistrates' Court (in towns and cities). Their court registers, up until 1900, are usually kept by the District Archive. Their court registers after 1900 are usually kept by the local Assize-Court. There are one hundred Assize-Courts in the country, listed in the telephone directory.

To find your way through the court register, which can often be very thick, you first look up the index listing all sentences, giving information about things such as name, occupation, address and crime sentenced, and also the number of the sentence, which can then be looked up in the register.

The court register can sometimes be handwritten in a way that is difficult to interpret. If so, you go to the typed copy of the court register, kept by the local Appeal Court. There are Appeal Courts in Umeå, Sundsvall, Stockholm, Jönköping, Göteborg and Malmö. Among the records of the appeal court are also the court registers of the sentences of the Appeal Court itself.

Cases of particular importance are finally taken up by the Supreme Court, established in Stockholm in 1789. The Supreme Court Register has been printed since 1873 in *New Legal Records*. The death of engine operator J.L. Lundin, e.g. is described in this journal of 1901, sentence 36. Other important sentences concerning conditions at factories are *New Legal Records* 1907:17, 1908:24, 1909:85, 89, 1917:92, 1920:13, 1923:33, 1934:187 and 1944:134. The sentences are described in an old-fashioned but clear, often florid language, giving an alarmingly clear picture of the conditions.

In his *Judicial Sociology* (Lund 1972), Wilhelm Aubert shows how to analyse a law or a sentence from the point of view of different social groups. The book is mainly intended for people with legal training and may initially seem daunting — but it is fundamental and well worth the effort of reading.

Private Legislation

Most people don't end up in court very often. But you face your employer and his deputies every day.

The Oxie and Skytt Assize Court could fine Lars Strandqvist and the others 15 kronor. The court could fine Leonard Norling a tenth of his total annual income.

But the employer could fine him his whole annual income by taking his work away from him.

The law courts are obliged to pass sentence according to the law of the land, once upon a time instituted by the king himself, then by king and parliament and now by parliament alone. The employer passes sentence according to his own law, instituted by himself.

But surely private people can't go around instituting laws just like that?

Of course they can. The right of ownership gives them the power to do so. They can certainly not own people, just things. But the power over things such as land, buildings and machinery also gives them power over the people who do not own the factories in which they work and earn their living.

As soon as the Slite cement factory was completed, its owner and manager, Fredrik Nyström, instituted the laws he wanted to apply at the factory. He called his law *Regulations at Slite Cement and Lime Company* and had it printed at the Gotlänningen printers in Visby in 1919. The Nyström law, following a pattern quite common in those days, established, amongst other things, the following:

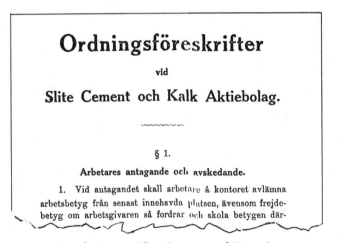

Ordningsföreskrifter

vid

Slite Cement och Kalk Aktiebolag.

§ 1.

Arbetares antagande och avskedande.

1. Vid antagandet skall arbetare å kontoret avlämna arbetsbetyg från senast innehavda platsen, ävensom frejdebetyg om arbetsgivaren så fordrar och skola betygen där-

Regulations at Slite Cement and Lime Co.

§1 *Employment and dismissal of workers*
1. On employment, the worker should give the office a reference from his latest employer as well as a character reference if requested by the employer, and the references will be kept by the office, until the worker is dismissed or resigns.

2. During the first 14 days after the employment of a worker, no notice needs to be given by the employer or worker.

3. From the 15th day after the employment of a worker, a notice of one week should be given mutually by the employer and worker.

4. For temporary redundancy for a period of up to 14 days, no notice needs to be given.

§4. *Absence from work*
1. Without permission or due cause, the worker must not fail to appear for work and can be dismissed immediately if he does.

§8. *Storage lockers and notices*
2. Posters and notices must not be displayed at the factory without the approval of the employer for each single case and in places indicated by the employer.

§12 *Penalties*
Except for the case mentioned in §4, the employer is entitled to dismiss immediately without notice:
1. Anyone who, in spite of being cautioned, still fails to observe the fixed hours for commencing and finishing work, or fails to appear at work without due cause or does not maintain an orderly behaviour;
2. Anyone who refuses to do the work given to him by a foreman on behalf of the employer at the factory, provided the worker is able to do it, or anyone who does not obey the orders given by the foreman regarding the work.
3. Anyone who appears at the factory under the influence of alcohol or brings alcoholic drinks to the factory or drinks them there;
4. Anyone who can be proved to instruct or try to force another worker not to fulfil his obligations according to this agreement...

Notice the last word. Nyström suddenly calls his law an "agreement". Legally, this is exactly what it was. Legally, Nyström was not instituting law — he and his workers were instead equal partners who had entered a voluntary agreement. Legally it was only a coincidence that the agreement did not take this shape:

§1. *Acceptance and dismissal of employers.*
1. To gain access to manpower, the employer should give the trade union office references from the workers he lately employed, and also a character reference if requested by the union, and these references will be kept by the office until the employer is dismissed or resigns.
4. For the temporary absence of the work force for a period of up to 14 days, no notice needs to be given.

§8 *Lockers and notices*
2. Posters and notices must not be displayed by the employer at the factory without the approval of the trade union for each single case and in places indicated by the union.

§12 *Penalties*
Except for the case mentioned in §4, the union is entitled to cut off the supply of manpower immediately without notice:
1. Any employer who without due cause fails to find work for his work force and does not behave properly;
2. who refuses to carry out improvements, ordered by the union on behalf of the workers, provided he is able to carry them out, or anyone who does not obey the orders given by the union regarding the work
3. who appears at the factory under the influence of alcohol or brings alcoholic drinks to the factory or drinks them there;
4. who can be proved to instruct or try to force another employer not to fulfil his obligations according to this agreement...

But in reality the agreements never looked like this. They still don't. In reality the parties are not equal and never have been. The right to ownership of means of production, guaranteed by the government, gives the power to one party. Whoever has the power dictates the terms. In that way, the employer's will becomes the law of the factory.

• What "regulations" and other private laws have been applied over the years at your factory?

Aids: The Slite Cement Regulations of 1919 I found at the District Archive in Visby. Other places where you can look for these things are the Collection of Small Prints at the Royal Library (Chapter 6) and the records of the local trade union and old workers.

So far, legal research has shown surprisingly little interest in the private legislation of employers. It would be rewarding to compare the regulations of different factories, different fields of industry and different parts of the country.

The Labour Court (LC)

The Labour Court (LC) was set up by the 1928 legislation for collective bargaining, by a Conservative majority in parliament, strongly opposed by the Social Democrats. The LC consists of two chairmen and six jurors, two of whom are appointed by trade unions and two by employers' organizations. The professional legal experts are therefore in majority, which has been used mainly to safeguard employers' right to private legislation and administration of justice at the factories.

The function of the Labour Court is that of a Supreme Court on issues connected with the interpretation of collective agreements. Before the LC was set up, the trade unions in certain fields had insisted on some kind of participation in decisions regarding the employment or dismissal of workers and other conditions at the factories. Now conditions took a step backwards. The Labour Court legal representatives applied not only the collective bargaining legislation but also an unwritten law, which gave all power at the factories to the employer alone.

The year the LC was set up, 1928, Fredrik Nyström was in a very difficult situation (see Chapter 7). Three years before, Skånska Cement had forced him to accept a cartel agreement that stifled the factory's development in the domestic market. On the export market, prices were going down. To cope with the crisis, Nyström was prepared to give up some of the power he had allocated to himself in the "Regulations" of 1919. Among his documents in the Visby District Archive is a letter from him to the local branch of the union, in which he appeals for cooperation along the following principles:

1) An effective rationalization, which must make sure that an export increase will not lead to losses. A condition for this is naturally better use of working hours and, if necessary, cutting down other production costs of cement intended for export.

2. Long-term agreements with permanent employment for all workers, whose work is part of the production, for the whole term of the agreement.

3. The forming of a factory committee, in which you are represented by a suitable number of members, with the task of discussing mutual issues in full confidence with the management. It is understood that this committee will follow the budgeted costs regarding production and sales of cement.

In other words, the *letter* offered security of employment and insight in return for increased work load and lower pay. The resulting *agreement* is full of expressions such as "intimate cooperation", "understanding", "sincerity", "good will", etc.

But the main issue, the security of employment, was here much more vaguely expressed than it had been in the letter:

> To attain these aims, the company will strive (underlined in pencil in the Labour Court copy of this agreement) to export excess production that cannot be consumed within the country and thus secure the workers' position throughout the year.

"Strive". Exactly. However, the part of the agreement referring to a reduction of the company's expenses for wages was formulated in clear figures. This helped the company through another couple of years, but in 1932, Nyström sold it to Skånska Cement.

The new Managing Director, Arendt de Jounge, started his appointment on 1 November 1932. On 5 November he called for the workers' representatives. There was no more talk of insight into financial calculations. The workers were simply told that it was necessary to reduce operation. By the time they left the meeting, the lists of redundancies had already been posted.

The workers took the matter to the Labour Court. They told the court what had been said and promised when the agreement was written:

> ENGSTRÖM: I risked my position among the workers to bring about this agreement. I did it because I believed that it would guarantee work every day. If not, we would never have been able to get support for it from the workers.
>
> In the committee we distinguished between those who were to be given permanent employment and the others. Not only the term of employment was decisive, but family conditions, land owned etc. The non-permanently employed would be "exposed to redundancy". Why else would we have distinguished between permanent employees and others?
>
> In the past year, it must have been difficult for the employer to supply full-time work, but the employer said

"they had to" as per the agreement. Only after Mr De Jounge's appointment on 1/11, was there a change. He did not know what the agreement was about. The workers and the whole community became very embittered.

KARLSSON: Some reduction of wages, but compensation in the form of pension and permanent work all year round. We accepted the agreement only because of the security of work all year round.

CHAIRMAN: Did you express this as a condition? Did you express it like this?

KARLSSON: It was never mentioned that we wouldn't have permanent work all year round.

CHAIRMAN: Did Captain Nyström promise you that?

KARLSSON: Yes.

CHAIRMAN: It is not expressed as a guarantee. Did you not notice that?

KARLSSON: When we were all supposed to cooperate. I interpreted it as the company giving us work permanently.

SEDELL: Permanent employees, as I see it, should have work all year round, the whole idea of cooperation was based on mutual trust.

CHAIRMAN: Was full work for the workers guaranteed?

SEDELL: Yes. Once someone asked what would happen if work was wanting. The answer was, in that case some other production work would start.

CHAIRMAN: Did you consider the wording of the agreement to give a secure guarantee?

SEDELL: The way I understood it, we were guaranteed work all year round. If not we'd never have accepted the agreement. It's the interpretation I conveyed to my mates.

CHAIRMAN: Did you base that interpretation on statements about mutual understanding in the agreement?

SEDELL: I asked directly. The answer was, if work was wanting at the cement factory, they'd find other work for us...

So far the workers' stories were noted in pencil by the Labour Court clerk and kept at the Law Court office. The workers still trusted their former boss and expected him to stand by the agreement. Therefore they asked Nyström to give evidence in the Labour Court.

But Nyström was now employed by Skånska Cement as the manager of their Visby factory. He was the prisoner of his former opponent. Among his documents at the Visby District Archive there is a letter from the Building Materials Federation where this certificate is spelled out to him:

...that as the agreement was made, it was never negotiated or mentioned, and certainly not intended that any guarantee for permanent employment with the company under all conditions should be given. — The so called "permanent employment" from the company's side only referred to employment with priority to work depending on the supply of work. — It would be particularly valid, if the certificate could include a statement of the following or similar wording: "I therefore consider the claims made by the workers in the summons unfounded in every respect." Such a certificate, if it can be obtained, should naturally not be shown to the workers before the beginning of the case.

Nyström was thus instructed to stab his former workers in the back. He may have written the requested certificate but it has not been kept. This is what he told the Labour Court:

NYSTRÖM: The company committed themselves to strive to supply work. I would have done this personally...I don't feel that I committed the company to supplying work but only myself personally (independent of the company) to strive towards it.

THE BUILDING MATERIALS FEDERATION: Would Nyström have considered himself entitled to reduce operation in spite of the agreement?

/Nyström evades the question. The question is repeated./

NYSTRÖM: The agreement wouldn't have stopped me, but personally I would have tried to avoid it.

The Court never seems to have asked itself how the workers were to know when Nyström's words were on behalf of the company and when only "personally (independent of the company)" on behalf of himself. The Court ruled (sentence 1933:20) by the wording of the written agreement and gave Skånska Cement the right to dismiss even permanently employed workers. All was back at the 1919 regulations.

Skånska Cement has lost two cases in the Labour Court. In the sentence of 1932:118, the company was ordered to pay out 28,800 kr immediately to eight workers as holiday pay. In the sentence of 1949:79, Skånska Cement's subsidiary in Degerhamn was ordered to pay 1 kr per shift as a wage supplement to workers at the raw mass mill when two cement mills were running.

These three sentences are fairly typical. Each time it was the workers who served a writ on the company — as in 80% of the cases handled by the Labour Court. The workers won the minor cases that only referred to a krona or two — as happened in 65% of the cases. But the workers lost the major, principally important case, the one referring to the right to work. That's what usually happened.

Not until the 1970s has the attitude of the Labour Court regarding private legislation of employers in factories been seriously questioned. The Åman legislation, working environment and workers' participation legislation has given the LC other things to do. But the capital amassed and developed under the protection of the LC is still "private property".

Private property is an excellent invention in its right context. I own my old shoes. You own your home. Private life is the natural area of private ownership. The government is right to guarantee us this right.

But the government is not right to guarantee the owner's power over the things outside the area of private life, where it robs other people of their freedom. The basic absurdity of our society is the fact that capitalists can buy and sell the places where other people work. Some thousand capitalists own most of the Swedish production apparatus, because they were allowed to write their own laws for too long. When will we seriously start questioning that?

- What conflicts at your place of work have been taken to the Labour Court? What does the sentence say about the conflict? What further material is there on the conflict at the Law Court office, among the trade union records, in the memories of old people?

Aids: All Labour Court sentences have been published annually since 1929 in *Labour Court Sentences*. Four different registers for each annual edition make it easy to find sentences referring to a certain company, a certain branch of industry or a certain place.

Protocols of negotiations, letters, agreements and other documents are kept by the Labour Court Chancery, Stora Nygatan 2, 103 11 Stockholm. Tel: 08/23 67 20. Anyone can go there and ask to see them.

Critical views on the Labour Court sentences can be found in the chapter by Per Eklund and Sten Edlund in *Cross-Sections. Seven Research Reports Published for LO's 75th Anniversary.* (Sthlm 1973).

• Who owns your factory? Why?

Aids: See Chapter 12.

24. UNEMPLOYMENT

Work was regarded as an obligation long before it was regarded as a right. Up until 1885 it was on principle considered criminal to be unemployed. Even in the 1920s, conservative circles considered the main reason for the unemployment to be the lassitude and unreasonable pay claims of working class people. This is a description of the slow breakthrough of a modern attitude to unemployment:

ÖHMAN, Berndt
Swedish Labour Market Policy 1900-1947. Halmstad 1970.

ÖHMAN, Berndt:
LO and the Labour Market Policy after the Second World War. (In: Cross-sections) Sthlm 1973).

This is an account of the whole theoretical and political discussion. But unemployment is still regarded from above. It is seen as a general social problem — not as a problem for people with a certain occupation, at a certain company, at a certain place.

The picture becomes a little clearer when you study the statistics. The first government count of unemployment is recorded in:

UNEMPLOYMENT
in Sweden, the winter 1908-1909. (The Institute of Commerce. Work Statistics H:1.) Sthlm 1910.

On 31 January 1910, another unemployment count was carried out (Work Statistics H:2). Both investigations give the following information about unemployment among gypsum and cement workers:

	Winter 1908-1909	31.10. 1910
Total number of unemployed	79	236
Number of able-bodied men	79	233
Organised	59	206
Non-organised	20	30
Without temporary work	76	221
With temporary work	3	15
Born in the place of count	25	50
Born in other places	54	186
Registered at place of count	76	229
Registered elsewhere	3	7
Average age	35	36
Unmarried	24	57
Married	54	174
Divorced and widowers	1	5
Single	19	53
1 person to provide for	14	22
2 persons to provide for	13	29
3 persons to provide for	9	40
4 persons to provide for	10	38
5 persons to provide for	6	22
6 persons to provide for	6	19
7 or more persons to provide for	2	13
Number of people affected by unemployment	268	678
Unemployment caused by		
lack of work	74	202

Illness	0	0
Conflict	3	26
Military service	1	2
Own resignation	1	2
The duration of employment		
2-3 weeks	3	35
3-4 weeks	14	20
4-5 weeks	10	21
5-6 weeks	8	14
6-9 weeks	12	76
9-13 weeks	3	12
3-4 months	12	10
4-5 months	7	13
5-6 months	5	2
6-9 months	3	23
9-12 months	0	2
1 year and above	1	3
Number of unemployed days per worker	-	77

Note that the amount of men without work due to the ordinary type of unemployment was many times that of those who did not work due to conflict. On 31 January 1910, 202 workers had been unemployed for an average of seventy-seven days each. That is 15,554 lost working days. Since the daily wage in the cement industry varied between 3.24 and 4.31 (see Chapter 26),a calculation brings the result that unemployment on this occasion had cost the unemployed cement workers between 50,000 and 67,000 kronor in lost earnings.

This was not considered a social danger, because only the workers suffered from it. The strikes, however, threatened the employers and so were considered much more serious.

For certain places the investigation also records the local picture of unemployment. On 31 January 1910, 239 people were unemployed in Limhamn, 162 of whom from the cement factory. Visby had ninety-nine unemployed workers, eighteen of whom were cement workers, Södra Möckleby Parish (where Degerhamn is) had twenty-nine unemployed workers, nineteen of whom were cement workers.

For a closer look at unemployment and its significance to workers, places and companies, it ought to be divided into three different types depending on the cause: season, market forces and structural changes.

Season

It used to be common in most fields that workers had to carry most of the cost when demand for goods varied in different seasons. When construction ceased during the winter, the cement factories too closed, and those workers who were not needed for repairs were made redundant for longer or shorter periods, leaving them to fend for themselves.

The significance of seasonal unemployment to the profits of the companies has, as far as I know, never been investigated. But it wouldn't be hard to do. You multiply (as in the example above) the number of redundancies in one special year by the period of redundancy and average earnings. The result equals the amount of money saved by the company by the redundancies. Or in other words: the losses imposed on the workers in the shape of seasonal unemployment. This amount instead became part of the company's profit.

Opinions differ regarding the attitude to this part of company assets. I think it should be seen as a form of saving which ought to give the same rights as shareholding.

From the socio-economic view, it doesn't make any difference if a shareholder saves 10 kr monthly to buy a share at the end of the year or if a worker saves 10 kr monthly to cope with the lack of earnings during a month of forced redundancy around Christmas. In both cases the company gains the same sum. In both cases, the same resources are made available for investment.

Legally, however, there is a tremendous difference. The saving of the shareholder makes him a partner of the company with a seat at the meeting of partners and a right to profits on the capital for as long as the company exists. EUROC still pays out profits on money put into the company when it was founded in 1871.

The saving of the worker, however, gives neither rights nor profits. EUROC still haven't paid out a penny of the money put into the company by workers in the shape of seasonal unemployment since the company was founded in 1871.

- What has been the significance of seasonal unemployment in your job, at your factory? What difficulties occurred, what was done to overcome them?

- What losses have been imposed on the workers on different occasions by the company in the form of seasonal unemployment? What proportion does this constitute of the profits recorded by the company? If this money had given the same rights as the money put into the company by shareholders — how would the power over the company have been affected?

Aids: Another unemployment census was made in 1927. The trade union statistics and the industrial statistics give an idea of unemployment between these counts (Chapter 26). After 1955, Official Swedish Statistics give monthly accounts of the number of unemployed registered by the national employment agencies. As of 1959, regular work force investigations are made, including unemployment not registered by the agencies. The results are published in *Statistical Yearbook* and from 1973 in *Yearbook of Labour Market Statistics*.

Statistics, however, give only the extent, not the experiences of the unemployed, not the reality as they see it.

That history has yet to be written. The material can be found mainly among living people but also in trade union history (Chapter 3), accounts of local history (Chapter 5), among the workers' memories of the Nordic Museum (Chapter 17) and in literature.

Market Forces

Even when demand goes down due to "bad times" (perhaps better called "bad financial policy"), companies usually impose the losses on the workers. This is what happened to employment in the cement industry in the crisis of the 1930s:

These figures, taken from *Industrial Statistics* (see Chapter 26), show that the production of cement went down to almost half between 1930 and 1933. The number of workers in the cement industry was reduced by a third, although the Lanna cement factory started with fifty newly employed workers in 1933. At the other cement factories, over five hundred cement workers had thus been made redundant.

An average cement worker's annual earnings at this time was about 2,400 kr. We can thus calculate that the cement companies and above all Skånska Cement in 1933 saved about 1.2 million kronor by making workers redundant. During the whole crisis, losses of about 3.5 million kronor were imposed on the workers.

The administrative staff were, on the other hand, taken care of. It was reduced by insignificant numbers. And the shareholders were taken care of. Skånska Cement alone, in the four years with the highest unemployment, distributed 4.6 million kronor to their shareholders, i.e. 10-12% of the capital. In 1935, immediately after the crisis, the company could transfer by so called stock emission (distribution of 'free shares') a new joint capital of 6 million kronor to the owners.

Euroc still pays out the dividends on those 6 million kronor of shares given to owners in 1935. But Euroc has not paid

Year	Places of work	Administrative staff	Workers	Reduction/Increase	Production (mill.kr)	Reduction/ increase (mill.kr)
1930	9	133	1,418	-	22.2	-
1931	9	128	1,298	-120	18.7	-3.5
1932	9	129	1,131	-167	15.7	-3
1933	10	126	973	-158	11.8	-3.9
1934	10	124	965	-8	16.2	+4.4
1935	10	132	1,174	+209	20.6	+4.4
1936	10	137	1,278	+104	23.3	+2.7

out a penny of the million kronor that unemployed cement workers saved for the company during the crisis of the 1930s. Holders of the free shares of 1935 still retain the same voting rights as other shares at Euroc's meetings of partners. But the unemployment of the 1930s only brought continued powerlessness.

And yet some people say that history is dead and gone. Nothing could be more wrong. History still lives and thrives, receives its dividends and governs the large companies.

• How many people were made redundant in your town or village, in your job, at your factory, during the crisis of the 1930s? During other times of recession? What profit did the company make due to this? Who are now receiving the profits and exerting power over the savings thus made?

Aids: To calculate the unemployment at a certain company it may be necessary to go to the primary information on industrial statistics — see Chapter 26. How to find shareholders — Chapter 12.

Structural Changes

Naturally, there are no sharply defined lines between different types of unemployment. Seasonal unemployment is extended and becomes recessionary unemployment in bad times, and a recession can lead to structural changes that in turn cause unemployment. Take another look at the table of the effect of the crisis of the 1930s. At the end of 1935, production was back at the level of 1930, but employment had not increased to the same extent. Even clearer is the picture if we look at individual factories:

Town	Number of workers			
	1930	1935	+-	
Visby	161	86	-	75
Rest of Gotland (2)	346	151	-	195
Bromölla	92	66	-	26
Klagshamn	85	70	-	15
Limhamn	365	303	-	62
Skaraborgs Län (2)	261	334	+	73
Lanna	0	50	+	50
Öland	108	114	+	6
	1,418	**1,174**	-	**244**

The cement industry had lost 373 jobs, most of them in Gotland. In 1931, Skånska Cement took over the majority of shares in the Visby cement factory. By 1935, seventy-five jobs were gone, in 1940 the factory had closed down. Skånska Cement took over the Slite cement factory in 1931. Redundancies started immediately (See Chapter 23). Cementa took over Valleviken in 1933 and immediately stopped cement production. In 1935, Gotland had lost a total of 270 cement jobs or 53% of employment before the crisis.

The other jobs were axed at the Bromölla cement factory, taken over by Skånska Cement in 1929 and closed in 1940, and at the Klagshamn cement factory, taken over by Skånska Cement in 1934 and closed in 1939. And at Limhamn, which is now about to be closed as well.

At the same time, 129 new jobs had been created, above all at Skövde, where the work force had increased by sixty, and at Lanna, where the Coop had started a new cement factory with fifty workers. That sort of thing is called "structural changes" or "structural rationalization". In 1936, a government committee was appointed to investigate the rationalization "especially regarding workers' employment". In the cement industry they chose to study especially the Hällekis plant, which had been extended in 1931 to be the most modern and successful in the country.

The investigation was conducted by the rationalization company owned by the Confederation of Swedish Industry, the Industrial Bureau. An impartial expert was employed — the chief engineer of the Industrial Bureau, Tarras Sällfors, a leading figure in the battle for industrial rationalization. The company's replies to the questions of the investigation are kept in the National Archive. The manpower of the new factory had been reduced from seventy workers per shift in 1930 to thirty-three workers per shift in 1936. Productivity had increased from 176 kg per worker and hour to 363 kg. About fifty of the workers no longer needed at the factory had been offered work in other fields of industry. "It happens, however, quite often that workers prefer a period of unemployment to accepting such work as forest or farm work, which does not give the same high wages as industry."

The published text (SOU 1939:14) faithfully relates the data as given by the company. The effects in other parts of the country were studied in a special closure study, quoting the attitude of Skånska Cement equally without any criticism. It is repeated over and over in the official writing of the history of the company, latterly at its centenary in 1971. It will soon be the only truth that remains.

Closures

In its first hundred years of activity, Skånska Cement closed down seven Swedish cement factories. This is how the consequences were described in the centenary memorial:

LOMMA, closed in 1905. Two replacement industries were started "in consideration of all the workers settled in this village". (But Lomma entered a long period of stagnation which wasn't broken until it became a Malmö suburb in the 1960s.)

MALTESHOLM, closed in 1928. "In consideration of the workers and the community, operation did not cease until autumn 1928... About 50 older workers in Maltesholm were allocated a certain annual pension, whilst many younger men were transferred to other factories belonging to the same company..."

KLAGSHAMN, closed in 1939. The plans of closure "were complicated by difficult adjustment problems for the workers who had settled at the place and could not find any other work... Only in May 1939 cement production stopped completely at Klagshamn."

VISBY, closed in 1940, which "caused serious problems for some of the workers who had built their own homes in the city. To help their financial problems, the company made an agreement with them about some redundancy money" (According to the minutes of a Board meeting on 17/8/1940, this amounted to 20-25 kr monthly for fifteen workers. By the 1975 monetary value this is 83-103 kr. monthly.)

VALLEVIKEN, cement production stopped in 1933, factory closed in 1947. "The Board wants employees and workers to get their own homes, and plots had been allocated for this purpose." But the plans were only partly realized by the time of the closure. During the Second World War the company proved totally unviable and in the spring of 1947, the factory closed down.

LANNA, closed in 1966. "There were no social problems, some of the workers who lived in buildings owned by the company were offered the chance to buy them at favourable prices."

The closure of HÄLLEKIS was decided in 1975. What will

they say about that in the next memorial? LIMHAMN, KÖPING and STORA VIKA seem to be next in turn. How will these closures be described by the historians of the company?

These minutes were among Fredrik Nyström's documents in the Visby District Archive.

Ruins of the Maltesholm cement factory, built in 1928.

I do not suggest that all cement factories should be kept going forever wherever some capitalist once thought of building one. I only suggest that the closures have brought losses for which not only the shareholders but more so the workers and the rest of the community had to pay.

I stopped at Maltesholm to have a bite to eat and ask the way. I came across some survivors from the closed-down cement factory, now old age pensioners. They were even now furious at the mention of the company that, according to them, had killed the community. Even fifty years later they were filled with hatred against the managing director who, according to them, betrayed the factory to Skånska Cement while De La Gardie was away. But Judas was duly punished. He ended up a beggar. He went round Hälsingborg as a drunkard. In the end he hanged himself.

Shot himself, according to some. They see it as God's finger or Divine Justice. Who else can they hope for to intervene?

The following are facts: The old workers at Maltesholm were given "a certain annual allowance" which ceased long ago. The Maltesholm shareholders, however, were given Skånska

Cement shares at a value of 1.4 million kronor, which, in 1970, via six stock emissions, had grown to 5.4 million kronor. These shares still yield the same profit and power as the other EUROC shares.

Isn't it time to give the shareholders "a certain annual allowance" and let them go?

- What factories have closed down where you live, within the concern where you work? What was the result to the owners of the closed factory? To the workers? To the community?

Aids: Books on closures and other labour market problems can be found in *The Swedish Labour Market 1950-1968: A Bibliography of Research and Debates*. (The Institute of Labour Market Issues, Sthlm 1969).

A more detailed discussion of methods and results within different areas of problems is given in two books from the Institute of Social Research: Leif Grahm, *Swedish Labour Market Research from the Sociological Point of View* (Vänersborg 1973) and Harald Niklasson e.a. *Swedish Labour Market Research from the Socio-Economical Point of* View (Falköping 1973) (inventory of Swedish Labour Market (Research 1-2).

These two books are very useful. But they do have limitations significant of the attitude of the researchers. Only topical research is dealt with — the historical aspect is completely ignored. No attempts are made to explain the aim of the research to those directly involved — i.e. the workers themselves. The workers are only regarded as the objects of research. There is no place or company index for a reader interested in knowing what research involves himself. It is never even suggested that the workers themselves might be able to contribute to research or control it.

---

25. HOUSEKEEPING

Karl Malmqvist was a labourer at Öland Cement AB in Degerhamn. In the autumn of 1932, he was thirty years old, married, with a three-year-old son. The family's winter provisions consisted of 200 kg of potatoes, 12 kg of cabbages, two cords of birch firewood, three litres of jam and four litres of syrup, together worth 55 kr. The last week of November Karl Malmqvist earned 34 kr 86öre.

How do we know all this? The Malmqvist family, together with five other families of workers at the Degerhamn Cement Factory, took part in a so called household budget survey carried out by the Ministry of Social Affairs. The result of this survey was published in *Living Conditions and Household Habits in Towns and Industrial Centres Around 1933* (SOS, Social Statistics, Sthlm 1938).

Anna Malmqvist was the one to keep the household accounts. Here, forty-five years later, she is reading a copy of the household accounts.

The survey was carried out like this: Individual families of workers and clerical staff in different parts of the country were told to keep accounts of their incomes and expenses over a few months. These accounts, or, as they were called, "household books", have been kept by the archive of the Central Office of Statistics. In the Malmvist household book, we can see that their expenses the last week of November were as follows:

Goods	Amount	Cost
Milk	10.5l	1.54
Butter	0.5 kg	1.28
Margarine	1 kg	1.10
Eggs	0.5 kg	1
Beef (stewing)	1.5 kg	1.35
Salt pork	0.8 kg	1.04
Sausage	0.9 kg	1.19
Smoked sausage	0.3 kg	0.90
Herring	1 kg	0.38
Cod	1 kg	0.35
Flour	3 kg	0.99
Rye bread	2.6 kg	1
Rusks	0.5 kg	0.50
Prunes	0.5 kg	0.45
Sugar	2 kg	0.90
Sweets		0.15
Coffee	0.5 kg	1.80
Cocoa		0.45
Spices		0.21
Paraffin (Astral)	3l	0.74
Wick, carbide		0.39
Tablecloth (embroidery)		0.75
Milk saucer		1.85
Shelf liner		0.10
Underwear (men's)		2
Sewing needles		0.30

Goods	Amount	Cost
Soap		0.25
Washing powder		1.29
HP instalment, record player		15
Total outgoings		39.25
Income		34.86
Deficit		4.39

This was quite a normal week. They always consumed 1.5l of milk daily and 3l of paraffin weekly. The family usually bought half a kg of butter, half of coffee and some rusks to have with the coffee. The cost of margarine, flour and sugar were quite normal, too. Only the monthly instalment of the record-player pushed the outgoings higher than the income this week. The family paid for that out of their savings and still had 70 kr left at the end of the week.

That was fortunate, because Christmas was coming up with increased expenses. At first the Christmas drink was bought, 2l of Akvavit at 3.75/l. That week the outgoings were only 23.16 kr. The following week the Christmas ham was bought, 2.6 kg, at a price of 3.38 kr. Further, 1.5 kg of Christmas ling at 1.20 kr, half a dozen oranges at 75 öre, three packets of washing powder and half a kg of soap for the Christmas cleaning, and 2.5m of flannel for a Christmas present for the husband. Together with the trade union fee of 4.40 kr, expenses amounted to 53.15 kr.

The week beginning 11 December brought some extravagance: 1.5 kg of butter mixed with margarine, 5 kg of flour, half a kg of icing sugar, one packet of figs and 2 hg of Christmas tree sweets. 11m of curtain material cost 9.50 kr, Christmas cards with envelopes and stamps 4.68 kr, and, as a Christmas present for the wife, 1 dozen spoons were bought at 8.50 kr. Altogether 55.17 kr.

The last week before Christmas, the Akvavit store was complemented by another 2l of Akvavit, one bottle of mulled wine, 1.5 dozen bottles of beer and a tin of anchovies. Further, 1 kg of rice for the Christmas porridge, 1 kg of apples, 1 dozen oranges, half a kg of raisins and nuts and two packets of candles. The expenses amounted to 52.68 kr.

So far Karl Malmkvist's income had been normal: 35.27 kr one week, 37.50 kr the next, 36 kr the third week. But at Christmas production stopped, and with it the income. The last week he earned 30 kr. After that he was unemployed.

It was not quite so easy to stop the expenses. After Christmas he had to pay his social security contribution: 6.90 kr. The subscription to the newspaper had to be renewed: 5 kr. The little boy needed a pair of shoes for going to a children's party: 4 kr. Altogether expenses of 27.50 kr.

The New Year began with continued unemployment. 3 January was Karl's thirtieth birthday. Seven people for supper. Anna had to buy 30cm of linen and new woollen stockings at 2 kr. The roast beef cost 2.53 kr, the cigars 1 kr and soft drinks for the children 60 öre. Apart from that they were very careful. Weekly expenses: 23 kr 43 öre.

Third week of unemployment: They lived on some mincemeat and 4 hg of sausages. But the trade union fee and a birthday present pushed the expenses up to 30.66 kr.

The fourth week of unemployment: They bought no butter, no margarine, no sugar. Total expenses: 17.53 kr, 7.20 kr of which was the inevitable life insurance premium, and 2.25 kr or a textbook in community affairs for the study group.

Fifth week of unemployment: This week they bought no paraffin and lived on herrings, oat porridge and peas and pork. The expenses were kept down to 13.77, 60 öre of which was for a notebook for the study group.

Sixth week of unemployment, operation was resumed the last two days. Income 13.87. The expenses amounted to 17.41 kr, 4.25 kr of which was for a new denim shirt for the husband when he went back to work.

The housekeeping book for the Malmqvist family is kept with thousands of others in the Central Office of Statistics.

How did they manage? Well, the family had savings of 25 kr when the unemployment started and an equal amount that they had lent which was later repaid. Karl had also worked as doorman at the dances in the civic hall all year, earning 5 kr a night and that money — 51 kr — was paid at Christmas. That was a kind of saving as well. In all, they had saved 101 kr. 15 kr were given to him and he borrowed 30 kr. The rest of the lost income was covered by eating less and cheaper foods in January.

But even so the next few weeks were very lean. The first working week they lived on half a kg of mincemeat and half a kg of pork sausages. Expenses 15.31 kr. The second working week they managed to push down expenses to 11.98 kr, 1 kr of which went into the workers' commune. It went on like this for weeks until their economy was again sound.

This is how Karl Malmqvist and his family in the New Year of 1933 saved 200 kr for the shareholders of Ölands Cement AB.

The Housekeeping Survey of 1969

The Housekeeping Books give a very clear and vivid picture of living conditions for Swedish families at different points in time. The latest investigation of this kind was made in 1969, when three thousand randomly selected households were asked to keep accounts of their expenses. The households were divided into ten different groups, the lowest with an annual income of 9,000 kr, the highest with an annual income of over 60,000 kr. The published report *The Household Budget Survey of 1969* (Statistical Memoranda P 1971:9) describes the consumption of the households of the different groups, distributed into 999 different pieces of goods or services — anything from baby equipment to plots for graves.

It turns out that the consumption of potato flour only increases insignificantly, from 1.66 to 2.50 yearly, from the lowest to the highest income group. The consumption of cocktail snacks, however, is multiplied by ten at the same comparison. The expenses for shandy are unchanged in different strata of income, but the consumption of wine, liquor and cigarettes rises rapidly with the income.

The consumption of fuel is tripled, the costs for transport are multiplied by ten, and the money spent on cars is twenty-three times more in the highest than in the lowest income group. Generally, the household consumption can also be compared between families with and without children, between different age groups, etc.

In this way, the Survey tells us what increased equality means in forms of changed consumption. The figures of the tables in many places can be translated into amounts of defined products. You could make a display depicting the exact amount of cocktail snacks, of which you rob a high-income family by lowering its standard to the closest lower level. And how much the low income-earner would gain from climbing one step. And so on for 999 different pieces of goods.

These 999 columns show the final result of the battle for better pay. This is the battle-ground of the market forces. The household budget surveys are now used mainly by companies to calculate where they should be prepared to absorb future boosts of buying power. But they could also be used to calculate the effect of growth on the welfare of different people.

Economic growth assumes quite a different concrete impact if it benefits children of low-income families rather than increases the buying power of single people with high salaries. What impact? Look at the tables!

Who Brought Us Here?

The first Swedish household budget survey was printed in *Swedish Cost of Living 1915-14, 1-3* (SOS, Social Statistics, Sthlm 1917-21). Referring only to workers and clerks, it included merely about a hundred items and types of goods. Instead, individual families were described one by one with all their personal and local differences. How much pork did a Malmö worker eat in those days? How much coffee did a Västerås postman drink? Answers to such questions were published from 1913 and from 1923, 1933, 1940-1942, 1948, 1952, 1958 and 1969, are kept in the archive of the Central Office of Statistics.

The first question that springs to mind when you study these tables is: *Why* were the increasing productive forces used like this? *Who* brought us here?

We did ourselves, according to the ideologists of market economy. The companies only serve their consumers. The market can be compared to a constant referendum, where the consumers, independently and in detail, decide the nature of production.

There is a lot to be said against this statement, though it is true to a certain extent. Consumers decide far too much at the moment of buying.

When you're holding an item in each hand and choosing between the two of them, you decide which country should produce the goods, whether it should be manufactured as piecework or against an hourly wage, what the working environment should be like, what risks the workers should have to take, which factories should flourish and which should be closed down. You decide what finite resources should be consumed, what refuse should be left, and what influence it will have on other people's consumption. Briefly: you decide, although blindly, the total social consequences of production and consumption. This is called market economy.

Market economy gives us power in our capacity as consumers and not in our capacity as workers. It's a suspect form of power, since it's almost impossible to use sensibly.

It would be a little better if we were not limited to the alternatives selected for us by the product developers of the companies and buyers of large chain stores. Selected representatives of the consumers should also have some say in the products to be developed and sold. Each company should be under obligation to give a public motivation as to why they've chosen to manufacture and sell a certain product.

Vague references to "what the customers want" should not be accepted. The motivation ought to include a precise description of the consumer needs the product aims at satisfying and the social side effects that can be expected. The motivation should also include definite information on the conditions of production and consumption of resources. They should form the basis of criticism and debate around the product policy of the company.

But today no other reasons are required than the fact that a product is profitable. Many useful and necessary products are unprofitable and so wiped off the market. Often a product is more profitable if it is manufactured under dreadful, humiliating conditions — which helps wipe out products manufactured under more humane conditions. And it is we ourselves who are appointed to control this competition, by buying or not buying.

It's a terrifying power, granted to us by the market economy. I think we ought to refuse it. Because the moment of buying is really the worst possible occasion to decide about other people's working conditions.

- Have any of your predecessors, in the job, at your factory, taken part in the household budget surveys? What picture do they give of living conditions in your town/village?

Aids: In the first survey, workers from Södertalje, Uppsala, Nyköping, Eskilstuna, Mjölby, Åtvidaberg, Jönköping, Huskvarna, Nässjö, Alvesta, Hemse, Kristianstad, Malmö, Landskrona, Hälsingborg, Ystad, Trelleborg, Falkenberg, Göteborg, Lysekil, Trollhättan, Åmal, Arvika, Karlskoga, Västerås, Sala, Hedemora, Ludvika, Gävle, Söderhamn, Bolnäs, Skönsberg, Sollefteå, Luleå, Boden, Malmberget and Kiruna participated. Most towns and centres have taken part on some occasion, and more or less all workers' occupations are represented.

The complete titles of all household budget surveys are under the title "Prices and Consumption" at the back of the Statistical Yearbook. The Housekeeping Books are in the archive of the Central Office of Statistics, see Chapter 26.

- Who are the consumers of the product you manufacture? Does it mean different things to people with low and high incomes?

Aids: Cement is not included in the list of 999 products and product groups in the budget survey (except as part of other materials for repairs to buildings). But most products can be found in the 1969 survey, showing the consumption of each individual household and the total consumption in Sweden, distributed over different groups of income.

You need data about prices to be able to convert the expenses in kronor and öre into amounts of different products. Prices as of 1913 are listed in *Retail prices and index calculations* (SOS) and as of 1931 in *Consumer prices and index calculations* (SOS).

- According to the laws of market economy, people as consumers, should control people as workers. In what way does consumer demand affect your work? In what way do you as a consumer affect the situation of other workers? Are there any better ways?

Aids: Håkan Lindhoff and Folke Ölander discuss the influence of consumers on the product development of companies in the book *People and Companies in the Communication Society* (Lund 1971). Their ideas ought to be developed further. At present, the company management plays consumer demands off against workers' demands and workers' demands against consumer demands. The workers who manufacture a product ought to meet the representatives of those who consume it and so plan product development and together make the same worker/consumer demand on the company management.

26. PRODUCTION

When Karl Malmkvist had been unemployed for a little more than a month, operation at the Ölands Cement Factory, was resumed, on 27 January 1933. That year, the factory maintained operation for 322 days. 29393 tons of cement were produced, at a total value of 855,355 kr. (In other words, cement was worth 29.12 kr/ton.)

Employers and administrators amounted to eleven. The factory had ninety-eight workers, six of whom were women and eight men under eighteen. In all they worked 217,763 hours (or 2222 hours per worker).

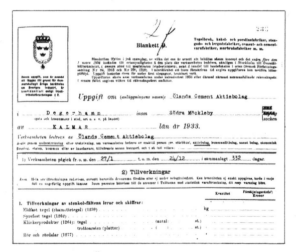

Data on production at Ölands Cement AB in 1933 were sent to the Institute of Commerce and are now in the archive of the Central Office of Statistics.

(So in that year, Karl Malmkvist and the other cement workers at Degerhamn produced 2,999 tons of cement each. They produced 0.13 tons/working hour. Each worker produced cement at a value of 8,733 kr, or 3.93 kr of cement/working hour.)

That year the Degerhamn cement factory consumed 2.9 million Kilowatt hours of electricity. (That was 9715 Kilowatt hours per ton of cement and 13.2 Kilowatt hours per working hour.) The main fuel was coal. They consumed 6527 tons (and produced 4.5 tons of cement for each ton of coal). (The coal consumption was 66.6 tons per worker or 30 kg per working hour.)

How do we know this? It is in the primary information for industrial *statistics*. (The figures you have to calculate yourself on the basis of these statistics have been given in brackets.) Each industrial company was and is under obligation to give such data on special forms. The completed forms from the period before 1923 are kept in the National Archive. For the period after 1923 they are in the archive of the Central Office of Statistics.

Industrial statistics go far back. The Institute of Commerce began to demand information on "manufacturers" as early as 1793. Compilations of these gathered data have been printed in annual reports since 1830. Cement appears for the first time in industrial statistics in 1874. As from 1890, we know how many tons of cement were produced in Sweden each year:

Year	Workers	Production thousand (tons)	Production per worker (tons)	Increase (+) Reduction (-) (%)
1890	1150	35	30	-
1895	831	57	69	+130
1900	1336	126	94	+36
1905	1298	168	129	+28
1910	1291	258	200	+55
1915	1375	306	223	+12
1920	1663	281	169	-24

Year	Workers	Production thousand (tons)	Production per worker (tons)	Increase (+) Reduction (-) (%)
1925	1525	446	293	+73
1930	1418	611	431	+47
1935	1174	740	630	+46
1940	1185	701	592	+6
1945	1218	1214	997	+68
1950	1428	1936	1356	+36
1955	1783	2550	1430	+5
1960	1694	2862	1689	+17
1965	1624	3696	2276	+35
1970	1595	3998	2510	+19
1975	1430	3345	2340	-7

The number of workers has remained more or less static. The production has increased hundredfold. In 1890, a cement worker produced thirty tons of cement in a year and in 1975, 2340 tons. The annual production per worker was seventy-eight times that of 1890.

The increase has varied in different periods, and at sometimes production has even shown a reduction. But on average, the production per worker has increased by 34% in each five-year period.

- How has production increased in your job, at your place of work?

Aids: The industrial statistics. The annual reports were called *Factories and Manufacturers* (Contribution to official Swedish Statistics, series D) until 1910, after that they are called *Industry* (Official Swedish Statistics). Data on individual companies can be found in the primary material for industrial statistics. The primary material until 1923 is in the National Archive (see Chapter 7); after 1923 in the archive of the Central Office of Statistics (Karlavägen 100, 102 50 Stockholm. Tel: 08/ 14 05 60, friendly and helpful staff.)

In the early 1900s, industrial statistics also included information about occupational accidents. As of 1960, data are given on certain production costs (divided into raw materials and types of energy) and as of 1970, also on the so called processing value.

Wages

What proportion of this increased production went to the workers? What wages has the cement industry paid over the years?

We have seen some scattered examples in chapters 13 and 15. The fundamental investigation of the history of Swedish workers' pay is unfortunately only available in English. That is:

BAGGE, G. e.a.
Wages in Sweden. (Wages, Cost of Living and National Income in Sweden 1860-1930. Volume 2.)
London 1932-25.

The researchers have gone through old pay-rolls from a large number of companies in different fields of industry, including the cement industry. The following figures were given for the Limhamn cement factory for skilled workers, i.e., the generally best paid group of workers. The production figures have been taken from industrial statistics:

Year	Hourly wage (Öre)	Annual wage (Kronor)	Annual production per worker	Annual wages in percent of annual production
1890	24.9	858	1600	54
1895	27.3	882	1900	46
1900	32.7	1000	3100	32
1905	36.3	1262	3800	33
1910	43.1	1361	6600	21
1914	47.1	1083	7500	14

In these twenty-four years, the value of production per worker increased by 370%. The skilled workers' annual wages increased by 26%. At the beginning of the period he received 54% of the production value as wages. At the end of the period only 14%.

A more comprehensive description of one of these years can be seen in *Working and Pay Conditions for Factory Workers in Limhamn in 1905*. (A memorandum from the Institute of Commerce, Dept. of Work Statistics, 1906.) In it we find a very precise description of wage distribution (See pages 228 and 229).

The figures of the Institute of Commerce show no great differences of hourly wages between different groups of workers. Still, the wages showed great individual variation, depending on the age and capacity of the worker. Concerning the annual wages, only one category, the coal-drivers, stand out from the rest with much higher wages.

As a comparison, we could mention that their employer, R.F. Berg, in 1905 was taxed at 25,784 kr. The highest paid workers earned 6.6%, the lowest paid 3.6% of their employer's taxable income.

Wages in Sweden described the wages at the Limhamn cement factory and many other fields of industry are recorded by the SAF statistical office in *The Wages of Workers in a Number of Fields of Swedish Industry: An Investigation for the Period 1914-1920*. (Sthlm 1916-1922).

Tab. 3. (Forts.) **Inkomst per timme för fabriksarbetare i Limhamn, fördelade efter specialitet och ålder.** [Cementfabriken.]

	Antal arbetare med en inkomst per timme af									Inkomst per timme.		
	under 20 öre.	20—25 öre.	25—30 öre.	30—35 öre.	35—40 öre.	40—45 öre.	45—50 öre.	50 öre och däröfver.	Hela antalet arbetare.	Högst. (Öre.)	Lägst. (Öre.)	Genomsnitt. (Öre.)
Arbetare i åldern 20—65 år fördelade efter specialiteter.												
Råmaterialsarbetare	--	—	1	2	9	45	14	—	71	49	25	41
Ringugnsarbetare .	--	—	—	3	9	14	--	—	26	43	34	39
Schaktugnsarbetare	—	—	—	1	4	29	7	—	41	47	32	42
Koksugnsarbetare .	—	—	—	—	—	—	5	1	6	50	47	48
Cementmjölnare. .	—	—	—	—	2	11	9	—	22	48	36	43
Cementpackare . .	—	—	--	1	2	27	2	—	32	48	33	41
Kolkörare	—	—	—	—	—	3	6	—	9	46	41	45
Lossare och lastare	—	—	—	—	—	2	9	—	11	49	42	46
Tunnbindare . . .	—	—	2	9	13	9	1	—	34	45	26	37
Järnarbetare . . .	—	--	2	4	8	4	—	1	19	51	26	35
Träarbetare	--	—	1	1	4	4	—	—	10	42	25	39
Murare	—	—	3	2	3	—	—	—	8	38	28	32
Maskinpersonal . .	—	—	—	1	2	10	1	—	14	47	33	40
Diverse arbetare .	2	2	5	6	7	3	2	1	28	52	10	33
S:a och medeltal	2	2	14	30	63	161	56	3	331	52	10	40
Dessutom förmän .	—	—	—	1	—	4	2	4	11	58	33	47
Samtliga arbetare (utom förmän).												
Under 15 år . . .	14	—	—	—	—	—	—	—	14	12	8	11
15—20 år	25	2	—	3	2	2	1	—	35	45	10	20
20—25 »	—	—	3	6	6	13	5	—	33	47	26	38
25—30 »	1	—	—	3	15	30	3	—	52	49	14	39
30—35 »	—	—	1	1	6	36	8	1	53	52	26	41
35—40 »	—	—	—	4	8	25	12	—	49	49	30	42
40—45 »	--	—	1	5	7	22	12	—	47	48	29	41
45—50 »	1	—	2	3	10	16	8	1	41	51	10	40
50—55 »	—	1	2	5	8	10	7	1	34	50	24	39
55—60 »	—	—	3	2	2	6	1	—	14	46	25	36
60—65 »	—	1	2	1	1	3	—	—	8	44	20	34
65—70 »	—	4	4	—	—	—	—	—	8	29	20	25
70 år och däröfver	1	2	1	—	—	—	—	—	4	28	17	22
S:a och medeltal	42	10	19	33	65	163	57	3	392	52	8	37

*Table 3. Income per hour of factory workers in Limhamnn,
distributed according to skill and age. (The cement factory.)*

Tab. 4. (Forts.) Årsinkomst för fabriksarbetare i Limhamn, fördelade efter specialitet och ålder. [Cementfabriken.]

Arbetare i åldern 20—65 år, fördelade efter specialiteter.	Antal arbetare, som arbetat minst 240 dagar, med en årsinkomst af											Genomsnittlig årsinkomst med en arbetstid af			
												240—270 dagar.		270 dagar o. däröfver.	
	under 400 kr.	400—500 kr.	500—600 kr.	600—700 kr.	700—800 kr.	800—900 kr.	900—1,000 kr.	1,000—1,100 kr.	1,100—1,200 kr.	1,200 kr. och däröfver.	Hela antalet arbetare.	Antal arb.	Kr.	Antal arb.	Kr.
Råmaterialarbetare	—	—	—	—	1	—	2	3	33	21	60	8	1,079	52	1,181
Ringugnsarbetare .	—	—	—	—	—	—	—	4	9	11	24	1	1,123	23	1,187
Schaktugnsarbetare	—	—	—	—	—	—	1	1	15	19	36	1	1,078	35	1,237
Koksugnsarbetare .	—	—	—	—	—	—	—	—	—	6	6	—	—	6	1,707
Cementmjölnare. .	—	—	—	—	—	—	—	5	2	11	18	3	1,083	15	1,227
Cementpackare . .	—	—	—	—	—	—	—	3	4	9	16	2	1,079	14	1,225
Kolkörare	—	—	—	—	—	—	—	—	1	7	8	—	—	8	1,335
Lossare och lastare	—	—	—	—	—	—	—	—	1	10	11	1	1,165	10	1,371
Tunnbindare . . .	—	—	—	—	2	1	3	7	7	4	24	2	901	22	1,081
Järnarbetare . . .	—	—	—	—	1	1	1	4	3	5	15	2	831	13	1,162
Träarbetare . . .	—	—	—	—	1	—	—	1	2	4	8	—	—	8	1,167
Murare . . . .·.	—	—	—	1	1	2	—	1	2	—	7	2	729	5	1,032
Maskinpersonal . .	—	—	—	—	—	—	1	2	4	7	14	3	1,112	11	1,231
Diverse arbetare .	1	1	—	1	4	2	3	4	3	3	22	3	956	19	980
S:a och medeltal	1	1	—	2	10	6	11	35	86	117	269	28	1,014	241	1,190
Dessutom förmän .	—	—	—	—	—	—	1	—	—	10	11	1	1,460	10	1,386
Samtliga arbetare (utom förmän).															
Under 15 år . . .	—	—	—	—	—	—	—	—	—	—	—	—	—	—	—
15—20 år	7	1	2	1	—	2	2	1	—	1	17	5	680	12	570
20—25 »	—	—	—	1	2	—	—	7	2	7	19	8	920	11	1,202
25—30 »	—	1	—	—	—	—	4	7	15	14	41	4	1,071	37	1,153
30—35 » . . : .	—	—	—	—	1	—	1	2	18	23	45	1	1,105	44	1,203
35—40 »	—	—	—	—	—	1	1	2	12	22	38	—	—	38	1,240
40—45 »	—	—	—	—	—	2	1	6	15	17	41	3	1,086	38	1,199
45—50 »	1	—	—	—	—	1	1	3	11	18	35	2	1,115	33	1,204
50—55 »	—	—	—	—	3	—	3	2	10	13	31	4	994	27	1,214
55—60 »	—	—	—	—	3	1	—	3	3	3	13	4	1,009	9	1,059
60—65 »	—	—	—	1	1	1	—	3	—	—	6	2	1,066	4	823
65—70 »	—	—	1	3	2	2	—	—	—	—	8	1	651	7	728
70 år och däröfver	—	—	1	1	—	1	—	—	—	—	3	—	—	3	688
S:a och medeltal	8	2	4	7	12	11	13	36	86	118	297	34	954	263	1,144

Table 4. Annual income of factory workers in Limhamn, distributed according to skill and age. (The cement factory.)

The SAF statistics are interesting, as they give a very precise account of the different jobs in the cement production of the time. The SAF divide the workers of seven different cement factories into the following categories:

Cement Factory Workers

15 slurry works watchers
4 milk silo watchers
52 clinker workers
57 rotary kiln workers
74 millers
12 crushers
41 dampeners
3 hoisters
53 driers
4 drying tower stokers
133 cement packers
26 cement distributors
6 weighers
25 sack adjusters
1 mill stone sharpener

Lime and Clay Pit Workers

13 excavator operators
5 stone blasters
601 limestone workers
23 stone drivers
130 lime burners
16 agricultural lime workers
4 lime slashers
4 lime works workers
12 lime unloaders
103 excavators
54 clay workers
3 slate workers
10 switchers
8 flint stone cutters

Cement Barrel Workers
113 coopers
59 barrel factory workers
24 auxiliary workers
34 boys in the barrel factory

Engine Staff
23 engine operators
31 stokers
2 motor operators
47 coal and peat-drivers
40 greasers
1 belt watchers

Craftsmen and Equal Workers
10 machine repairers
9 electricians
67 iron and machine workers
30 smiths
9 platers
58 wood workers
8 masons
38 helpers
1 saddler
7 apprentices

This diversity must be partly due to the fact that different factories use different names for the same concept, such as "train driver" and "engine driver". Some of the jobs in the lime pit have nothing to do with cement production, but even so, it's an impressive list. The cement production of that time was a rich world of different little jobs.

The hourly wage is recorded by the SAF annually for all these different categories of workers, for ordinary time, for overtime, period wage, piecework rates and average wage, as well as the highest, the lowest and the average annual income. We shall now follow the average hourly wage and the annual wage for a rotary kiln burner. After 1914 we can also follow the change in monetary value. Under the heading of "Converted" I have converted the wages into the 1975 monetary value, using the same method as in Chapter 13.

Year	Hourly wage	Converted hourly wage	Annual wage	Converted annual wage
1914	0.48	4.26	985	8737
1915	0.46	3.55	1487	11465
1916	0.46	3.14	1522	10380
1917	0.52	2.81	1763	9538
1918	0.80	3.06	2598	9924
1919	1.19	3.94	3211	10268
1920	1.37	4.52	3408	11246

Comment: In 1914, operation stopped for four months.

The real value of the hourly wage, it appears, went down strongly during the First World War and was not reinstated until 1920.

In Chapter 13, we investigated Ernst Wehtje's income in the same period. It may be of interest to compare the burner's annual wage with the taxable annual income of the Managing Director:

Year	Burner's annual wage	MD's taxable income	The burner's annual wage in percent of the MD's taxable income
1914	985	84000	1.2
1915	1,487	101000	1.5
1916	1,522	107000	1.4
1917	1,763	132000	1.3
1918	2,598	140000	1.9
1919	3,211	152000	2.1
1920	3,408	226000	1.5

Only on one occasion did the burner's annual wage rise up to 2% of Wehtje's taxable income. From 1929, annual wage statistics are published in the series *Official Swedish Statistics* (SOS), first entitled *Yearbook of Wage Statistics* (1929-1951) and then entitled *Wages* (1952).

The first edition of the *Yearbook of Wage Statistics* gives the following information on nine cement factories. The figures refer to male workers:

Average number of workers in the active period	1776
Average working hours per year and worker	2324
Piecework	41.6% (It is interesting to see the proportion of piecework falling quite steadily until 1940, when it starts rising again.)
Annual average wage for ordinary working hours	2412

Including overtime, payment in kind, etc.	2522
Average daily income	9.05
Average hourly time wage for ordinary hours	0.92
The same, piecework	1.26
The same, average	1.07
Average hourly wage including overtime, payment in kind, etc.	1.09

In government statistics we can no longer distinguish between burners and other groups but have to accept an average figure for all male workers in a cement factory. I choose to follow the average hourly and annual wages (including piecework supplements and payment in kind) every five years from 1930. In 1970 and 1975, the figures also include lime workers, which makes it more difficult to calculate the annual wage. I have also converted the figures into the 1975 monetary value. In the last column, the average cement worker's annual wage is shown in per cent of the taxable income of the MD of Skånska Cement.

Year	Hourly wage	Converted hourly wage	Annual wage	Converted annual wage	Worker's wages as percentage of employer's income
1930	1.80	5.81	2442	13138	0.7
1935	1.06	6.06	2350	13442	1.0
1940	1.33	6.21	2764	12908	0.8
1945	1.78	6.78	4024	15331	1.2
1950	2.54	8.69	6075	20776	1.8
1955	3.63	9.73	8346	22368	2.4

Year	Hourly wage	Converted hourly wage	Annual wage	Converted annual wage	Worker's wages as percentage of employer's income
1960	6.12	13.34	15564	33927	7.0
1965	9.38	17.17	23068	42216	7.1
1970	13.78	20.06	25200	-	-
1975	24.50	24.50	42500	42500	-

All along the workers' wages remained a fraction of the employer's income. In the 1930s and 1940s, it was at times less than 1%. In 1960 and 1965, after Elam Tunhammar had succeeded Wehtje, we were back in almost the same relationship between workers and director as in R.P. Berg's days.

The difference is the fact that after 1940, progressive income taxation claims more and more of the high incomes. This affects the final result considerably — but perhaps not as much as you may think. One example: According to the tax tables shown in the 1965 Taxation Calendar, the average cement worker that year took home 17,850 kr after tax. The Skånska Cement managing director took home 106,000 kr. So even after tax had been deducted, the worker's pay was only 17 % of the director's salary — disregarding all the advantages such as interest deductions and untaxed capital increases which the director was better able to benefit from.

The hourly wage of cement workers has increased sharply, even in fixed terms. By the 1975 monetary value, the 1914 hourly wage was worth 4.26 kr. In 1975 it went up to 24.50 kr. In other words, it has doubled five times in sixty years.

But it took time. The 1930 hourly wage was only 36% above that of 1914. In 1940, the hourly wage was 46% higher than in 1914. In 1950, the hourly wage had doubled since 1914. That was after thirty-five years. The swift pay developments only came in the 1950s and 1960s.

Production for a long time increased more sharply than the wages:

Year	Production per worker (Kronor)	Change (%)	Annual wage (Kronor)	Change (%)	Annual wage in percent of annual production
1930	15700	-	2442	-	16
1935	17500	11.5	2350	-3.8	13
1940	28100	60.6	2764	17.6	10
1945	45100	60.5	4024	45.6	9
1950	66600	47.7	6075	51.0	9
1955	85900	29.0	8346	34.7	10
1960	105100	22.4	15564	86.5	15
1965	152000	44.6	23068	48.2	15
1970	200600	32.0	25200	9.2	13
1975	342700	70.8	42500	68.7	12

The sharp increases in production in the first twenty years did not lead to corresponding increases in pay. Not until the second half of the 1950s, when pay increased by 86.5% and production by 22.4%, did the cement workers recoup the same proportion of the production value as they had had in 1930 — and in 1914. Since then this proportion has again been lost.

The directors who granted themselves fifty, even one hundred times the income of the workers, did all they could to keep costs down. Wages in the cement industry were always below (and for a long time very much below) the national average for a male industrial worker — in spite of the swift development of productivity in this field.

Why? In the official history published at the centenary of Skånska Cement, the matter is given this explanation:

Cement workers for a long time came under the so called low-wage category. One reason for this may be the fact that among the members of the Building Materials Federation were a large number of brickworks with relatively low profitability, and the Cement company, in spite of its dominant position, by loyalty to these other members, had to help keep down the workers' claim for better pay — an unfavourable effect of the so called national agreements, which were now strived for within different occupational groups.

In other words, the cement company with its relatively high profitability would have been able to meet the workers' claim for better pay, but instead chose to refuse them, not due to any mean mercenary or other similarly crass reason. Oh no, the low pay policy was simply an "unfavourable effect" of the national agreement. It was loyalty towards the Federation comrades that forced the company to keep the workers' wages down at the same level as the unprofitable little brickworks...

What shameless hypocrisy! The low-wage policy was certainly not "unfavourable" to Skånska Cement! On the contrary, the company greatly profited at the expense of the cement workers' poverty.

Don't grieve things past, they say. But in this case things are not past. The money is still there. Some of it has been invested into technical equipment to make further increases of production possible. Some has been invested in other companies. All of it today constitutes the capital of the industrial company Euroc.

This capital was gathered just like this — krona by krona, day by day, decade by decade, when the company management seized it from the country's cement workers by paying them lower wages than motivated by the production increases.

That's how history still lives in the capital. One day the workers of this country will reclaim their history.

- What were the wages of your predecessors, in your job, at your place of work? Compared to other workers? Compared to the director of the company? Compared to the production increases?

Aids: The industrial statistics, the wage statistics and all other Swedish government statistics are conveniently available on open shelves at the library of the Central Office of Statistics, Karlavägen 100, 102 50 Stockholm. Tel: 08/ 14 05 60. The large county libraries are also usually well provided with statistics. If something is missing — just order it!

Swedish government statistics were published in 1860-1910 mainly in the series *Contributions to the Official Swedish Statistics (BSOS)* and from 1911 in *Official Swedish Statistics (SOS)*.

Particularly interesting are the special investigations of certain groups of workers such as mechanic workers, published by the Institute of Commerce entitled *Work Statistics* (1899-1912) and *Memoranda from the Institute of Commerce*, Department for Work Statistics (1903-1912). The work statistics for 1913 were taken over by the Ministry of Social Affairs who, amongst other things, investigated hygienic conditions in the cellulose industry (1915), forest workers' working conditions in Värmland, Dalarna and Norrland (1916), dockers' conditions (1916) and the Swedish cottage industry (1917).

How do you find your way in these statistics? To what extent can you trust them? How have they been used by different researchers? These questions are answered, unfortunately too briefly, by Birgitta Odén in *Statistics for Historians* (Uppsala 1970). A more comprehensive, more pedagogical book is needed, which could give many clear examples of the information that can be found in old statistics.

Today more than twenty thousand pages of official statistics are published each year, apart from those produced by local government, organizations and industry. Erland Hofsten gives a guide to modern statistics in a *Guide to Swedish Statistics* (the 7th ed. came in 1971).

Official Swedish statistics are often planned as if they were intended to directly obstruct any unwelcome conclusions. Wage statistics are one example. To avoid comparisons between workers and administrators, their wages are shown in different volumes, hourly wages for workers, and monthly salaries for administrators. They ought to make comparisons easier by giving the annual income in both cases. To avoid comparisons between the workers' production and their wages, wage and production development are shown in different books. On the contrary, such comparisons should be encouraged.

27. INVENTIONS

The huge production increases in the cement industry are due to the efforts and inventiveness of numerous people. The two names mentioned above all are two Englishmen: Joseph Aspdin (1779-1855) and Isaac Charles Johnson (1811-1911).

Joseph Aspdin was a Leeds mason. In a purely practical manner, he invented a new method for making cement. He mixed the dust from English limestone roads with clay and water to a paste. The mixture was left to dry and then broken into pieces that were burnt in a lime kiln until all its carbon dioxide was driven out. The burnt pieces were then ground to a fine powder, which Aspdin termed "Portland cement". To produce Portland cement in the modern sense of the word, Aspdin would have burnt the mixture until it melted, "sintered". This occasionally happened by mistake, but such pieces were considered unusable by Aspdin who discarded them.

Anyway, this method gave the best cement that had been available so far and his son, William Aspdin, ran a little cement factory at Rotherhithe outside London, where he jealously guarded his father's secret. In order to mystify the manufacture to the workers he had, the story goes, a secretive chest in his office. Every now and then he would take a handful of flour from the chest and throw it into the kiln.

Isaac Johnson, the son of a cement factory worker, was determined to uncover the secret. He made systematic tests with different proportions of lime and clay and applied different burning temperatures. He found then that, if he burnt the mixture until it melted, his cement had even better properties than Aspdin's product.

In 1844, the first modern Portland cement was released on to the market. In Germany, production started in 1850, in Russia in 1856 and in Denmark in 1868. In 1869, the Swedish technician Otto Fahnehjelm toured England and France in order to study different types of cement and their application. His travelogue was printed by the Prospects of the Engineers' Association in 1870. The following year, the engineer A.W. Lundberg was sent by the Institute of Commerce to Germany and England. His travelogue *On the Preparation of Portland cement* (Sthlm 1871) in detail describes the production methods of twelve foreign cement factories.

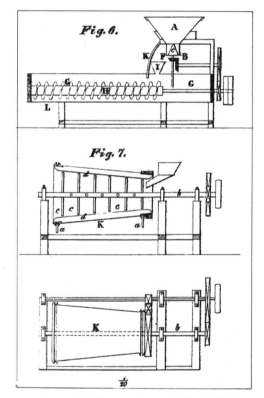

Early concrete mixers. An illustration to Fahnehjelm's travelogue in the Prospects of The Engineers' Association in 1870.

In Sweden, Portland cement at this time was still an imported luxury item, used only where its special properties were absolutely essential, especially when building under water. *The Book of Inventions: A Survey of the Development of Industrial Work in All Areas* was published in six volumes in Stockholm 1873-75. The fourth volume is about the "chemical treatment of raw materials". On the first page the goddess of Chemistry appears, engulfed by the steam from test tubes and retorts. The "Swedish cement" she had managed to produce with her magic wand was, however, not very good. Made of alum slate, it had to be ground with water at the building site "in an ordinary mortar mill" and then used at once "since the air makes it deteriorate quickly". But there was hope:

A factory for manufacturing Swedish cement, based on better foundations than before, is being constructed in Sweden at this moment, but has not yet started to supply the market with any product.

The production methods at the new factory were described by R.F. Berg at the Engineers' Association's discussion on Portland cement on 23 February 1897. At Lomma, as in all cement factories at the time, production was based on the principle of brick moulding. Stones were baked of lime white and clay, packed in kilns, burnt and then ground into powder.

But a new idea had already been born. In 1877, the Englishman Thomas Russel Crampton was granted a patent for his rotary cement kiln. It was developed further by another Englishman, Ransome, in 1885, and ten years later was given its modern form by Hurry and Seaman in the US. The slurry was poured straight into the kiln, without any previous brick moulding or packing, and from the opposite direction, burning oil or pulverized coal was blown in. The rotary kiln came to Europe in 1898, when F.L. Smith installed one in Aalborg. In 1902, the Klagshamn cement factory was equipped with Sweden's first rotary kilns, 23 metres long. The *Technical*

Journal presented the revolutionary method in two articles in 1903 and 1904:

When the balls of slurry had reached the lower burning zone, they shattered and then again formed little balls, their size varying from that of a pea to that of a walnut. This is where the Enormous strength of this method lies: *The raw material forms itself to a size and form suitable for burning and grinding.* The hard work of moulding, drying and piling the raw bricks into the kilns and then crushing them is thus avoided. Yet another advantage is achieved: you obtain a product more evenly burnt through than that be achieved with moulded bricks, which mostly become too hard burnt on the surface and too softly burnt at the core, which is another indicator that the raw materials are not used as well as possible.

The Goddess of Chemistry raises her wand. Title page of the fourth volume of The Book of Inventions, 1873.

This was the foundation laid for the technology of modern cement industry. Klagshamn remained alone with the new manufacture technique for five years. Then it had a wide breakthrough. Between 1907 and 1909, rotary kilns were installed at Limhamn, Hällekis, Maltesholm, Ifö and Visby.

At about the same time, reinforcement techniques evolved. The idea of combining metal and cement was born almost at the same time as the cement. The Frenchman Lambot exhibited a concrete rowing-boat at the Paris exhibition in 1855. It had been reinforced with an iron skeleton. Then inventiveness flourished further. In 1867, gardener Joseph Monier was granted a patent for a flower pot of iron wire surrounded with founded concrete. A new possibility was born: reinforced concrete.

Earlier on, new building materials had outshone each other. Cast iron from wood, wrought iron from cast iron, steel from wrought iron. But iron and concrete complemented each other — iron had the tensile strength lacking in concrete, and concrete had the compression strength lacking in iron. Together they reinforced each other's best properties.

Now that concrete has become almost equal to brutality or at least to drabness, it is difficult to understand the bold dreams once born out of reinforced concrete. The designers were no longer stopped by the limitations of the material needed for their design. This freedom was inebriating.

The first technician to master this freedom, both in theoretical and practical terms, was the Franco-Belgian Hennebique. He used it to build soaring newel staircases, protruding balconies, hanging gardens — air castles of cement. He was the first to lift the concrete from the ground with the magic of a geyser.

At the turn of the century, both the technical methods to mass produce cement and the technical methods to combine cement and metal were available for previously unbelievable constructions. Since then the cement kilns have become even longer — 75 metres in 1914, 145 metres in 1938, 170 metres in 1967. And the bridge spans have grown — the Skuru bridge from 1914 is 72 metres, the Traneberg bridge, built in 1934, was the longest in the world with 181 metres, the Sandö bridge in 1943 was another world record with 269 metres. But these feats were based on the fundamental principles that had had their breakthrough at the turn of the century.

Looking back at the development, we find it straight and obvious. But in reality it was of course full of dead ends. If you want to look at them more closely, you ought to go to the library of the Patent and Registration Authority at Valhallavägen 136 in Stockholm.

This is a public library, you just walk in. Available here are the descriptions of all Swedish patents since 1885, when a small patent agency was set up by the Institute of Commerce. There are two ways to find what you're looking for:

You can partly look in a series of annual editions of the *Patent Index*. First you locate the heading of "cement" and then under "clay, brick, cement and stone industry" find brief descriptions of all the patents of a certain year within a certain area plus the numbers of complete patent descriptions. Each volume also contains a name index, listing the people or companies that have been granted patent rights. All the well-known Swedish and foreign company names can be found here as well as many unknown small businesses.

You can also see in the "Class list" what class the particular product you´re interest in comes under. Cement came under class 36 and later class 80. Once you know that, you can go straight to the complete patent descriptions which have been arranged into their classes.

It turns out that forty years after the invention of Portland cement, many people were still busy inventing it. Some of the early Swedish cement patents looked like this:

Number	Brief description
357	Damp "slurry" and fuel separately or mixed, are successively thrown into the cement kiln in the place where the charge is burning most lively. (W. Joy.)
1439	So-called "bog-lime", clay and possibly silicon are mixed in a clay mill with water added. The mixture is then moulded into bricks, dried, burnt and ground. (O. Sundgren.)
1634	Quick and slaked lime is mixed with burnt, pulverized slate. The mixture is then hard burnt again and pulverized. (C.J. Widmark.)
1921	2-4% sulphuric acid is added to a small part of the lime, or an equal quantity of concentrated sulphate solution, with or without iron oxide. The mixture is dried, pulverized and mixed with the rest of the cement mixture.
2009	The lime is burnt twice separately without mixing and then pulverized. (Widmark.)
3038	Dusty substances, rich in clay, are added to the finely ground cement and [Till det under sintringstemperatur brända och fint pulveriserade cementet tillsättas stoftfina, lerrika ämnen (C. von Forell).]
5348	The raw mixture is stemmed before burning with granulated, unground blast furnace slag. (A. Stein.)

This lot is taken from the first ten years. It isn't easy to know what were purely wild suggestions and what were industrially valid ideas. At Degerhamn especially many experiments failed. They were trying to find their way, and these attempts brought ideas that were later dismissed, because they didn't work under the present circumstances or they did not work with prices of that time. But they are still included in the records of the Patent Authority, as in a gene bank, and one of these days, some of them may reappear in new guises.

Generally, it is exciting to see all the thousands of directions that development could have taken but didn't. It's a marvellous experience to be taken back to a period when our everyday products were bold conquests and new discoveries. Once you start to leaf through the inventions of the nineteenth century, you find all sorts of strange machines that you simply can´t miss. The most difficult thing about the Patent Authority library is to tear yourself away from it.

When you read the patent descriptions and the technical literature on cement production at that time, you hardly ever come across a worker. The technicians go to great lengths to admit that tips and loans have been provided by other technicians and scientists. But they seldom or never suggest that they may have learnt something from the people carrying out the practical work.

Does this mean that the technicians completely lacked the ability to benefit from the workers' experiences? Or have they quietly taken over the workers' contribution and claimed them as their own? No one knows the answer — the contribution of workers to technical development is as yet unexplored territory.

In technical literature, workers appear only as the anonymous "workforce". The ambition is to employ a work force as small and unqualified as possible. In the description of a new procedure, there may be a suggestion of also creating a new occupation, as in this issue of the Technical Journal about Klagshamn:

The burner is now able to obtain a reductive or oxidizing flame in the kiln, of a length of between 2 and 20 metres, thanks to different additions of coal or air and the possibility to control the draught. We also know that the addition of slurry is extremely easy to control (using different inlet nozzles) and that the kiln can be stopped at any moment. This shows also that an experienced burner would have no difficulty at all in producing clinker exactly as it should be.

Thomas Alva Edison's Swedish patent of a rotary kiln, forty-five metres long, which can take four-five times the amount of material of earlier kilns, thus reducing fuel consumption and improving the durability of the kiln lining. A drawing of this kiln is overleaf.

Working conditions are hardly ever mentioned in these descriptions. Quite often though, an indirect picture is given of people's conditions when the working conditions of the machinery are described. One example from the last page of the *Book of Inventions*:

The *cement industry* works with a number of different

machines, mills, fans etc., for which group operation is beneficially applied. In this field, working conditions are particularly demanding, since the fine cement dust is bad for the engine bearings. Strangely enough, it appears that enclosed engines are often the more unfavourable, since these will suck in the air through the journals as they cool, due to the air thinning effect. The cement dust will then come in with the air and thus render the bearings unclean.

What guided technicians when they considered the dangers presented by cement dust to the engine bearings but disregarded the dangers of cement dust to the human body? What guided inventors when they presented thousands of different suggestions that are now buried at the library of the Patent Authority? What guided the selection among the presented proposals?

Ultimately they were guided by the profitability of the capital. The owners' keenness to invest capital determined what technical possibilities should be developed further, and thus also determined the nature of the proposals presented. Technology changed working conditions and created new situations. But the owners, not the workers, had the power over it.

Today's cement workers' representatives are members of both the labour safety committees and the Boards. Technicians are forced by new legislation to accept that dust renders human lungs as unclean as the engines' journals. But these new facts are not reflected in the library of the Patent Authority. There it becomes obvious that the fundamental situation after all is unchanged.

The capital garnered, krona by krona, from the cement workers of this country (and all other workers as well) still controls the direction of technology in all its more important aspects. And it will go on doing so, until the workers themselves take over the means of production.

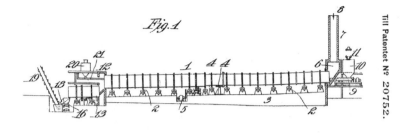

- How were the product and the machines with which you work invented? What problems were they supposed to solve, what were the alternatives?

- How are your job and your place of work described in technical journals and books? How are the workers' contributions to the technical development of your job described?

Aids: The patent descriptions and the indexes are printed and, like all other books, can be ordered by the county library.

The Book of Inventions, describing the then production of most industrial products, was published in several different edited versions 1873-75, 1889-91, 1901 and 1909. The last edition, written entirely by Swedes, came in 1938-39. It was replaced by *Technical Sciences* (Sthlm 1920-30) and *Handbook in Chemical Technology* (Sthlm 1948).

The best insight into the technical discussions of the time is given by the *Prospects of the Engineers' Association's* (1866-90) and in *Technical Journal*, which first came out in 1870. Both include industrial descriptions and in the beginning also breath-taking, beautiful pin-up machine drawings — first-class technical artwork.

Most fields of industry have their own trade journals, such as *Scandinavian Journal for Clay and Stone Industry* (1904-08), *Stone and Cement* 1908-17, *Concrete* (1916-1956) and *Cement and Concrete* (1926-1972). Old journals are easy to look up in Bernhard Lundstedts *Swedish Periodical literature* 1645-1899 and modern ones in the *Swedish List of Periodicals* 1970-71 (Sthlm 1971).

Foreign trade journals sometimes include descriptions of Swedish factories — e.g. Degerhamn is presented with many photographs in the German journal *Zement* 23.7-27.8 1925. A list of foreign periodicals is in *Concrete* nr 2, 1954.

Books with interesting illustrations on cement production include *Portland Cement* (London 1904), *The Manufacture of Portland Cement* (Dublin 1922) and *A Hundred Years of Portland Cement* (London 1924), all by A.C. Davis. The pre-history is written by P.E. Halstead in *The Early History of Portland Cement* (The Newcomen society for the study of history of engineering and technology, Transactions, vol. 34, London 1963). A descriptive list of old cement literature is *Some Writers on Lime and Cement* by Charles Spackman (Cambridge 1929).

Tage Bilde's book *Cement and Concrete* (Stockholm 1940) is a Swedish summary. It was part of the Technical Popular Library, which describes most fields of industry in a number of volumes. Elias Cornell gives a ravishing account of the application of cement in *Building technology* (1970).

28. FACTORY PLANNING

Who planned your factory? What did they think of your job?

The chief engineer, Mr T.A. Bergen, was the director of the AB Industrial Agency's technical department. He wrote the first Swedish handbook of factory planning: *Basic Planning, Design and Construction of Industrial Premises According to Rational Principles* (Confederation of Swedish Industry, Sthlm 1918). He believed the factory should be like one large machine:

> The premises must be seen as a part of one large industrial machine, in which each worker and tool has a defined task. Its aim should be to make possible the harmonious cooperation that will produce the best possible efficiency at the lowest possible cost.

T.A. Bergen had many disciples. One of them is Stig Tolestam, who wrote *Industrial Plant Technology* (Lund 1969). Tolestam expressed his main idea like this:

> The aim of industrial planning is to achieve, with economical and rational methods, a plant that gives the best possible financial return, as regards method, equipment, raw materials and staff, also considering time and resources available.

During the fifty years spanning these two statements, Swedish society has changed fundamentally. We now have political democracy, electricity, motorcars and pensions. National produce, standard of living and educational standards have doubled manifold.

However, the very power behind this development, the factory, has remained remarkably untouched by the changes it has created all around it. Factories are still being built for machines and procedures, not for people. Bergen, in 1918, puts the workers on par with tools. In 1969, "Personnel" is put on par with equipment and raw materials by Tolestam. A human being is something you are in your spare time, if you feel like it. In the factory, however, you're only supposed to provide the "best possible financial returns".

The most comprehensive motivation of this attitude is given in Sten Ödeen's introduction to the *Handbook of Industrial Plant Technology* (Sthlm 1949). A factory is and should be different from all other buildings, writes Ödeen. Because factories are *production plants*. Their main aim is to use human labour and material resources to produce necessities or means of production. All other buildings — homes, hospitals, schools, theatres, shops etc. — are *consumer plants*. Their main aim is to supply the means to satisfy needs. Therefore they call for entirely different designs.

This division is of course slightly schematic, Ödeen emphasizes. Even production plants include certain consumer functions, such as creating a suitable environment for the human labour force. *"But one should note that this is done, not in order to satisfy certain human needs, but in order to create better working conditions, which makes a better production result possible."*

Or, in even less ambiguous terms: the functions of consumer plants are as it were "human". In the production plants, however, "the only function of the worker and their human needs, is to enable the technical means of production".

Why? Because the production of goods is not the main purpose. "In its deepest sense this aim is only a technical expression of the fundamental function — which is economical."

Capital is required to create and run a production plant. Those who have the capital strive to place it in companies that make the highest profit. The real function of the production plants is thus to give the best possible return on the capital invested in the company. *"This main aim must never be disregarded when a production plant is planned and erected,"* Stig Ödeen points out.

Examples of the expressions these ideas took in the form of concrete buildings can be found mainly in journals for the building trade — from 1910 in the *World of Construction* and the *Building Journal*; from 1922 in *The Builder* and from 1930 in *The Building Industry*.

In *The Builder* of 1932, number 9, the now closed factory at Hällekis is presented as *The New Cement Factory at Hellekis: A Carefully Planned and Designed Industrial Plant.* The plans were made up by the Skånska Cement engineers in cooperation with the sister company Skånska Cement Foundry and with machinery from F.L. Smidth in Copenhagen. Two different suggestions were made for the kiln house. One was in reinforced concrete and would cost 600 kr per metre of building. The other, preferred, version consisted of an iron skeleton with bricks and was estimated at 560 kr.

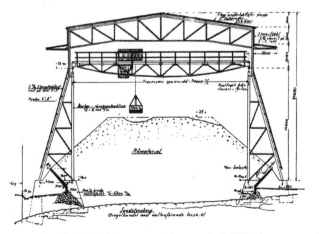

A Drawing for the Hällekis cement factory in 1932. A cross-section through the raw material store. From The Builder 1932:9.

When the details were designed, the aim was mainly to be independent of all external walls, so that these could be erected afterwards if operation had to start before the premises were completed. As for materials, the least possible number of different types was recommended, in order to bring costs down to a minimum.

And so on, page up and down. It gives a very clear picture of the perception of problems and solutions to these problems. All the time, two processes — production and construction — are prioritized. Not once do the plans approach the notion that they are building a place for people to work in.

In the mid-1930s, two new kilns were installed in Limhamn. The planning is described by Molle Nilsson in *A Lecture at the Cement Technical Meeting at Strömsnäsbruk and Malmö on November 16-17, 1938*. (Malmö 1938). The new buildings were planned by the same firms as at Hällekis. The various parts for the kilns weighed up to forty tons, and a special crane had to be built to lift them. Inside the kilns, 2,600 metres of chain were first mounted according to a vertical system and 1,765 metres according to the so-called American system. However, the result was not good enough, so the vertical system had to be reduced in favour of the American. This adjustment brought a much better result. From the kilns the clinker was brought by a roll chute to a jaw crusher and then on by a conveyor belt to the clinker silos. "Perhaps it should be mentioned that the lift shaft, which is 8.5m deep and reaches 6m below the water surface, is made of armoured cement and has proved totally watertight."

But what did the lift shaft look like? What was it like as a place of work? Perhaps it was the little windowless hole, called the "shithole" which is still left at the Limhamn factory? Nowhere in this lecture is a word mentioned to suggest that they expected any people to work in the planned factory.

The Köping cement factory was presented by the engineers Ivar Häggbom and Börje Lambert in a special brochure, *The Skånska Cement AB Industrial Plants at Köping and Forsby*.

One problem that the planners had to deal with here was building on loose clay of varying depth. The kiln house had to be founded on concrete piles, twenty to twenty-five metres high. Apart from that, the design of metal, bricks and asbestos cement sheeting was similar to that at Hällekis and Limhamn. As before, not a thought was wasted on the people they were building for.

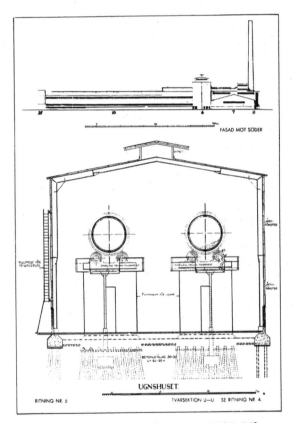

A drawing of the Köping cement factory in 1939. When you read drawings for new buildings it's often wise to check the drawings of the existing buildings. Drawings often improve reality.

The most comprehensive description I have managed to find of the planning of a Swedish cement factory is that of Stora

Vika, in the periodical *Concrete* in 1949 and *The Builder* in 1950. For the first time, mention is in fact made of certain staff rooms, such as the changing room and canteen and the housing area adjacent to the factory. The company even employed an architect to design the facade and a gardening expert to select particularly dust-hardy plants for beds around the canteen and office block.

But in the factory itself the production procedure still reigns — as supreme as ever. About the workers — not a word.

Every day that has passed in the thirty years since Stora Vika was built, someone has been sitting by the coarse crusher, in the small cabin which no one thought of proofing against vibrations and noise. Someone has been watching the fine crusher. Someone has been sitting in the cabin by the rope railway. Someone has driven the traverser across the materials store. Someone has worked in the noise from the mills.

Human beings have been working in this factory every day for thirty years — but the planners described their plans without them even being mentioned.

This is history. History still alive.

It lives in the "shithole" in Limhamn and in all other places of work, such as Stora Vika, where work is still in progress and hopefully will continue for many years to come.

But even when all these factories are closed, history will live in the shape of the capital saved by Skånska Cement by the building they did without considering human beings. A few bob were saved on the little cabin by the coarse crusher, a few bob on the fine crusher works, a few bob on the mill house; at every spot in the factory they saved a few bob. This money did not disappear. It has grown with the accumulated interest over thirty years and is still part of the Industri AB Euroc's capital.

This capital may seem immense. In September 1977, the journal *The Business World* estimated the company's net worth at between 110 and 114 million kronor. All of it has been saved in the manner described, krona by krona, at different places of work, inside and outside the company.

Of course capital is a good thing to have. The only question is: who should have it?

Some people consider it right and proper that the capital goes to the shareholders since they ordered the savings. That is called capitalism. Others believe that the capital belongs to the worker since it was amassed at their expense. That is called socialism. We still live in a capitalist society.

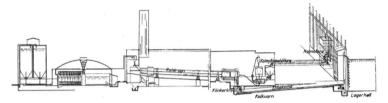

A drawing of the Stora Vika cement factory in 1949.

•   Who planned your place of work? How did they think, what did they want to achieve? What was their idea of your job?

Aids: Find out the year your factory was built and check in building journals and periodicals of your trade if the factory is represented. The year in question can be ordered by the county library if it's not already there. Staff journals and local press usually have less informative descriptions, but should be checked. Drawings and other documents relating to the factory planning are probably in the archive of the company or the building contractor.

A critical discussion of Stig Ödeen's and other factory planners' philosophy is included in my book *Change of Work* (Sthlm 1975). I have also, together with the architect Jan Henriksson, written a handbook in factory planning for, mechanic workers: *Flats on the Workshop Floor* (Örebro 1977).

By the legislation on workers' participation and working environment, workers of the 1970s for the first time ever have been given a certain possibility to take part in the planning of their own places of work. Some intense method development is in progress. Most promising of this seems, at the time of writing, the methods of Jesper Steen and Peter Ullmark in *How Can the Employees Change their Environment?* (The Architectural Section of the College of Technology in Stockholm, 1976.)

The basic handbook in factory planning for workers is *Planning*, published by the Labour Safety Committee and the Correspondence School (Sthlm 1976). A public enquiry has investigated what can be done to *The Working Environment of the Steel Industry* (SOU 1975:83). Factory planning at sawmills is discussed in *The Development of Sawing Sheds* (The Architectural Section of the College of Technology in Stockholm 1976), which is based on, amongst other things, the cross-scientific investigation *The Working Environment in Sawmills* (Report AM 101/75, the Labour Safety Committee, Sthlm 1975). Practical guides, which have a certain amount to offer to factory planning in other fields of industry, can be ordered from the Sawmill Industry Committee for Working Environment Issues, S. Blasieholmshamnen 4A, 111 48 Stockholm. The need for continued investigations are mapped out in *The Planning of the Physical Working Environment* (Sthlm 1975).

29. PSYCHOLOGY

Factory planning has been dominated by experts of technology and economy. But there are also experts on human beings and on inter-human relations. What have they done for industry? Have psychologists not exerted a counterweight to engineers?

Generally speaking, no, they haven't. When psychology in the late 1880s became an independent science, the natural sciences were chosen as a model. The natural scientists had cooperated with industry and created a new technology. The psychologists were now hoping to follow suit and create "psycho-technology".

Psycho-technology in Sweden was introduced by the leading American psychologist Hugo Münsterberg. In his book *Psychology and Industry* (Confederation of Swedish Industry, Uppsala 1917) he drew up the following guidelines"

First of all we ask: *How can we find those people whose mental capacity makes them most suited to the work they are to do?*

Secondly: *Under what psychological conditions can we ensure the most satisfactory work return from each individual?*

And finally: *How can we exercise influence over people in ways most beneficial to the interests of certain branches of industry?*

Or, in other words, we want to appoint the most suitable person, get him to achieve the best possible work and ensure the best possible effect of it.

Münsterberg was a far-sighted man. Whenever later psychologists have bothered to take any interest at all in work and industry, it has been to find answers to these questions and achieve these three aims. The answer to Münsterberg's first question was aptitude tests. The answer to the second question was productivity tests. The answer to the third question was marketing psychology.

Aptitude Tests

The first person to have applied psychology to industry seems to have been the father of work studies, F.W. Taylor. In 1896, he reorganized the work in one of the largest ball bearing factories in the US. 120 girls were working there, 10.5 hours a day, checking bearing balls. Taylor realized that the work above all required quick reactions. He knew that psychologists had just learnt to measure this capacity.

He therefore employed a psychologist to test the girls, select the quick ones and discard the "torpid" ones. Unfortunately this meant, writes Taylor, "that many of the most intelligent, diligent and reliable girls had to go, because they did not have quick enough reactions and powers of resolution."

The new selective method together with other measures gave the result that thirty-five girls working 8.5 hours a day at high speed could do the job of the previous team of 120 girls working 10.5 hours daily. The work force with the highest performance quota did the job in less than a quarter of the time originally required. Such results naturally appealed to Swedish employers as well.

The Sandviken Ironworks seems to have been the first to import psycho-technical methods. When they introduced time studies in 1918, they noticed great variation of capacity between different workers. If ten workers, of about the same age and experience, did the same relatively simple job, the worst one could achieve 140 and the best one 340 units per hour. Repeated studies in different factories confirmed that the best workers achieved two to three times more than the worst. All the company management had to do was to employ the best ones. But to be able to do just that, they needed an instrument which could predict the future capacity of the workers.

In 1928, Professor Poppelreuter and some other German psycho-technical experts were called to Sandviken. They produced a list of so called aptitude tests, designed to investigate the following characteristics:

- Eyesight
- Colour-sense
- General skill
- Combination ability
- Speed
- Reactivity
- Sense of proportion
- Sense of balance
- Preciseness and sense of order
- Mechanical capacity
- Constructivity
- Practical ability
- General intelligence
- General physical constitution
- Tenacity and endurance
- Adaption

They also tried to define the work requirements, the demands made by the employer on the worker for a certain task. Labour, for example, was described like this: "The work is not qualified but may require a certain versatility. It requires physical endurance and awareness of accident risks."

The work description was then translated into such qualities as those measured by the aptitude tests. To be accepted for labour, a worker should have at least the average score for the following qualities: quick reactions, sense of balance, practical ability, physical endurance and good physical constitution.

Between 1928 and 1940, over 2500 workers and applicants were tested with these methods at Sandviken. The test results were passed on in secret memos to the personnel office and the company management. The reports finished with final judgements like: "Considerably above average. Quick, precise, tenacious, mechanical, constructive, skilled. Strong and intelligent. Calm, confident, ambitious. Suitable foreman material." Or, for the tests with less satisfactory results: "Considerably below average, generally; difficulties to follow instructions. Colour-blind. Not mechanical or constructive. Could possibly be used for some kind of unskilled labour."

In 1937, the Swedish Employers' Federation's Company Management Institute began to cooperate with psychologists at Uppsala University to produce aptitude tests for industrial use. Rudolf Anderberg and Gunnar Westerlund in a number of reports published by the Confederation of Industry have shown how tests were devised for the employment of weavers and spinners in the textile industry (1938), examiners in the china industry (1940), crane operators and foremen (1943) and tram drivers and conductors (1945).

These tests did not measure as many qualities as those in Sandviken. And it was enough (e.g., in the textile worker study) to characterize the applicants as A or B men, i.e., as acceptable or unacceptable in a competitive situation.

In 1945, only ten-fifteen Swedish companies still used psychological aptitude tests on a regular basis. This year a committee was appointed by the Technical Science Academy to co-ordinate the tests. In 1952, the *Personnel Administrative Board* was formed. This Board always describes itself as a "neutral independent organization", in other words it was formed on the initiative of the Swedish Employers' Federation, its board members were appointed by the same body and it receives annual financial subsidies from it. Moreover, this board is naturally financially dependent on the satisfaction of its clients.

A form for memoranda from the psycho-technical dept. of Sandviken Ironworks.

The clients in the 1950s and 1960s were mainly large companies. The activities culminated in 1966 when 14,000 aptitude tests were carried out under the control of the PA Board. Thirty-nine of these were done at the Limhamn cement factory to select staff for the new computerized kilns.

After 1966, the number of aptitude tests at the PA Board has decreased. Instead, *aptitude analyses* have increased. The difference could be described schematically like this: An aptitude test is based on the employer's requirements of manpower and seeks to establish which person of a number of applicants would be best able to fulfil these. An aptitude analysis makes a similar examination but from the point of view of the applicant's employment requirements.

In both cases, the work opportunities and their nature are regarded as given. The worker is tested to show whether he fulfils the requirements of a certain employer (aptitude tests) or to see whose employer's requirements he can fulfil (aptitude analysis).

The employers and their jobs, however, are not tested.

- Are there any aptitude tests for your job? Have they been applied at your place of work? What was the result?

Aids: During the first ten years, the PA Board regularly published lists of the jobs for which tests had been devised. The 1962 list included the following:

automat controller, automator, miner, driller, operator, factory mechanic, attendant excavator, iron worker, cold header, power station attendant, coil winder, engine driver, machine attendant, engine operator, offset printer assistant, paper making machine operator, paper making machine attendant fitters, sample makers, mechanics, turret lathe operators, quick tank attendants, service engineer, serviceman, forest machine operator, sewing machine mechanic, checker, post office engineer, telecommunications installer, telecommunication checker, truck driver, television checker, mechanical engineer, workshop checker, chief fitter, chief roller.

No such lists have been published after 1962. The information department of the PA (P. O. Box 5157, 102 44 Stockholm. Tel: 08/14 14 00) will tell you whether aptitude tests have been devised for certain occupations and whether aptitude tests have been carried out at a certain company.

In connection with the description of the work requirements, the PA Board psychologists occasionally voice modest opinions regarding a defective working environment and organization. In Limhamn, e.g., they pointed out that the instrument panel

---

was difficult to survey and that the order situation between the burner and foreman was unclear. It is impossible for an outsider to assess the extent of such criticism, since the PA Board consultant reports are secret. Their possibilities are of course restricted, because the criticism has to be such that the companies are willing to pay for it.

Test the Test!

"Do you wish you didn't get anxious and harassed so easily?"

If your answer to that question is yes, you are considered to be slightly less valid than if it is no. "Validity" is an imagined degree of "availability of energy necessary for nerve processes in the brain". A person with low availability of such energy is considered to be quiet, careful, meticulous, diligent and tense. A person with plenty of such energy is instead considered confident, free, capable and calm.

"Do you prefer books giving a colourful picture of reality to those containing well-formulated thoughts?"

If you answer to this type of questions is yes, you are considered to be slightly less stable than if it is no. "Stability" according to the psychologist Henrik Sjöbring's theory is the individual's ability to act by habit, to be cool, comfortable, abstract and skilled.

"When you are bored, do you like to think of something exciting to do?"

If your answer to this type of question is yes, you are considered to be slightly less solid than if it is no. "Solidity" has to do with the endurance of your involvement. The most solid person according to Sjöbring's theory would be far-sighted, mature, collected and impossible to influence.

These three types of questions were asked to people applying for the job as burner at Limhamn in 1966. Imagine the situation. There are thirty-nine of you applying for the job. Thirteen are accepted for training. With the blessings of the union, the company has called in a psychologist to ask these questions.

M N T-SKALAN

(Marke—Nyman: Temperamentskala)

KONFIDENTIELLT

Ert namn: _____

Ert födelsedatum och år: _____/_____ år _____

Ert yrke: _____

Ert kön: man
(stryk under)   kvinna

Ert civilstånd: ogift
(stryk under)   gift
           frånskild
           änka/änkling

51. Tar ni gärna självständigt initiativ på er arbetsplats? .... Ja Nej

52. Har ni lätt för att påverka och övertala folk? .... Ja Nej

53. Brukar folk säga om er att ni döljer era känslor så att det är svårt att förstå sig på er? .... Ja Nej

54. Anser ni att man bör undvika den moderna tendensen att klä sig ledigt men litet slarvigt? .... Ja Nej

55. Betraktar ni er själv snarast som en reserverad och litet kylig person än som en hjärtlig och varm människa? ...... Ja Nej

56. Har ni lätt för att få förtrolig kontakt med barn? .... Ja Nej

57. Tycker ni ibland att ni inte orkar med lika mycket som de flesta andra i er bekantskapskrets? .... Ja Nej

Example of a test given to applicants for the job as burners at Limhamn in 1966.

He knows why he asks them. You don't. He knows how to interpret the answers. You don't. He knows what qualities in you the questions are devised to measure. You don't. He can evaluate the strange, doubtful theory on which the questions are based. You can't. All you can do is say yes or no, and you have no idea which answers ruin your chances of becoming a burner.

You have to make do with guessing. Does the employer want workers who feel anxious and harassed? Probably not. Does the employer want workers who like colourful descriptions of reality or workers who like well-formulated thoughts? Difficult to tell. After all, the job will be done in reality. If only you knew what the psychologist were after, you would also know what to reply. But the whole point is, you shouldn't know what he's after. The point is, he, not you, controls the situation.

In future you shouldn't have to be quite so exposed. The workers' legal right to participate will give the unions a chance to influence the choice of workmates and foremen. But should they accept that these are selected with psychological aptitude tests? What explanation should they then demand in advance to assess whether the aptitude tests are suitable? How do you test the test?

Test psychologists do not like to explain their methods. The secrecy is excused by the fact that the tests would be useless if they were generally known and discussed. But there are several points in an aptitude test that the psychologist can and should explain in advance. Ask for written explanations that can be checked.

These are some of the questions you could ask:

1. On what description of the job is the aptitude test based?
At Limhamn, only a sketchy description was given of the job, because the factory for which workers were required had not yet been built. It is important to check that aptitude tests are based not only on the employer's description of the job. Completely different aspects may be essential from the worker's point of view. The work descriptions may also be inaccurate for other reasons, they may for example be outdated or may not agree with conditions at your particular place of work.

Never accept an aptitude test without checking that it is based on a correct description of the job.

2. How has the work description been translated into qualities?
At Limhamn, the psychologists thought that a burner, judging by the sketchy work description, needed the following qualities: ability to form conclusions, sense of figures, understanding of instructions, technical ability, attentiveness, emotional stability, energy resources, self-confidence, endurance, independence, accuracy, need for human contact, and skill in human contact and involvement in his work.

It is not at all self-evident that these are the very qualities that, in the sequence given, produce the best burner. In retrospect all parties agreed that "ability to co-operate" was the main quality they should have looked for. Never accept an aptitude test without checking how the work description has been translated into qualities!

3. With what methods are the qualities measured?
Those who applied for the job as burners at Limhamn were tested by 9 different tests, including the MP, EPPS and MNT. Today these tests are considered outdated and other combinations of letters, such as the EPF, are more topical. In 1966, it was practically impossible for the tested persons, even afterwards, to find out what these letters were abbreviations for, why the questions had been asked, and how the answers had been interpreted.

The union now ought to ask these questions in advance. But it is not good enough to ask only the test institute itself for information about its tests. They are all keen to sell their services and, for natural reasons, prone to overestimate their methods. The National Trade Union ought to employ a psychologist independent of the test institutes to write a comprehensible handbook giving an account of the different tests used on the Swedish labour market. The handbook should also critically evaluate the different tests from the point of view of the workers.

In the absence of such a book, the next best thing is to demand to see the manual for each test to be used. The manuals are usually written in a language which is incomprehensible gibberish to an outsider, but it does at least contain some basic information.

The manual to the questions at the beginning of this chapter is called *Manual of the MNT Scale*. MNT is an abbreviation for "Marke-Nyman, Temperamental Scale". The list of literature in the *Manual of the MNT Scale* refers to an essay in the *Socio-Medical Journal* (annual ed 37, pp. 123-130) by G.E. Nyman and S. Marke and to the same authors' work *Sjöberg's Differential Psychology* (Lund 1961). In it you can read more about the background of the test. Never accept an aptitude test without finding out the methods that will be applied and theories on which they are based.

In certain special cases, an aptitude test may still appear to be motivated, even after it has been tested on these three points. But I believe those cases will be very rare.

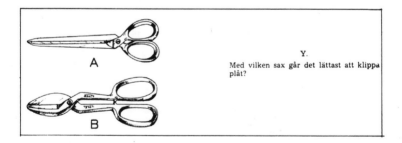

Bennet-Fry: Mechanical-technical test, Form BB. Example of a test used when selecting burners at Limhamn in 1966. Which pair of scissors is more suitable for cutting plate?

Productivity Investigations

Let us return to Münsterberg and his three questions. The second question -"under what psychological conditions can we ensure the most satisfying work return from each individual?" — has also given rise to many investigations.

The most well-known are the so called Hawthorne investigations made in 1927-1932 under the guidance of Elton Mayo. Researchers found that group work, professional pride and influence over the work situation led to increased production. Most productivity investigations, however, have referred to more restricted questions, such as: How does a worker's productivity change during the day? With work periods of different duration? With shift work? The effect of lighting, ventilation and noise on the workers' productivity has been carefully examined.

Let's take noise, which is of particular interest to the cement industry. A text-book which was very common and influential in the 1960s — *Work Psychology* by Edwin E. Ghiselli (Sthlm 1938) — gives an account of a number of investigations that have given contradictory results. Some studies indicate that noise leads to reduced production, others indicate that workers who stay in the noise for long enough will adjust to it and so resume their previous production capacity. The only thing that seems to have been properly established is the fact that noise disturbance often depends on the workers themselves.

Tired, bored or maladjusted workers, or workers who find the work difficult or uninteresting, complain most of disturbing noise. In many cases these complaints should only be seen as rationalisations (excuses). These workers complain of disturbing factors simply to conceal their lack of success at work to themselves and others. In a working environment without any disturbing noise they would soon find something else to complain about. (p. 310).

If this is what future employers were taught by science, there's no great hope that they might soundproof the cabin at the coarse crusher or erect walls between the mills in the mill-house.

The long-term effects of constant noise we don't know much about, Ghiselli pointed out. "Generally, personality disturbance is considered to appear in workers who have spent a lot of time in very noisy factories, such as punching workshops or weaving mills. However, these conclusions were only based on occasional observations and so must not be taken as final."

I see. But in that case, why haven't they looked into the matter? Is it the purely scientific interests that decides that disturbances of the production ability are more worthy of research than long-term damage to the workers? Of course not. The direction the research takes is reflected by the power balance in society.

It has proved valuable to the employers to assess the extent to which workers' productivity is reduced by noise. It has been uncomfortable to them to assess the long-term damage that could be caused by noise. And the psychological research for work has long been adapted to such judgements.

Only rarely has the question been asked: *How should the work be adjusted to suit the workers?* In that area, very little research has been done.

Edmund Dahlström and Bertil Gardell e.a. gave a first impression of this in *Technical change and work adjustment* (Sthlm 1966). One of the most important examples of such research is Bertil Gardell, *Production Techniques and Happiness at Work* (Sthlm 1971). The investigation was carried out at the Olofström Works, the Mörrum Works, Gruvön Works and Billerud Works. The main question was this: Is it true that a free and qualified job gives the worker greater satisfaction than a limited, unqualified one?

In order to answer that question, Gardell started by dividing the different jobs into classes, depending on the freedom they provided and the demands they made on knowledge and own initiative.

He then examined the workers' reactions to these jobs. He gauged their involvement in the job, the physical strain, the feeling of influence over the way the job was carried out, the togetherness within the working group and the contact with workmates.

The reply to the main question of the investigation was: YES. The large majority of workers find monotonous, restricted jobs unsatisfactory — and this feeling increases, the more disintegrated, one-sided and enforced the jobs are.

Gardell's conclusion is a recommendation to create places of work that give the workers a chance to participate and act in a qualified manner. These changes should apply to the entire work situation — organization as well as production techniques.

Workers have known this for a long time. But Gardell's research was not without impact. Just as America remained "undiscovered" until the first European arrived, the bad conditions in industry are not seen as "discovered" until a researcher has confirmed them.

In our society, decision-makers listen much more to a researcher's view of the workers' experiences than to demands expressed by the workers themselves. A researcher has to collects the experiences of the workers, for them to assume weight and reality for the decision-makers. This task is not unimportant.

- Have any psychological investigations been carried out at your place of work? What was the aim? What was the result?

Aids: Work psychological investigations which have been published since 1954 are listed in *Personnel Administrative Index*, published by the PA Board.

The most comprehensive Swedish handbook in work psychology is *Man and Work* (Sthlm 1950), in many places

---

terrifying reading. In 1969, a group of Marxist researchers attacked the work psychology in *The Art of Training men* (4th revised edition, Vänersborg 1971). The discussion led to a re-evaluation, the result of which is recorded in e.g., *Behavioural Science Work Research* (SOU 1973:53] or in *Psychology in Society* (Lund 1975).

The reply to Münsterberg's third question — the marketing psychology — won't be discussed, in this context. See e.g. the chapter "What is economical psychology" in my book *Self-evident matters* (Sthlm 1970).

30. RESEARCH

Does not the psychological science lose its impartiality when it starts serving industry?

Even Münsterberg asked himself that question. He replied that one had to distinguish between means and end. As long as the researcher supplied only the means, he remained impartial. To decide the end, however, was up to the client. The choice of the end was not the business of the impartial researcher. Not even if it was a question of taking part in torture, should the researcher give up his factual, non-evaluating attitude:

> The psychologist can recommend methods with which to press a confession from an accused, but the question whether it is right to press people to confess is not to be answered by the psychologists.

In the same way, the psychologist should avoid taking a stand regarding the aims of industry:

> The psycho-technician can serve certain aims of industry, but it is not up to him to determine whether these aims are the best. — The psycho-technician therefore stays outside today's industrial conflicts. It is not up to him to determine whether the ideas of trusts or trade unions are the most suitable for selecting workers.
>
> The psycho-technician can indicate how publicity for a certain product should be handled, but it is not up to him to determine whether it can be considered desirable for society to increase the sales of this product. If a sociologist were to voice the opinion that it would be better if less unnecessary goods were sold, and that the aim ought to be

to protect the consumer rather than assist the producer, the psycho-technician would have nothing to retort against it. His interest should be concentrated only on finding the appropriate psychological means which could lead to this end. He does not take sides, neither for producer nor consumer, neither for the Capitalist nor the worker....

Briefly: Münsterberg's psycho-technician is as impartial as a herring salesman. He stands in his scientific store, serving his customers in turn, whether it is the Pope or Satan himself, as long as they pay for his scientific services. And who have been able to pay?

In this scientific store, work psychology has lingered for too long. With the best of intentions, for sure. Even Münsterberg meant well. This is how his book ends:

No aim could possibly be greater for the economical experimental psychology than this adjustment of the work to the individual's mental capacity, which means that dissatisfaction with work, depression and dejection will be replaced by enriched satisfaction and harmony.

Beautifully put. Almost every psychologist since Münsterberg's time has said the same thing. But the workers never had the power to order research. The workers never had the resources to commission researchers. And so Münsterberg's cynical willingness, rather than his illusory expectations, came to affect the relations between psychology and industry for more than half a century.

But it would be unfair to point the finger at the psychologists. They only took after natural scientists and technologists, inventors and engineers. During this investigation of the cement worker's job we have seen that many other specialists had a similar attitude. Vocational guidance counsellors and textbook writers, historians, museum staff and architects, not to mention factory planners — they all, in one way or another accepted Münsterberg's idea of the neutrality of research.

Isn't it about time we changed that? Isn't it time research was given new clients?

The Power of Research

A few years ago I conducted a little experiment. I toured a number of Swedish universities and took part in their seminars. I produced a black leaflet from the Uppsala University Contact Secretariat and read out the following:

THE CONTACT SECRETARIAT
Modern society depends completely on science. No social sector is unaffected by the advances of research and technology. To the greatest extent this applies to the Swedish working classes.

Scientific regeneration often takes place in libraries and laboratories. A certain degree of solitude and quiet is a condition for regeneration. Therefore, it is an important task to encourage new thoughts and ideas, to convert them into action. We must seek contacts and links between the representatives of researchers and society and the representatives of the working people, and establish a network to be used for exchange in both directions. We must get to know the needs of the working classes, the working classes must get to know our resources.

This is the double function that the university wants to try to fulfil by its contact secretariat. It is an attempt to keep roads open between university and society.

TORGNY SEGERSTEDT
CHANCELLOR OF UPPSALA UNIVERSITY

COOPERATION WITH TRADE UNIONS
The trade unions know best the workers' requirements. The contact secretariat therefore regards cooperation with trade

unions as only natural. But nothing stops individual workers or groups of workers to contact the secretariat directly.

DIFFERENT FORMS OF COOPERATION
"Commissioned research" means that a local or central trade union gives a commission to a university department. If the workers want to do their own research in a department, it's called "visitors' research". The advantage then is the workers' participation in the activities of the department and the access they gain to qualified guidance and equipment, "Exam workers" can also be employed for a shorter or longer period. Finally, the contact secretariat has special subsidies to make pre-investigations, which in turn can be used to apply for further research grants. "In that way even a small local trade union branch without resources for commissioned research can have its needs for research satisfied by the agency of the contact secretariat."

So this is what I read out. It was interesting to see the reaction among the students. Their astonishment turned into incredulity. They felt more and more that there must be something wrong with this text, that the Chancellor of Uppsala University could never have written such a thing, that the document I was quoting from must be a forgery...

What created these suspicions? Contacts with the trade union movement is in itself not unusual in research. Within several branches of research it's actually part of the routine, to ensure you have the support of the union before you start a research project that in any way affects working life. It also happens that union representatives are members of reference groups for different research projects.

But doing research directly commissioned by the workers and in cooperation with them — that's a different matter. Then the workers would seize the initiative. They would select the framework for the project and the problems. The fact that the Chancellor of Uppsala University (who has devoted some of his research to proving that the working classes do not exist) should want to put his university at the service of the working-classes — that was incredible. To let the university go out to the workers with an open offer to put research resources at their disposal — this appeared to my listeners so bizarre that most of them were soon convinced that I was reading from a forged document.

It was forged, of course. There was a leaflet. But a few words here and there had been changed.

The members of the seminar generally had no difficulty in pin-pointing these. Most of them realized that wherever I read "the working classes" it really said "industry" (whose existence Torgny Segerstedt has never tried to deny). Where I had read "trade unions" it had really said "business associations". Where I had read "workers" it said "companies", i.e., "company management".

As soon as these little adjustments had been made, the text was no longer strange or worrying but only what could be expected from a Swedish university.

The discussions showed that many researchers were as unhappy with this as I was. Many of them would prefer commissions from the working classes to those from industry. Especially at the Centre of Inter-Disciplinary Studies in Göteborg I felt a great interest in such contacts. But what could they do?

A few miles north of Göteborg is a little town called Surte. The glassworks founded there in 1862 was bought in 1960 by the PLM concern. In the spring and summer of 1975, the employees started to wonder if all was well at the works. They wrote to the PLM managing director Ulf Laurin to ask him how the future of the glassworks was planned.

On 2 October 1975, the Works Council at the Surte Glass Works had a meeting and decided to appoint a conference group with representatives also for the other PLM glassworks. The group was given the task of distributing production between the three factories.

The group had two meetings of two days each on the 8th and 9th of October and on the 13th and 14th. The company management presented some compact, impenetrable figures. The workers' representatives had no chance to confer with their union or with outside experts, since the company management had insisted on strict secrecy for the whole conference.

The company management almost immediately neglected the original task of the conference groups, to distribute production between the three works, and instead began to discuss which of the three works should be closed. It soon appeared that the management had already decided on Surte.

Then the workers' front split up and the representatives of the two works that were not threatened supported the management. The majority thus decided that the Surte Glass Works should be closed.

The decision was made by the PLM Board on 17 October. The Works Council at Surte was told on 21 October. Only then the conference delegates were free from their imposed silence. A workers' committee was appointed to investigate the possibilities of saving the works.

The decision opposed by the workers had been made on the basis of extensive investigations by the PLM concern. The workers had no corresponding investigating capacity at their disposal. They lacked not only the right to decide about their own future but also any firm foundation for their own judgement of the decision made by the company management on their behalf. They had many queries and suspicions — but no factual material to set against the company. What could they do?

So here, separated by only a few miles, were a group of workers with a desperate need for research and a group of researchers looking for new commissioners. On 8 December they found each other. Originally the workers only asked for an environmental assessment of glass as packaging material. But finding that the Centre had experts who could also be used for other issues, they extended the commission. Twelve researchers from the Centre began looking into the work.

They took up issues such as: Was the decision of closure necessary? What did it imply from the point of view of environment and resources? What consequences would it have for those affected? What were the alternatives?

The research group's report was given in *Report from Surte, January 1976* (Kungälv 1976). The conclusions can be summarized as follows:

The material presented by PLM to the employees does not show unequivocally that the factory necessarily had to be closed. On the contrary, there were reasons to suspect that PLM had other undisclosed intentions, such as moving production abroad or forcing a transfer from bottles to cans. From the point of view of environment and resources, returnable glass is obviously to be preferred to cans. The consequences of the closure to the workers, to the town and the county, is in opposition to the declared aims of occupational and regional government policy. There is a realistic alternative to closure: nationalization. Another alternative would be for society to restrict the expansion of metal as packaging material.

The report did not save the works. Scientifically, the results were not epoch-making — no more than the majority of research results created on the initiative of industry. But the report contained a new starting-point, from which I can see immense possibilities opening up.

Torgny Segerstedt in his leaflet on the contact secretariat talks about the necessity of keeping roads open between university and society. But "society" is not just industry and authorities. Society is also people, groups and classes, who lack not only the right to decide about their own future but also the necessary basis to judge the decisions made by others on their behalf.

In such a society, research, whether researchers want it or not, is a power factor. How should this power of research be applied? To increase further the differences in financial and political power? Or as a counterweight to other power centres in society?

The Surte report gives a reply to these very questions, and it calls for a follow-up from others.

• Do you and your workmates have problems that you need professional researchers to help you solve? Do they refer to employment, technology, work organization — or what?

Aids: The universities are in Umeå, Uppsala, Stockholm, Linköping, Göteborg and Lund. University branches can be found in other places as well. Addresses are in the telephone directory. Each university publishes a catalogue with information on departments, researchers and lecturers.

Most university departments now have researchers who will be delighted to take commissions from the working classes. The recently formed Working Life Centre (PO Box 5606, 114 86 Stockholm, tel: 08/22 99 80) will be pleased to help make the contact for you.

The Centre for Inter-Scientific studies of man's conditions at Göteborg University (Mölndalsv. 85, 412 85 Göteborg. Tel: 031/81 04 00) has taken on several similar commissions after the Surte report. Commissioned by the Lomma workers, they have for example written *The Asbestos Cement Industry: A Pre-Study* (stencil 1976). An English example of direct cooperation between researchers and workers is the so called Lucas report presented in *The Lucas Workers' Battle for Purposeful Production: Purposeful Work* by Leif Dahlgren e.a. (Stockholm 1977).

The Conquest of the Company

The Surte workers took an interest in research only when the crisis was already acute. By then it was too late. Research is not mainly a defensive but an offensive weapon. It's more suited for conquest than for defence.

In this book I have made suggestions mainly for historical research. The central theme of the book is that *history still lives*.

We have seen numerous examples of this. We have for instance studied the monotonous reappearance of death and its constant surprises in the reports of the Factory Inspectorate. We have seen who took the risks. The company made money on it. And the money is still there.

The Hällekis workers lived with the dust for sixty years after the electrostatic filter was invented. Each year the company saved a few bob on not installing an electric filter. The money is still there.

The cement factories were built without a thought spared for those who were to work in them. In each place in these factories the company saved a few bob. The money is still there.

The company directors offered their workers housing quite different to their own homes. The company saved money this way, and the money is still there.

The Labour Court looked after the employer's right to control work and sack his workers freely. Each time this right was applied, the company saved some money. That money, too, is still there.

When the worker Karl Malmkvist was not needed at the factory in the low season, he was sent home to fend for himself. The company saved money on that. The money is still there.

In bad times hundreds of workers were made redundant. On each one the company saved a few thousand kronor. The money is still there.

When factories were bought and closed at Maltesholm, Klagshamn, Visby, Valleviken, Ifö and Lanna, the losses were imposed on the workers. The company saved money. The money is still there.

But it is not mainly by redundancies that the workers made money for the companies. It's by producing. Time studies and piecework increased the pace. The company made more money. The money is still there.

New inventions multiplied production many times. But the cement industry kept wages down to protect unprofitable little brickworks. In that way the company saved a penny per worker each working hour. The money is still there.

That is — not all of it is there. We have seen that quite a lot of it was spent keeping owners and directors at a standard of living way above that of the factory workers. We have seen some of the money disappear out of the country as their heirs settled in Switzerland or the South of France.

But most of the money that the company saved at the expense of the workers is still in the company and called the capital. History lives in the capital.

Sixty years after the conquest of political democracy, the Swedish Workers' Movement is now to preparing to conquer economic democracy. Private owners will no longer be able to buy and sell other people's places of work. Private property will be referred to its right place: private life. The capital saved over the years and over the centuries at the expense of workers will no longer give a few owners the power over future generations of workers.

Those who have the economic power have so far had control of the research concerning the companies. They have defined the picture of themselves. They have defined the picture of the company.

Therefore many workers do not know their own predecessors. They know nothing of the history living in the capital. That history must first be explored, concretely and locally, in one company after another. Those who are to conquer the company must also conquer the picture of the company. A new picture must be created, a picture that has the work and the workers at the centre.

In this book we have searched far and wide for such a picture. In no science can we find a complete one. It must be created by the workers themselves. It has to be built up by the cooperation of workers and scientists. In thirty different areas have we found materials and methods, which anyone can use to trace their own history and that of their workmates.

THE BAREFOOT RESEARCHERS

Nowadays you always hear that it was the NARKODAT scandal in 1987 that started the so called barefoot research. That is to take a much too simplistic view of the matter. The term "barefoot research" appeared as early as 1978. It's at the middle and end of the 1970s that the roots of "barefoot research" can be found.

First of all we ought to point to the economic crisis hitting the Capitalist world at that time. It was the first major crisis after the Second World War. In Europe millions of people were unemployed. In Sweden the ground trembled even under the largest, most solid companies.

This new insecurity was a shock to many people. When jobs were uncertain, they wanted to know why. When production stopped increasing, they wanted to know how the result was distributed. When power was no longer successful, it became seriously questioned. It is significant that the first barefoot groups were formed in the places worst hit by the crisis.

The conditions were there. Education in the 1970s was certainly still very authoritarian, with the emphasis on studying a prepared, already established curriculum. But in places the active search for knowledge was encouraged. Students were taught not only to reply but also to query. Team cooperation was on its way to becoming a natural form of work.

In the arts, attention still focused on a few performing stars in the areas of literature, music, theatre and visual art. But a new concept of culture was being formulated, stressing active participation rather than consumption.

Such an attitude to culture was expressed as early as 1972, in a memorandum from the Arts Council. There is still no mention of research, which is assumed to be an activity exclusively reserved for specialists. But in the long term, research could not remain unaffected.

The rapid social changes of the last fifty years had transformed even the immediate past into an unknown, exciting continent. To many people this was the cause of some nostalgic retrospection. One Swedish novel in three published in 1975 had an historical theme. Thus the past took its revenge in the era of future research.

A new *historical awareness* was beginning to break through. The Vietnam War had taught a whole generation that history must be studied if the present is to be understood and the future to be influenced. To them the past was not a refuge from today's demands. They knew that history bears arms.

Today we can state that hardly any have come true of the predictions drawn up by the prognosis makers of the 1970s. The insight they seemed to convey was false. But the new picture of the past that has grown up thanks to the barefoot groups became significant, both scientifically and politically.

The interest in history went hand in hand with the interest in local affairs. This was interpreted by many as a recoil from the concern for the Third World in the 1960s, a shrinking awareness of the world. But it was more like a reaction against the abstract questions that had long affected both research and political debate. "Concrete things are always local," was a typical watchword of the barefoot movement.

This was not a way to ignore the rest of the world. It is obvious that the problems taken up by early barefoot groups in Säffle or Sandviken had often first been observed in developing nations. The difference was that, in Säffle, something could be done about them.

Even the NARKODAT scandal, which undoubtedly had great significance for the barefoot movement, had its predecessors in the Third World, such as the CAMELOT project in the mid-1960s, when North American universities sought Latin American assistants in an extensive investigation of the reasons for "social unrest". It turned out that the investigation was commissioned and paid for by the US military force. The Latin American researchers were in reality to function as spies against their own people.

The conflict surrounding this project in Latin America caused an increased awareness of research as a source of power creating dependence. Many Latin Americans concluded: We must learn to control the research of other people, so that we can find out what we need to know, not what they need to know to control us. And above all, we must learn to do our own research. We must learn to use the methods which at present give our opponent the upper hand.

The NARKODAT scandal brought a similar awareness to Swedish workers. They suddenly realized that for decades they had been the object of research that they had never asked for, conducted in a language which wasn't theirs, and often leading to conclusions not in their own interest. It was research for experts, authorities and company managements. But if the workers wanted to know something about their own jobs, about the products they made, about the company where they worked — where could they go? If workers wanted to commission research — how would they go about it?

The main contribution of the barefoot movement is related to the struggle for power over the companies in the 1980s and 1990s. It soon turned out that the picture of the company created in the capitalist era had survived the legal right to participate and workers' profit-sharing funds. An entirely new image had to be created. In this case, too, historical facts had the greatest explosive power. The barefoot movement's conquest of company records in the early 1990s dealt the fatal blow to Swedish capitalism.

In light of the later successes of the movement, it is easy to underestimate the difficulties faced by the first barefoot researchers. When they started to appear at libraries, archives and scientific institutions, they often came two by two to support each other in the foreign environment. Preserved documents show how they tried to strengthen each other's morale:

> Don't think that a person with higher education knows everything. Most of the things we have found out are new not only to you but also to university students and their teachers. It's fundamental that you realize this: nobody knows everything. Each person is a specialist in his own field.
>
> So are you. If you have worked in your job as we in ours, you have a specialised knowledge which no other researcher has. This knowledge is a mine which you could learn to exploit. When you do research, you are not trying to catch up on a lead given to others free, through education — no, on the contrary, you are exploiting the knowledge that you alone possess, you are finding out about things not known by anybody else, you are combining pieces of knowledge which others have only in fragments.
>
> To make this more clear concrete examples are needed. We have them. But not until you yourself begin to research will you really know what we're talking about.

Today we smile at these keen reassurances. But the class society of the 1970s was no playhouse. To think of a Swedish worker going to a scientific institution had long seemed as preposterous as a black man in the American South taking advantage of his civil rights. Courage was needed.

The reaction of the research establishment at first was mainly one of suspicion. The very term "barefoot researcher" is evidence of that. It was originally a derogatory term, implying that these researchers like the Chinese "barefoot doctors", did not have academic qualifications. In that way they wanted to emphasize the difference between "amateur research" or "workers' research" as it was also called, and "proper research".

Quite naturally, some of the research of the early barefoot researchers was imperfect. Anything else would have been impossible. All the handbook literature that later grew up to guide beginners and show how material can be traced and processed, how research can be applied to concrete problems in political and trade union work, all of that was lacking in the early days of the barefoot movement.

In spite of being aware of the shortcomings in their work, the barefoot researchers were always opposed to the established sciences' claim for exclusive right to the word "research". An early document shows why they took this stand:

> To "study" is to absorb knowledge already documented e.g. how to pronounce the words of the English language. Not long ago it was believed that only a few people with special "good brains" could study. These days most youngsters spend twelve years at school.
>
> "Research" means finding out about things not previously known, or combining previously known things in a new way so that the knowledge becomes more useful to those who need it. The idea that only a small elite can manage this is still generally accepted.
>
> "Research" is a word with prestige. People with power and influence therefore are trying to reserve it for their own activities. In a society with marked gender roles they say that he "does research" while she "is working for her degree" — although both of them may be doing the same thing. The company's marketing experts are "researching a new product" when they try to dress up failure. The workers, however, "have a little study group" when they investigate what the new working environment legislation means to their place of work.
>
> These expressions, determined by gender and class, tell a lot about the nature of our society. But factually, they are not justified.
>
> "Research" simply means "investigation". Different people are of course more or less skilled and experienced when it comes to carrying out different types of investigations.

But university education does not give a monopoly of these qualities. Anyone can learn how to investigate.

These simple truths were first accepted by the county libraries which became the natural centres of barefoot research.

County libraries in those days were simple book collections almost entirely without any political service. Today it seems incredible that during the first half century of democracy in Sweden, we accepted the elitocracy which was a consequence of the fact that only national administration and industrial bureaucracies had investigative resources for political activities. The demands of the barefoot movement were behind the first information and research appointments at the county libraries in the 1980s, which in due course led to the modern library's investigation departments.

Even to universities the barefoot movement has been very important. I must here restrict myself to a few main points.

The extensive specialization of work in the industry of the 1970s had affected science too. Social sciences e.g., were divided into about twenty different "subjects", the limits of which were as unclear as they were jealously guarded. Each new technical approach and each new object of research tended to give rise to a new "subject", which once established constituted a kind of lifetime prison for the researchers dealing with it.

Suppose that a twenty-year-old took an interest in a certain book by Wilhelm Ekelund. He learnt a scientific method to find out what the book was about and why. To continue his research he had to be prepared to stay in exactly the same place by the scientific conveyor belt, making the same manual movements on constantly new texts, which might not even interest him anymore, until he was old enough to retire.

The barefoot researchers had problems to solve instead of methods to guard. They wandered back and forth across the academic boundaries and so helped pull them down.

They also brought valuable experiences from industry. A university in the 1970s could be compared to an immense factory with conveyor belts radiating in all directions, each delivering some kind of true knowledge to an immense peripheral storeroom, where customers were expected to ramble, picking among the goods to assemble for themselves a motor-car or a sewing-machine or whatever they needed.

The barefoot researchers began by assembling such oddments. But they soon realized that the old method was impractical.

To academic research, the breakthrough of the barefoot movement also meant a change of commissioners. Before 1975 it was extremely rare that a research institution received a commission or accepted a job from working-class individuals or groups. The all-dominant commissioners were the Ministry of Defence, industry or the public authorities. Researchers who wished to put their work at the disposal of the working classes generally tried to guess what type of research would benefit them.

The professional specialists who, before the emergence of barefoot research, were the only ones to devote themselves to science, lived in a world almost totally isolated from the workers' world. The pupil could become a student and the student a professor — even in social sciences — without any kind of social experience beyond the scholarly institutions.

To many academics the barefoot researchers became their first chance of real contact with people from a social class different from their own. These contacts paved the way for the system of regular and obligatory changes of work, which is now routine in all Swedish universities.

As the barefoot movement became accepted by the society it helped reshape, the prefix "barefoot" became increasingly rare. After 2020 we come across it almost exclusively in historical descriptions of the emergence and development of the movement. By now the term "barefoot research" has almost disappeared from our language.

INDEXES

This book has three different indexes: one materials index, one author and title index and one name and subject index.

Material Index

This index shows the different types of materials mentioned in the book and in what archives and libraries information on the material can be found.

Author and Title Index

This index contains authors' names and titles of books and periodicals mentioned in the text.

Name and Subject Index

This index contains the names of all people, places, companies and organizations mentioned in the text and gives an account of the subjects dealt with in the book. The index does not include Skånska Cement, Cementa, Euroc or their subsidiaries, nor subjects mentioned in the previous indexes. The names of workmates are given under each location name. Nils Persson of Brömolla would thus come under Brömolla and Nils Persson of Lomma under Lomma.

AFTERWORD: AFTER WORDS, ACTIONS
Gareth Evans

When Sven Lindqvist died in May 2019, the Anglophone response to this significant literary loss was notable precisely for its *lack*, its silence. There was no flurry of reports or tribute pieces. It took some days for his death even to be acknowledged, and then only in the United States and online at first. Indeed, his primary British publisher, despite a number of written entreaties, not only failed to mark his passing and celebrate his achievement, but kept his author page details determinedly in the prior present tense for over a year. Giving the benefit of the doubt, one might feel this is how all great authors should be treated — their work lives on (and by association so do they, as it were), remaining perennially relevant. However, the blanket failing to honour Lindqvist — at the moment of his departure — as one of the most formally inventive, insightful, politically urgent, rigorously exploratory and creatively cross-disciplinary writers of our times suggests otherwise.

The first and one of the very few obituaries in the UK press came three weeks later, both initiated and written by Tom Overton for the *Guardian*. The self-declared progressive newspaper did not have a text prepared (a time-sensitive common practice for dailies when considering well-known public figures in their later years). Overton is the archivist, anthologist and now biographer of the late John Berger, who was very much a kindred spirit to — and correspondent with — Lindqvist, although it appears that they never met in person.

This is not to say Lindqvist's work in his lifetime went unacknowledged or unappreciated in the English-speaking world. He was critically acclaimed by fellow writers and peers in his various chosen fields, and generated a form of network influence not dissimilar to that of Berger — or W.G. Sebald — for those to whom he mattered. However, it feels like he never quite established that critical mass of impact in English, tipping him into that status of a "given", named as a shortcut indication of a subject or position. Might this have been due to the fact of translation (I have a fierce hostility to such an opinion, as the English language reader still encounters their own language in the act of reading!) or because Lindqvist refused to let "liberal" Western countries off the hook when it came to their deeply ingrained colonial, imperial, racist and extractive pasts and presents.

Which is why the publication of this new edition — and the first in English — of his *Dig Where You Stand* is so refreshing. Not only because, on being approached with the proposal to publish, Repeater Books embraced the idea and need for it so rapidly and enthusiastically. Not only because it brings into the language a hugely topical text on solidarity in labour and workers' relation to place, property and power both economic *and* social — one that had an enormous international impact in practical terms on its original publication. And not only because, for an Anglophone reader already familiar with his work, it provides a useful bridge between the earlier translated books of committed reportage in China and Latin America and Lindqvist's later works on racism, bombing and the desert. It is also because its production embodies many of the values Lindqvist himself argues for in his work — what we might call "engaged collaboration".

It feels important very briefly to put this on the record, as it demonstrates simply and clearly that there are other ways to do things, working together for a shared and worthwhile outcome, just as Lindqvist's book identifies. And especially as Sven himself, although he did not live to see publication, knew it was underway. In late 2018 the scholar, publisher and critic Sukhdev Sandhu (a great friend of Repeater) and I approached Lindqvist and his wife Agneta thanks to Michael Morris, co-director of the arts production agency Artangel, with whom Sven had worked in 2012 on *A London Address,* part of *A Room for London*.[1] We had noticed that the fortieth anniversary of *Dig Where You Stand*'s publication was approaching and proposed a first English edition via our own small presses. Sven thanked us kindly for our interest and told us a parallel desire was active with Andrew and Astrid. We spoke, shared our common interest and learnt of a translation already extant but unpublished. From there a plan to co-produce developed. Sven's death and Covid both shifted and delayed that process. Sukhdev's introduction to Tariq at Repeater ensued in January this year (at time of writing in August 2022), which would have seen Sven's ninetieth birthday, and immediate acceptance followed. Now, just over a year later, the book exists. I have noted this to show how publishing rarely does but sometimes *can* work, and to share that with readers.

The direction of travel that human society appears to be taking is far from energising and can often fill a conscious witness to the attendant destruction with despair. *Dig Where You Stand* offers both a potent brake on that passage and a modest but crucial rerouting. I'd like to extend my huge thanks to Sven in absentia for his trust in the proposal, to Agneta for her warm approval and support, to Andrew and Astrid for their impeccable delivery, and to all at Repeater Books for turning the idea into a wonderfully produced, activating and necessary reality.

---

1 https://www.artangel.org.uk/a-room-for-london/a-london-address/#sven-lindqvist

Andrew Flinn is a Reader in Archival Studies and Oral History at University College London and a member of the Raphael Samuel History Centre.

Astrid von Rosen is Associate Professor (docent) at the Department of Cultural Sciences, University of Gothenburg.

Gareth Evans lives in London. He is a writer, editor, event/ film producer and hosts the Screen at Home programme for the *London Review of Books*.

ACKNOWLEDGEMENTS

We would like to thank Sven Lindqvist for his remarkable and enduring text, and both Sven and Agneta Stark for their permission, trust and belief in our realisation of this publication.

We are hugely grateful to Tariq Goddard, Josh Turner and all at Repeater Books for their understanding of this book's importance and their exemplary production. It has been a pleasure to work with them.

We thank Swedish-born translator, author and playwright Ann Henning Jocelyn for so willingly updating the manuscript, and all those who have endorsed this edition.

Astrid and Andrew warmly thank colleagues, friends and students at University College London (UCL), University of Gothenburg (UGOT) and the broader academic community, as well as practitioners and other participants, for generously committing to *Dig Where You Stand* workshops, seminars, symposiums, conferences, publications and teaching activities. At UGOT we wish to acknowledge Catharina Thörn's long term and very stimulating *Dig Where You Stand* engagement. At the Centre for Critical Heritage Studies a special thanks goes to those working for the Archives Cluster. Mats Malm has been a key person throughout the publication process, and Alda Terracciano has provided case studies helping to demonstrate the relevance of the "Dig" approach. In addition to the above Andrew would like to acknowledge the contributions of all those at UCL involved in the *Dig Where We Stand* project in 2011, members of the Community Archives and Heritage Group, and particularly Peter Box, Nicholas Lloyd and Sharon Messenger for all their inspiration and long discussions about

Dig Where You Stand and "history from below" practitioners and movements.

Gareth would like to thank Sukhdev Sandhu for his essential and generous introduction.

Andrew Flinn and Astrid von Rosen, with Gareth Evans

Repeater Books

is dedicated to the creation of a new reality. The landscape of twenty-first-century arts and letters is faded and inert, riven by fashionable cynicism, egotistical self-reference and a nostalgia for the recent past. Repeater intends to add its voice to those movements that wish to enter history and assert control over its currents, gathering together scattered and isolated voices with those who have already called for an escape from Capitalist Realism. Our desire is to publish in every sphere and genre, combining vigorous dissent and a pragmatic willingness to succeed where messianic abstraction and quiescent co-option have stalled: abstention is not an option: we are alive and we don't agree